MW01252833

# Unlikely Friends

# Unlikely Friends

## *Bridging Ties and Diverse Friendships*

James A. Vela-McConnell

LEXINGTON BOOKS
A division of
ROWMAN & LITTLEFIELD PUBLISHERS, INC.
*Lanham • Boulder • New York • Toronto • Plymouth, UK*

Published by Lexington Books
A division of Rowman & Littlefield Publishers, Inc.
A wholly owned subsidiary of The Rowman & Littlefield Publishing Group, Inc.
4501 Forbes Boulevard, Suite 200, Lanham, Maryland 20706
www.lexingtonbooks.com

Estover Road, Plymouth PL6 7PY, United Kingdom

British Library Cataloguing in Publication Information Available

**Library of Congress Cataloging-in-Publication Data**

Vela-McConnell, James A., 1967-
  Unlikely friends : bridging ties and diverse friendships / James A. Vela-McConnell.
    p. cm.
  Includes bibliographical references and index.
  ISBN 978-0-7391-4874-7 (cloth : alk. paper)—ISBN 978-0-7391-4875-4 (pbk. : alk.
paper)
  1. Friendship. 2. Interpersonal relations. 3. Difference (Psychology) I. Title.
  BF575.F66V45 2011
  158.2'5—dc22                                                    2010040055

♾™ The paper used in this publication meets the minimum requirements of American
National Standard for Information Sciences—Permanence of Paper for Printed Library
Materials, ANSI/NISO Z39.48-1992.

Printed in the United States of America

*In memory of Platon Coutsoukis,*
*whose unreserved acceptance and friendship*
*demonstrated the very bridging ties*
*at the heart of this book.*

# *Contents*

| | | |
|---|---|---|
| Acknowledgments | | ix |
| Introduction: Some of My Best Friends | | 1 |
| 1. | Friendship and the Fabric of Society | 15 |
| 2. | Structuring Friendship Opportunities | 45 |
| 3. | Social Boundaries in the Context of Friendship | 101 |
| 4. | Interpersonal Techniques for Managing Social Boundaries | 129 |
| 5. | "Bridging the Gap" Through Friendship | 167 |
| Afterword: "Some of My Best Friends Are . . ." | | 195 |
| Appendix A: Researching Friendship Diversity | | 205 |
| Appendix B: Friendship Pairs | | 221 |
| Bibliography | | 225 |
| Index | | 237 |
| About the Author | | 241 |

# Acknowledgments

This book would not have been possible without the contributions and support of numerous individuals. Foremost among them are the research participants who took time out of their busy lives to participate in multiple interviews and shared with me intimate stories of their friendship. Engaging in these conversations is certainly the most rewarding aspect of conducting research. You provided much inspiration and motivation to me. Seeing the quality and depth of your relationships gave me hope that bridging ties can counterbalance the societal disconnection so many sociologists observe and lament.

Over the years in which this study was undertaken, a number of student research assistants contributed to the research process in a variety of ways, including Lori Cain, Melissa Gaulke, Mandy Froiland, Natalie Shai, Tracey Lange, Melissa Marano, Xia Xiong, and Jenny Nacey. Your help shaved one or two years off of the data collection and analysis process. Thank you! The data collection and analysis is perhaps the most straightforward part of conducting research; then there is the writing process. Lars Christiansen, Dru Dunwoody, Doug Green, and Eric Gronberg all read the first draft of the complete manuscript and provided much support with their feedback. In addition, I must thank four anonymous readers who were quite rigorous in the review process. The final product owes much to their insight and advice. Annette Gerten, Jessica Nathanson, Tim Pippert, and Kathy Swanson all read portions of the manuscript as well and provided many helpful comments and ideas and Diane Pike helped me wrestle with different ideas for a title. Thank you all very much! And I would be remiss if I failed to mention Kathleen Odell Korgen. Our collaboration in the early stages of our respective research projects provided much assistance in the formulation of my initial ideas and research strategy.

Finally, and of most importance, I wish to express my deepest gratitude to my partner Matthew McCright for his enduring support as I brought this book to fruition. I am truly grateful for your patience and capacity to help me persevere and complete this work.

# *Introduction*

# Some of My Best Friends

How people live and who they are will be determined more by their friends than by their mothers or their superior line managers. We find out who we are as people with and through our friends. Friendship is about hope: between friends we talk about our futures, our ideals and larger-than-life meanings. There is an idealism in strong friendship because it is detached from the fixtures of role, status and custom (Pahl 2000, 165).

The phrase, "Some of my best friends are . . ." is all too typically used by individuals wanting to demonstrate their liberal credentials. "Some of my best friends are . . . gay." "Some of my best friends are . . . black." People say, "Some of my best friends are . . ." and then fill in the blank with whatever marginalized group which they care to exonerate themselves. However, depending on the listener, this can come across as rather shallow and seems to indicate that the friendship is merely there in order to score points with other liberals rather than for any inherent value in the friendship itself.

But perhaps this is not a fair assessment. What about those instances where there are indeed close friendships between individuals on different sides of some social boundary? In those instances where such friendships really do exist, there is a very important phenomenon occurring: friends are breaking the social distance that social psychologist have noted separates the two individuals and that usually prevents the emergence of any kind of close relationship (see, for example, Vela-McConnell 1999; Vander Zanden 1987; Moreland 1985; Lauderdale *et al.* 1984; Wilder and Shapiro 1984; Gonzales, *et al.* 1983; Byrne 1971; Shibutani and Kwan 1965; Newcomb 1963, 1961 & 1956; and Speier 1941). These unlikely friends have "gone against the odds" which say that relationships are usually based on similarity in terms of demographics: the same race, the same gender, the same sexual orientation, the same class, and so on.

Examining such friendships requires that we acknowledge the system of privilege and marginalization in our society and appreciate its impact on individual perceptions. Identity research has shown that those parts of our identities that serve to marginalize us—or set us apart—become a central aspect of our conception of self. Because these characteristics marginalize us, we have to deal with them all the time. So, there are plenty of people out there who say things like "Blacks dwell on race too much," or "The only thing that gays and lesbians ever talk about is sexual orientation." This is actually normal and understandable behavior on the part of these different groups. They are not the ones who make it the focus of their lives. Society—the rest of us—*makes* race or orientation or gender an issue *for* them—an issue that they cannot ignore, even if they wanted to. They have to face it every waking moment of their lives. So, these groups are highly conscious of these dimensions of their identity because it is the source of their marginalization—of being cut off from the rest of society. And this is the perspective of the marginalized: a race, gender, or sexual orientation-focused consciousness.

For those who are not marginalized, the experience is different. On the one hand, many whites, especially those who would define themselves as being open and friendly to people of all races—those wanting to demonstrate their liberal credentials—feel that the color of one's skin doesn't matter at all. They speak of color "not mattering" and of "color blindness." However, as Cornell West (1993) has so succinctly said, of course race matters. We have only to hear the stories of those from across the racial divide. Those who speak of color "not mattering" are falling into the trap of "symbolic ethnicity" as outlined by sociologist Herbert Gans in 1979 and again by Mary Waters in 1996. This entire debate has seen a resurgence since the election of President Barack Obama and continued through the intense debate surrounding the arrest of Professor Henry Louis Gates, Jr. in his home by Cambridge police: are we living in a "post-racial" America where race is no longer an issue, or is race still persistent and influential even though few (particularly among those who are white) are willing to name it? Then there are the whites for whom race *really does* matter. In fact, it matters so much that they too could be described as having a race-focused consciousness. This intense focus on race is tied up with hatred—hatred toward the "other" who is not like me. Between these two ends of the spectrum are those—perhaps a majority—who occupy the middle ground where they acknowledge the presence and impact of racism in the abstract sense, but who live their lives as if everything is okay or improving even as they unconsciously go on "alert" when crossing paths with unknown members of racial minority groups, particularly if they are being loud, or worry about a racial minority dating their daughter. Of course, the same could be said regarding gender, sexual orientation, class, or whatever socially constructed boundary one wishes to consider.

But what about another possibility for those living on different sides of a particular social boundary? What about an acknowledgment of race—a racially-focused consciousness—that is not caught up in the hatred and fear so often inspired when thinking of race? What about a similar acknowledgement of gender or sexual orientation? What about those who become good friends despite their differences? What about those who have moved beyond blindness (whether racial, gender, or what have you) and who have come to accept those around them for who they really are instead of wiping out their differences? What about those who have moved beyond having to protest to others "Some of my best friends are . . ." (and fill in the blank)?

There are those individuals from diverse backgrounds who have created a world, at least within their own private lives, that is not broken by the socially constructed boundaries of race, class, gender, sexual orientation, religion, ability, and age; people who have established deep, lasting relationships with others from very different backgrounds. As will be seen in chapter 1, however, past research on relationships indicates that such friendships are a relatively rare phenomenon. One question raised is "why?" and many sociologists have sought the answer to this question. However, another sociological question focuses more on the successes of the few: "How have you accomplished this? How have the two of you broken down the socially constructed boundary within your own relationship and bridged the social distance that separates you?" Unfortunately, research in this area of friendships is slim. With this gap in mind, I have set out to understand how people bridge the social distance between them within the context of their friendships. Because we live in a world in which there is increasing contact with diverse others, understanding how differences are bridged—regardless of which socially constructed boundary we happen to be speaking—is an important pursuit.

## My Best Friends

Some of the most creative sociologists are those who engage their sociological imaginations (Mills 1959), drawing ideas from their own personal lives when deciding upon a research topic. The point of such an exercise is to begin to see the connections between one's own biography and society itself: how does one's own personal life fit into and reflect the larger patterns of society? This exercise also highlights the perspective and possible biases of the sociologist. Despite the fact that our personal lives seem detached from the larger social processes going on in the world around us, we are very much caught up in larger social patterns. Our patterns of friendship, for example, are not random; nor are they entirely the product of our own decision-making. Instead, our social context provides us with certain opportunities and deprives us of others. The question is what do we do with the opportunities with which we are presented? At that point, individual decision-making enters the picture.

For example, when it comes to opportunities to befriend people who are different from me, I think that I have had more than is typical simply because of my social circumstances.[1] Of course, I didn't have to take advantage of those opportunities, and I probably didn't in every case. Nonetheless, I did take advantage of the opportunities in enough instances that I feel privileged to have made friends from many diverse backgrounds. The irony here is that, because it is my life and my own experience, I have never really thought there was anything special, unique, or different in my friendship pattern. Like many of us, I have taken the opportunities presented to me for granted simply because they were my "norm." That is my subjective experience. From an objective perspective, on the other hand, my experience with friendship does not fit the norm of our society due in large part to the fact that I am a minority. It was my realization of this point that piqued my sociological imagination. What was it about my social context that allowed for a relatively diverse group of friends? And how is it that these friendships have succeeded?

Before I can describe my experience with friendship, I need to identify myself and describe my own background. In some ways, I am privileged and in others I am marginalized. On the privileged side, there is gender (male), class (educated, upper-middle class), religion (Christian upbringing), age (middle—"in my prime"), and ability (I am able-bodied). These aspects of my identity work to my advantage as I try to make a life for myself. On the marginalized side, there is race (biracial, which means I don't really fit among whites or Mexican-Americans) and sexual orientation (gay). These aspects of my identity put me at a disadvantage in our society.

The United States is set up in such a way as to provide an advantage to those who are straight. The legal and tax systems, for example, privilege straight people by allowing them to marry and obtain legal recognition for their relationships. Straight people don't have to worry that they may face discrimination in the workplace or in housing, and they don't have to think twice about holding hands with their partner in a public place. Gay, lesbian, and bisexual individuals do not have these and many other privileges. In terms of race, I'm not Latino enough to "fit in" with other Mexican Americans even though—culturally speaking—I identify more closely with that group. And I don't really fit into the white group either. While I can certainly pass and most people treat me as white, with all the resulting privileges, my affiliation with that group begins to break down quickly when I start hearing talk about "dirty Mexicans," jokes about "wetbacks," and people conflating "Mexican" with "illegals," which happens a lot given how prominent the immigration issue is today. Identifying myself as a middle-aged gay man who is biracial, middle to upper-middle class, Christian, with no disabilities serves to give you an idea of where I am positioned within the stratification system in the United States. It is a somewhat odd position in that it is not status consistent.

Relating this background back to the question of friendship, in those areas in which I am privileged, I move in rather homogenous social circles. Conversely, in the areas of race and sexual orientation, I have interacted primarily with those who are different from myself. In other words, I've had the opportunity to befriend a diverse group of people, perhaps more opportunity than most; but those opportunities were not equally distributed across the various aspects of my identity. Becoming friends requires two things: (1) the opportunity to meet and interact and (2) the individual choice and effort to become friends, based on variables like shared interests, values, and what is commonly referred to as "chemistry." Take age, for example. Outside of our extended families, we live in a society that is very much age-segregated. Our educational system is set up according to age and our career trajectories are largely based on age as well (though we are more likely to call it "experience," the two are highly correlated). So, I actually have very few friends who are ten or more years my junior or senior, and this is where my experience is typical of many in our age-segregated society. The few friends I've made who are different in age were made once my education was complete and I had started my career, where one is perhaps more likely to meet people of more diverse ages, at least among those who are in more senior positions. What this example highlights is the relevance of social context: my social context has not provided me with many opportunities to befriend people of noticeably different ages. At those rare times when I do have the opportunity, then the element of choice or preference enters the picture—as reflected in similar interests and values, not to mention the chemistry mentioned above. Of those people I've met who are significantly older or younger, only one has become a close friend of mine.

The same processes are at work with regard to class, religion, and ability. First, do I inhabit a social context in which it is possible for me to meet many people who are different from me in terms of status? Not really. We live in a society that is highly segregated by class, so not many opportunities exist. Christianity dominates our society. And when you consider that I went to Catholic-affiliated schools for college and graduate school and currently work at a Lutheran-affiliated school, the odds are perhaps even slimmer that I'd meet people of other religions. Of course, there are non-Christians at all of these institutions, but the opportunities to meet and befriend them are still few. The same holds true for ability: I've had very limited opportunities to befriend those of different abilities because my social context does not include many who are different from myself in this area. In other words, like the majority of Americans, my social context is pretty homogenous in terms of age, class, religion, and ability, minimizing my opportunity to meet and befriend people who are different from myself in these areas. Again, it is only after opportunity itself is present that the element of choice or preference enters the picture: of the very few people who are different from me in these ways, with whom do I share enough interests, values, and chemistry to become friends? As it turns out, there is only one whom I consider to be a close friend who is different from me in any of these dimensions.

When it comes to race, gender, and sexual orientation, the picture changes dramatically. Starting with race, *all* of my good friends and even the vast majority of my acquaintances are different from me. This is one of many areas where the experience of racial minorities is vastly different from the white majority. It is much more difficult for racial minorities to live their lives apart from the white majority and so we are continually faced with racial differences. While I've met some people who are both white and Latino, they are very few in number. Perhaps because I pass as white and I move in largely white circles, most of my friends and close friends are white. In fact, having white friends is so common that I easily take it for granted. When reading the sociological literature on friendship patterns, however, it is immediately apparent that it is anything but common for the vast majority of one's friends to be of a different race than oneself. When one is biracial, however, it is difficult to *not* be friends with those of different races.

With gender there are far more opportunities to meet people of the opposite sex given that men and women comprise roughly equal portions of the population. There are other factors involved, however. Consider how sex-segregated our society is, not to mention the fact that, when a man and a woman get together, others expect there to be a romantic involvement rather than a strictly friendly relationship. The cultural norms guiding the interaction between men and women are so strong that many feel it is impossible for men and women to simply be friends. However, as a gay man, my position has been different. It is easy for me to befriend women because there is no possibility for a romantic relationship. In fact, for that reason, it is often easier to be friends with women than it is with men. If another man is gay, and assuming we're both single, we have to take the time to establish the nature of our relationship: strictly friends or romantic potential? Of course, it is rare to directly address the question, so much time and energy is spent trying to figure out where I stand vis-à-vis another gay man. If the man is straight, there's definitely no sexual attraction on his part and, while there may be no sexual attraction on my part either, he needs to be confident in knowing that. Again, a straight man is never likely to ask, nor am I likely to offer. Instead, we have to take the time to figure it out, or at least he does. And if he's not comfortable with gay men to begin with, he's not going to take the time. I have been friends and even close friends with straight men, but only very few. Like many gay men, most of my male friends are gay. And I have had many close friends who are women, both straight and lesbian. So, while not as diverse as my friendships in terms of race, my friendships in terms of gender and sexual orientation have been pretty diverse. Atypically so, in fact; and this depends largely on social context.

Again, the sociological literature to be covered in chapter 1 strongly indicates that we are not likely to have close friends who are demographically different from ourselves. So, while my friendship pattern seems completely normal to me, it does not fit what one would expect after looking at the data. Accordingly, my social circumstances and my choices have not fit the normal pattern.

In this way, I'm not typical. Being biracial and gay has a lot to do with it. Those are the areas where I'm most obviously not average. As a racial minority, I can't help but interact with a majority of people who are different in terms of race. As a sexual minority, the same holds true *and* it has consequences for my interactions with people along the lines of gender, as described above.

Learning that I didn't fit the typical friendship pattern is what raised my curiosity in this area and triggered my sociological imagination. While the pattern of demographic homogeneity among one's friends has been well established, what intrigued me was that I could deviate from that pattern so much and not really think anything of it. I've taken it completely for granted and it made me wonder about others whose close friendships did not fit the pattern. When I tried to find information about these atypical friendships, I realized there really was not very much at all known or written about them. That makes sense: they are in the minority, after all. But I think it's a very important minority to understand: those who have bucked the trend of homogeneity and have established close friendships with those who are demographically different from themselves. To me, that speaks to what is sorely lacking in our society: the ability to draw connections and build bridges between diverse groups of people. If we can't do that in our personal lives, how can we ever think we can accomplish it on a wider, societal scale where problems like institutionalized discrimination are built right into the social fabric? This is what inspired the research presented in this book: the idea that we have much to learn about bringing diverse groups of people together from those close friendships that do not fit the expected pattern, those unlikely friendships that actually pose a challenge to the status quo in our society and question the legitimacy of our system of social stratification based on qualities like race, gender, sexual orientation, class, religion, age, and ability.

## A Brief Methodological Overview

As my own experiences with friendship made clear to me, the consequences of our social structure and individual choices extend beyond the simple lack of opportunity for diverse individuals to meet and befriend one another. Our friendship patterns in which we are most likely to befriend those who are most like ourselves in terms of race, gender, sexual orientation, and so on—what is known as homophily among social scientists—has consequences for society as a whole. If most friendships are limited to those who are similar to ourselves, how strong can our social fabric be?[2] If, for example, we are still segregated by race in terms of our close, intimate social circle, can we really fool ourselves into believing that we live in a fully integrated society? De Souza Briggs identifies the social bonds between diverse groups of people as "bridging ties," and these ties are of crucial importance because they "mitigate against economic inequality" and such ties "are essential to the development of broader identities and broader communities of interest" (2002, 42-43).[3] These bridging ties are of crucial importance to a free and democratic society. It is the *absence* of such ties, however, that most previous research has emphasized, not the bridging ties that already exist. There is a paucity of systematic studies that concentrate on close friendships that serve as bridging ties between diverse groups of people. To begin closing this gap in our sociological understanding of friendship, this book directs attention to the minority of friendships that *do* serve as bridging ties. With this goal in mind, I have set out to address the following research questions:

(1) At the theoretical level, what do friendships crossing socially constructed boundaries (including race, gender, sexuality, class, religion, age, and ability) *have in common* in terms of the dynamics involved in bridging the gap between individuals who are different? At the same time, what makes the various social boundaries distinct from one another in the context of friendship?

(2) How do individuals define and interpret the relevance of socially constructed boundaries in the context of their close friendship?

(3) What role does the social boundary play in the initial emergence and development of the friendship?

(4) What circumstances encourage close friendships that cross socially constructed boundaries and what is the relationship between these circumstances and the individuals involved?

(5) What relevance do outside relationships have on the internal dynamics of the friendship?

(6) What are the interpersonal techniques used by the individuals in the friendship pair to circumvent or overcome the apparent obstacle posed by the socially constructed boundary?

The remaining question then is how did I go about studying these friendships that go against the major trends toward homophily in our society?

Since the friendships under study—friendships that break down socially constructed boundaries—are relatively rare, it was necessary to engage in an exploratory and descriptive project utilizing a qualitative research design. (For a much more detailed consideration of the research methods used for this project, please see Appendix A.) There have been other studies in this area of social psychology; however, there are limitations to this past research that I hope to rectify here. Past research focuses on a single demographic difference at a time, and more often than not, that difference is race, especially blacks versus whites (Rawlins 2009; Rude 2009; Tropp 2007; and Korgen 2002[4] are but three examples). Most past research focuses exclusively on children and young adults (such as Feddes, Noak, and Rutland 2009; Kawabata and Crick 2008; and Crystal, Killen, and Ruck 2008), especially within educational settings such as schools and residence halls (see, for example, Trail, Shelton, and West 2009; Shook and Fazio 2008; and Saenz, Ngai, and Hurtado 2007). Beyond that, much research is restricted to neighborhoods, work, or church environments (including Dwyer 2010; Stolle, Soroka, and Johnston 2008; Letki 2008; and Yancey 1999).

In addition, most of these studies are statistical in their analysis, which is highly useful in providing reliable and generalizable data, though such generalizability is restricted to the context of the study—a school, residence hall, neighborhood, and so on. Sampling is especially challenging when focusing on these friendships because of how uncommon they are: it is extremely difficult to identify the entire population of such friendships and obtain a random sample for inclusion in a survey that could then provide us with statistics that are generalizable to the entire population. Moreover, a statistical analysis is decidedly restricted compared to the rich data about human and interpersonal experiences to be gathered through qualitative methods. Intensive interviewing offered the most effective form of data collection given the nature of the topic and the depth of information that could be obtained from those being interviewed.

Even in those instances where researchers have pursued a more qualitative approach, the focus has been on only one of the friends involved (see Rude 2009) or the two friends were interviewed separately without the opportunity for a joint discussion on the topic (see Korgen 2002). This is especially incongruous since the focus of the research—friendship—is about a relationship between two people. Accordingly, the unit of analysis should not be restricted to the individual, but should include both members of the friendship pair *relating* to one another. Finally, as noted by Rude (2009), most research on friendship has actually been completed in the absence of a definition of friendship. It is therefore difficult to determine whether the term "friendship" has been used consistently across the many studies that focus on it. For this reason, I lay out a specific definition for friendship in chapter 1. Given the shortcomings of past research, I set out to complete a qualitative research project using intensive interviews to gather rich data from both parties in the friendship both separately and in a joint interview. These individuals ranged in age from late teens through retirement. Additionally, the friendships studied here are to be found in a variety of contexts—not just schools, churches, workplaces, or neighborhoods.

In terms of sampling and recruiting research participants, my goal was to have equal numbers of friendships representing several of the major socially constructed boundaries in our society. I originally intended that they would include race, class, gender, and sexual orientation as the primary focus of the study given their centrality in the study of social stratification. In addition, there would be a secondary focus on additional social boundaries for comparison purposes, including religion, age (where the friends are more than ten years apart in age), and ability. However, early on in the research process, it became apparent that identifying and recruiting friends who bridge the social boundary of class was amazingly difficult, and I have come to a renewed appreciation for how class-segregated we are as a society. This is a topic that will be taken up in later chapters. For now, it is sufficient to say that class had to be removed as one of the primary social boundaries studied. Instead, class was included among the secondary boundaries. The boundaries in this category are no less important than race, gender, or sexual orientation. In fact, given the challenge in identifying and recruiting friendships that cross class lines, that particular social boundary may be of crucial importance for future research. In this project, however, the secondary social boundaries simply provide the basis for additional comparisons.

In the end, I collected data on ten friendships that crossed the racial divide, ten crossing gender lines, ten crossing sexual orientation, and ten crossing the secondary categories of class, religion, age, and ability (see Table P.1). The total number of interviews was 120. (For a complete list of the research participants and the socially constructed boundaries they crossed, see Appendix B. This appendix will also be useful in keeping track of the interviewees throughout the book.)

Table P.1: Sample Size for Each Category

| Social Boundary Crossed | Pairs | People | Interviews |
|---|---|---|---|
| Race | 10 | 20 | 30 |
| Gender | 10 | 20 | 30 |
| Sexual Orientation | 10 | 20 | 30 |
| Class | 3 | 6 | 9 |
| Religion | 3 | 6 | 9 |
| Age | 3 | 6 | 9 |
| Ability | 1 | 2 | 3 |
| TOTAL | 40 | 80 | 120 |

From there, and using a referral or snowball process to identify and recruit research participants, I attempted to diversify the sample as much as possible. For example, in the friendships crossing racial lines, there are men and women, gay and straight, and people of a variety of different races. Many friendships include a white person, but others do not, including, for example a friendship between a black and an Asian person or a Latino and a Native American. Among the friendships focusing on gender, there are people of different races and orientations. Sometimes both are straight. Sometimes one is straight and the other isn't. Sometimes one is lesbian and the other is a gay man. The same is true for all the other categories: one will find much diversity within each even though the focus of the interviews was primarily on that single social boundary in question. This allowed me to ask participants to compare the relevance and impact of different social boundaries within their friendship. By maximizing the diversity within the sampled population, I was able to play up on a particular strength of qualitative, inductive analysis: it permits the researcher to create a more comprehensive theoretical understanding of the phenomenon in question. In terms of overall demographics, the sample was 44 percent male and 56 percent female (N=80); 80 percent white and 20 percent black, Latino, Asian, and Native American; and represented a full spectrum of ages, from 20 to 65+ years of age. In addition, the friendships included ranged from one year old to those lasting over 20 years. Of course, the findings from such a sample cannot be generalized in the same way that statistical data from a random sample can be. Then again, these friendships are rare to begin with and are not representative of friendships in general. Again, our focus is on the exceptions, not the norm.

In order to provide as comprehensive a picture of each friendship as possible, I decided to interview *both* of the friends. This is particularly important when considering that each one may remember different things about their friendship or remember events in their friendship differently. Moreover, each one would have a unique perspective on the role and relevance of race, gender, sexual orientation, and so on. within their friendship given that they would occupy different sides of the social boundary in question. As a result of these considerations, I interviewed each friend separately. I then interviewed the two friends together, using some of the same questions and adding a few new ones. The point of the paired interview was not to rehash the same information already provided in their one-on-one interviews, but to provide the two friends the opportunity to engage in a conversation with one another about the socially constructed boundary they've bridged—a conversation that I could witness. Thus, each friendship studied included three separate interviews. These interviews ranged from one to six hours in length, averaging between two and three hours each. The interviews were recorded and then transcribed.

## Overview of the Rest of the Book

This book will begin with a focus on friendship in general and the importance of bridging ties in fostering social cohesion. In chapter 1, I will examine how friendship is understood by social scientists, including patterns of friendship and our current understanding of why friendships tend to conform to the social divisions within our society. Subsequent chapters focus on the actual process involved in crossing the noted socially constructed boundaries as well as the relevance of those boundaries for the friendships. Chapter 2 examines the structural and contextual circumstances out of which these friendships emerge in the first place and the role the social boundary plays in the development of the friendship. The socio-cultural, institutional, group, and individual contexts are all very important variables that can prevent these friendships from materializing in the first place; but, if conditions are favorable in all of these contexts, friendships that cross socially constructed boundaries are possible.

Chapter 3 moves our focus within the friendships themselves, examining how the research participants see the impact of the social boundary on their friendship overall. This focus will take two different directions: What do socially constructed boundaries have in common? And what separates each social boundary, distinguishing it from the others? I will show that the interviewees assess the overall impact of race, gender, sexual orientation, and so on very differently. Even so, it is possible to place these very different social boundaries within a single conceptual model for understanding their relevance for friendships. The result is that friendships crossing socially constructed boundaries go through several rather predictable stages of development with regard to the impact of the social boundary in question.

Chapter 4 maintains the focus within the friendships themselves, examining the interpersonal techniques used by the two friends to manage the socially constructed boundary. While they are not always conscious of doing so, these friends are making a mutual effort to ensure that the social boundary does not cause problems within their friendship. Finally, in chapter 5, I take a step back and provide an overall assessment of what friendships crossing social boundaries have in common in terms of the dynamics involved. Again, we will hear from the interviewees themselves as they attempt to identify what has made their friendships possible, successful, and important in their lives. And we will see how these friendships challenge our system of social stratification by creating the bridging ties that connect diverse groups of people and strengthening the overall cohesiveness of society.

# Notes

1. What follows is an example of the autobiographical form of auto-ethnography (Ellis and Bochner 2000) in which the researcher him or herself becomes the subject of study.

2. As noted in chapter 1, the focus of this study was exclusively on platonic friendships. There is a growing body of literature on dating and marriage relationships between members of diverse groups. I chose not to focus on those relationships in order to focus on what I will describe in chapter 1 as "voluntary relations" that have no institutional support and recognition such as marriage. As argued by sociologists in the area of friendship, and as will be described in the first chapter, these relationships have a distinct character and relevance that is different from sexually intimate relations.

3. Here is the passage from Briggs in its entirety: "Bridging ties are important for two main reasons. First such ties mitigate against economic inequality and enhance productivity by improving access by out-groups to information, vouching, preparation, mentoring, and other keys to career success. . . . Politics is the second reason that bridging ties matter so much, especially for a large society becoming more socially diverse and institutionally complex. In classic rendering, crosscutting ties are essential to the development of broader identities and broader communities of interest. These are the social foundations of power sharing, without which the formal machinery of democratic government— competitive elections, freedom of assembly and of the press, and so on—tends to falter around the world. The absence of bridging ties undermines the reciprocity and learning crucial to democratic behavior" (2002, 42-43).

4. In the interest of full disclosure, Korgen (2002) and I actually began the conceptual work for our respective books together and presented a paper at the 49th Annual

Meeting of the Society for the Study of Social Problems (Korgen and Vela-McConnell 1999). At that point, however, Korgen and I set off in slightly different directions: Korgen focusing on interracial—and exclusively black-white—friendships while I decided to include multiple social boundaries within the same study. Given that we began our work together, however, the careful reader will note some similarities in methodological design and conceptual frameworks, although the final products are quite different from one another.

# Chapter 1

## Friendship and the Fabric of Society

*There's a fine line between friend and family. I mean family, you know . . . you don't choose your family. You choose your friends. I guess friends in some ways are even at a higher echelon than family, although you'd never break those family ties. You love your family, but sometimes you grow apart from the way your family is. I love my brother dearly, but you know, I don't think if we were in the same town, we'd spend an awful lot of our free time together. Maybe part of that is because we feel like we have that family tie. We don't have to work on that. But with friends, you're aware of the fact that you need to invest time in it to grow the friendship* [Bill, Interview 12A].

If it is the depth of the relationship that distinguishes a close friend, what then separates friends from family? We've all heard how "we can choose our friends, but we can't choose our family;" but what does this mean, exactly? Such a saying implies that we have certain obligations to family; obligations that we must meet even if we're not particularly close to or even like some family members. Similarly, we feel an obligation to "be there" for our friends, but the difference is that these relationships are entirely on a voluntary basis; so "being there" takes on a whole new level of significance when, and unlike with family, not being there is an option. For Bill, the fact that we're there for our friends even when the relationship is completely voluntary raises the status of these relationships even higher, in some ways, than our relations with family members. To be sure, dating and choosing a life partner is a voluntary decision in our society, but these relationships typically enjoy an institutional recognition by religion and the state that is not available to friendships and such recognition also provides structural support (such as employment benefits, tax laws, inheritance, and so on), a form of support that is not generally available for friends (Wiseman 1986; Rude 2009). In fact, friendship often takes a "back seat" to marriage, family, and even work relationships (Rawlins 2009, 131). For this reason, friendship bonds are considered by some to be fragile and "appear to have uncertain viability" (Wiseman 1986, 192).

However, it is the friends *themselves*—together with communal affirmation and support from their wider social circles—that nurture and maintain these relationships, something that requires active and ongoing participation by both parties. Given the absence of institutional recognition and support, friendships are fundamentally different from sexually intimate relations, particularly where marriage is an option. At the same time, friendships play an important role for social cohesion—the glue that holds society together. As noted by Spencer and Paul, "While the role of family in social cohesion has been acknowledged for centuries, friendship as a form of social glue has been given far less attention" (2006, 30). Because of the strong voluntary nature of these social ties, and, as will be seen below, their egalitarian nature, friendships are considered to be a particularly important form of "bridging tie" or "bridging social capital" that potentially plays a critical role in strengthening the fabric of society by providing the social glue that holds society together (de Souza Briggs 2007; Putnam 2000). Therefore, the study of friendship plays an important part in sociologists' larger understanding of social cohesion, a subject that has been central to the discipline since the founding of the field (Durkheim 1984; Tönnies 1988).

In this chapter, I will first briefly examine friendship itself, focusing specifically on what it is. As already argued, understanding friendship is key in understanding the larger issue of social cohesion, so we will then look at the sociological relevance of studying friendship. Nonetheless, patterns of friendship suggest that social cohesion is fractured along the lines of social inequality, such as race, gender, sexual orientation, class, age, religion, and ability. Accordingly, I will then turn our attention to the nature of social cohesion and those factors that serve to undermine it. Why do friendships reflect societal patterns of separation between diverse groups of people? Finally, we come to our central focus: friendships that serve to bridge the fracture lines in our society, challenging our system of social inequality and strengthening the overall cohesiveness of society.

## What Is Friendship?

Much has been written on friendship, and from a wide variety of perspectives, from philosophy, to biographical accounts, to research within the social sciences. Still, most attempts at writing about friendship have occurred in the absence of a common and precise understanding of what friendship actually is. Even psychologists and sociologists, who know the importance of defining the concepts they use and then operationalizing them for research purposes, have made the mistake of assuming that a common understanding of friendship exists and that, when people hear or use that term, they are all referring to the same kind of relationship. While sociologists have much to say about the role and relevance of friendship for society, there is no single understanding of what a friend is in the first place. This is even true for the layperson: everybody seems to know what is meant when we say "friend," but there is little consensus on the qualities of a good friend. Sociologist Ray Pahl notes that "while there is little common agreement on what counts as being a true friend . . . people will respond to given actions and behaviours by emphasizing and appreciating their quality: 'She was there when I needed her.' 'He was a really good friend.' However, there is no common agreement on any kind of qualitative scale. The notion of 'best friend' can be interpreted in different ways" (2000, 14). In fact, in today's world of social networking sites such as Facebook and MySpace, friends may not even have met each other in person and yet still consider one another to be in a close relationship. While such friendships are "easy to enter," they are nevertheless "easy to exit because of the lack of offline interaction" (Vitak 2008, 78; see also Rheingold 1993; Wellman and Gulia 1999). Are "virtual friends" who never meet in person really "true friends?"

One source of difficulty in defining friendship is that the use of this word is highly dependent on context. Its meaning has changed over time, so historical milieu is of crucial importance in understanding what is meant by the term. Moreover, it can be used differently in different cultural contexts or even personal environments. For example, what one person calls a "friend" another might label an "acquaintance." Many of those interviewed noted that we tend to overuse the word "friend" in our culture, to the point where we may even identify people we just met and whom we hardly know as "friends." At a cocktail party, for example, we may say, "Meet my friend Jane" when introducing a person we just met to a colleague who has walked up to say hello. The excessive use of the term "friend," many believe, can cheapen the word and make us lose track of what friendship truly entails. Dave is one of those who worries about the overuse of the word "friend."

> *Most people confuse friendship and acquaintanceship. It's kind of like dropping a rock in a pond and seeing the ripples. You drop the rock, the first ring that you get, those are your close friends and then the next ring out is generally what people would call their friends, but are really just acquaintances; and then from there goes their colleagues and then it goes to people whom they work with and then it goes to people that they've had some type of social interaction with. The farther out you get, the less close it becomes; but most people confuse that. Colloquially, people say, "Oh, this is my friend," even if they may have met once or twice. I think most Americans don't have a good definition of what a friend is to begin with* [Interview 6A].

Like Dave, many of those interviewed made a point of separating out a close friend from an acquaintance or someone who is merely a friend. "The word 'acquaintance' implies a relationship much less significant than a friendship. In acquaintanceship, very little is revealed about oneself . . . and typically the relationship is a surface one" (Bell 1981, 22).

Another source of difficulty in defining friendship harkens back to Bill's observation above: where exactly is the line drawn between family and friends in a world where a friend can become "a part of the family" or a family member might also be a friend? Recognizing that the meaning of friendship is context-specific is the contribution of sociology to our greater understanding of the term. Whereas, for example, psychologists might focus on how friendships develop, for sociologists "the fundamental assumption is that friendship is socially patterned and must be understood in context. Ties of friendship are inherently social rather than personal and friendship is not a fixed, universal relationship, but takes its shape and form from the specific context in which it develops" (Spencer and Pahl 2006, 40).[1]

We know that friends are much more than acquaintances and are different from family, but what does friendship actually mean? This was a key question asked in the interviews for this study. Of course, there were as many answers as there were people interviewed. While everybody had a different understanding of friendship, some much more detailed than others, no one person presented a complete picture of what friendship is. On the other hand, there were many common characteristics that came up again and again among those interviewed: intimacy, camaraderie, support, affection, development, reciprocity, chemistry, history, contact, shared values, and voluntary affiliation.[2] No one person included all of these characteristics in his or her definition of friendship, but most mentioned three or four. For a single friend to exhibit all of these characteristics represents more of an ideal image of friendship: "[T]hey are at once the expression of the idealized imagery that talk about friends summons up and the widely shared wish for just such a relationship" (Rubin 1985, 7).

Friendship is one of those things where "we know it when we see it." Nevertheless, given the above-noted absence of a common definition for what friendship is in the first place, it is important to establish one for the purposes of this research project. We will understand close friendship to be an active[3] and freely chosen platonic relationship between two equals demonstrating a high degree of commitment toward each other and relating to one another in a variety of ways.[4]

## The Sociological Relevance of Studying Friendship

While we all know something about friendship based on our own personal experiences, the literature on the sociology of friendship is surprisingly thin, particularly with regard to how friendship fits in with the larger society. In fact, a number of authors have noted the lack of research and writing in this area (Pahl 2000; Pahl 2002; Spencer and Pahl 2006; and Eve 2002). Perhaps this is due in part to the seeming familiarity of friendship. At the same time, other areas within sociology are seen as much more central to the discipline: inequality and stratification, community, and social organization to name a few. There are, nonetheless, a number of reasons why studying friendship is sociologically relevant. While it is a form of intimate relationship, friendship—unlike most forms of intimate relationships—is entirely voluntary and based on the equality of those in the relationship. In addition, while friendships can be reduced to a focus on only two people, such dyadic relationships are a building block of social organization and are caught up in an interlocking network of relationships that are fundamental to civil society. As such, friendships are very much a part of the larger social order and are therefore subject to its influence. The social trends that shape our society, such as the move from small, traditional communities to large, impersonal metro-complexes, influence all relationships, including friendships.

Unlike the vast majority of the relationships that exist within our society, friendship between two people represents a voluntary association between equals in the sense that these relationships are freely entered into, maintained, and terminated without the need for contractual arrangements. In our society, we learn that "you choose your friends, not your family." We live in a highly rationalized and bureaucratized world where most relationships are governed by contract and require some form of organizational recognition. Our work relationships are but one example. Other examples include our economic relations (trade) and membership within groups (whether the nation itself or our "voluntary" organizations); even marriages are based on a contractual arrangement, whether actually written down (as in a Jewish marriage contract or a pre-nuptial agreement) or simply verbalized through vows made before witnesses. Civil marriages require one to purchase a license and go before a judge and witnesses. What makes the contractual nature of these relationships most evident is that they require some effort to break the relationship. Friendships, however, require no such legal or civil recognition, contract, fee, or license:[5]

> Friendship in our society is strictly a private affair. There are no social rituals, no public ceremonies to honor or celebrate friendships of any kind. . . . In our society, no clear lines mark the beginnings of a friendship; often none mark the ending either. . . . [F]or us, friendship is a *non-event*—a relationship that just *becomes,* that grows, develops, waxes, wanes and, too often perhaps, ends, all without ceremony or ritual to give evidence of its existence (Rubin 1985, 4-5).

Still, while not institutionalized, friendships are perceived as valid relationships at an informal level among the members of one's larger social network and they may—and often do—occur within an institutional context such as the work or school environment.

Friendships do not exist in a social vacuum. While these relationships are voluntary in and of themselves, they are subject to societal norms that guide our choices in friends, how we interact with our friends, how we judge a good friend, and our expectations of a friend (Blieszner and Adams 1992, 2). Insofar as we look to and follow these norms of friendship, they are not entirely a matter of free choice. Because our friendships follow predictable patterns, whether we are talking about the differences between men's and women's friendships; friendships among young people, adults, or the elderly; or the stages through which a friendship progresses, friendships betray the influence of our larger society, its structures and hierarchies (Spencer & Pahl 2006; Blieszner and Adams 1992; Rawlins 1992; and Bell 1981). This dichotomous balance between its voluntary nature on the one hand and the constraints of society on the other makes friendships sociologically interesting. "In studying friendships, one focuses on the most voluntary and least institutionalized of all social relationships. To understand how choice and constraint interact in friendship contributes to understanding how they operate in other, increasingly voluntary types of relationships" (Blieszner and Adams 1992, 3).

Equality is another key characteristic of friendship: contemporary friendships exist between those who recognize and treat one another as equals (Pahl 2000 and Bell 1981). The equal status of friends implies that there is no power differential between them. For example, there is no dependency by one party upon the other; not that there won't be times of need where one person needs help or needs to rely on the other,[6] but in these situations either party would be able to provide approximately the same amount of assistance if their situations were reversed. It is important that neither friend feel that she or he is being taken advantage of by providing more than her or his share of support (Rude 2009). In those relationships where there is a power imbalance, such as the dependency of a child on a parent or a worker on a boss, the sense of obligation is then more binding and compelling and the dependent is expected to reciprocate with honor and respect at the very least. Consequently, the relationship itself is less voluntary. Moreover, when there is an imbalance of this sort between potential friends—such as work colleagues—contempt, resentment, and prejudice are a likely result (Hudson and Hines-Hudson 1999; Allport 1954; Rude 2009). Because modern friends regard one another as equals, they generally follow a particular social pattern in that friends often occupy the same status level within our larger society—a point that is central to the purpose of this book. Allan and Adams note that

> many commentators have referred to the characteristic equality which imbues friendships. Essentially this refers to the respect each gives the other as a person and the acceptance that, despite potential difference, each attaches equivalent value to the other. . . . But as part of this construction of equality, friends usually—though not inevitably—share social and economic characteristics in common. This itself fosters a conception of social identity. Like the birds that

flock together, the social location of our friends often serves to confirm our own self-identity. They help us authenticate our place in the world, our standing within the hierarchies and divisions of society (1998, 191).

When there are differences between friends, there is an understanding that they still share an equivalent status. On the other hand, given the status differences based on race, gender, sexual orientation, class, and so on in our society, it is difficult for many to have close friendships that cross those "hierarchies and divisions." The result is that we tend to befriend those who share the same social and economic characteristics as ourselves.

In fact, there is oftentimes social pressure preventing people from establishing friendships with those considered to be "beneath" or even "above" themselves (Rawlins 2009; Pahl 2000; and Hutter 1978). The reason for this is that friendships between status levels challenge the relevance and legitimacy of the system of social stratification. Rules against fraternization are one example. While it is true that any given friendship is a private relationship between two individuals, a *pattern* of such friendships that cross the lines of social stratification becomes a public statement that calls the stratification system into question in the first place. Such a pattern has the potential to create a counter-culture (Pahl 2000).[7] As such these friendships—while rare—pose a threat to the established and taken-for-granted order of society and have the potential to move our society in the direction of increased egalitarianism. "A truly friendly society would, of course, be a classless society, and so, logically, giving a greater centrality and salience to pure friendship could be a powerful force for social change" (Pahl 2000, 162). For this reason, understanding these friendships that challenge our system of social stratification is essential for those who hope to see a "truly friendly society."

Turning this point around, to the extent that we maintain status homogeneity within our friendships—even if unconsciously—our friendships become an important means for legitimating and reinforcing the class structure of society. In fact, one may argue that such patterns of homogeneity in our personal relationships actually determine the amount of social stratification existing in a society (Laumann and Senter 1976).[8] As already mentioned and as will be detailed below, friends thus are more likely to be similar to one another in terms of race, gender, sexual orientation, and so on. This makes the particular friendships under study here all the more interesting because they are between individuals who live at different points within our stratification system. The friends disregard that socially constructed and externally imposed status inequality and instead create their own sense of status equality. They honestly see one another as equals, without power differences between them. While there are norms that guide friendship patterns and choices (among many other dimensions of friendship), the wholly voluntary quality of friendship makes it much easier to deviate from those norms and challenge the larger society in which those norms exist.

Friendship at its most basic level is between two people. Dyadic relationships such as these are the fundamental building blocks of social organization

(Simmel 1950) because it is here that relationships and social bonds are established. Again, this is what distinguishes a sociological approach to friendship from a psychological one: sociologists examine friendship as a piece of the larger society, as a microcosm of society and subject to the same structural principles and processes. In many ways, friendships embody our society, echoing its stratification system by being largely restricted to those individuals with the same social status.

Still, it is equally evident that friendships between two people are not as complicated as society as a whole. It thus falls under the heading of social psychology or "microsociology"—the study of small groups, the individuals who inhabit them, and the social order created within them. One of the dominant theoretical perspectives within social psychology is that of symbolic interactionism. As the name implies, this perspective highlights the importance of symbols—such as the relevance of language, body language, gestures, and appearance—in our interaction with one another (Blumer 1986). All of our words and behaviors have meaning that is interpreted by those around us. Moreover, we share those meanings and as a result are able to understand and relate to one another. Through our interaction, we begin to create social order such that our interactions and relationships begin to follow a predictable pattern. From this perspective, we create the social world around us—including the divisions of race, gender, sexual orientation, and so on—but of course, we are not exempt from its influence. So, dyadic relationships do not exist in a vacuum. They are very much a part of the larger society around them. And while we have the power to shape that society through our interaction with those around us, we are also subject to the influence of that wider society.

The issue of equality as already discussed above serves as an example. Our friendship patterns generally reflect the social stratification system that exists within our larger society, indicating that even our personal relationships are shaped by outside influences. However, because of the voluntary nature of friendship, we can choose to befriend those from different status levels when the opportunity presents itself (though such opportunities are comparatively rare given the stratified nature of our society). To the extent that we consider and treat our friends as equals, we pose a challenge to that existing stratification system. If enough of these friendships are formed, then we will reach what Gladwell (2002) identifies as a "tipping point" that can overturn the system of stratification as it is currently shaped. In other words, though our larger social context has much influence on our dyadic relationships, what occurs within these dyadic relationships can accumulate and influence the shape of that larger social context. As such, dyadic relationships like friendship represent the building blocks of society as a whole, especially when one considers that our friendships are likely to outnumber our partners or spouses. They are an integral part of larger networks of social ties that form the foundation for society. Consequently, looking at friendship strictly from a microsociological perspective overlooks the larger, structural relevance of these dyadic relationships (Eve 2002).[9] A social psychologist should never lose sight of the fact that the micro social order is an integral part of the macro social order (Allan and Adams 1998, 183).[10]

The study of friendships—and in this case, friendships that exist between individuals who inhabit different positions within our system of stratification— has much to reveal about the structure of society. As will be seen in this book, our social context—our group affiliations, institutions, and society as a whole— exerts much influence insofar as it limits our opportunities to meet people, particularly those who are different from ourselves, and establish a friendship in the first place. So, while the focus will be on dyadic friendships, it is necessary to continually recognize and point out how these relationships are woven into the fabric of other relationships and the larger structure of our society. On the other hand, I will also include a look at how these dyadic friendships influence and shape the individuals and groups who exist outside of that relationship.

Given that friendships are very much a part of the social order of our wider society, placing the topic of friendship within a larger sociological framework is important (see Rawlins 2009; Grief 2008; Spencer and Pahl 2006; Pahl 2002; Pahl 2000; Nardi 1999; Allan 1990; and Fischer 1982a). As one of the most fundamental forms of relationship, friendship is based on the same social bonds that are crucial for the emergence and viability of society. We will now turn our attention to the social cohesion that holds society together.

## Friendship and Social Cohesion

[Friendship is] more apt than love to connect a whole person with another person in its entirety; it may melt reserves more easily than love does—if not as stormily, yet on a larger scale and in a more enduring sequence. Yet such complete intimacy becomes probably more and more difficult as differentiation among men increases (Simmel 1950, 325-326).

Georg Simmel's observation regarding the potential of friendship to forge social ties is tempered by the reality of differentiation that actually keeps many people from establishing ties of friendship, potentially undermining an important source of the social bonds that hold society together. Without these fundamental social bonds, society may begin to deteriorate. In fact, sociologists—particularly those taking the social disorganization perspective—have seen evidence of such deterioration from the inception of the field of sociology to today. From this perspective, it is understood that technological, demographic (including urbanization), and cultural changes (including rationalization and bureaucratization) produce disequilibrium within society and personal disorganization within the lives of individuals (such as mental illness and alcoholism arising out of stress and the breakdown of intimate social relations) (Rubington & Weinberg 1995). In other words, social change is creating conditions that promote the breakdown of our social bonds. The ultimate result is the emergence of a "society of strangers" and a corresponding breakdown in social relationships (Vela-McConnell 1999).

For example, when asked about what the interviewees liked least about their friendships, the most common response was that they don't get to spend enough time with their friend because they're both so busy. While Katie feels close to her friend Ed (who was her interview partner for this study), and despite the fact that she has many people she knows and calls "friend," she still feels lonely. When asked what the word friend brings to her mind, Katie poignantly responded:

> *It's funny that you ask that because I've had an ongoing struggle within myself, wondering, "Who are my friends?" I feel like I have a lot of acquaintances, as any other person would call them, but to me I consider them to be my friends. Pretty much anybody I know I consider a friend, you know. But when it comes down to who are my good friends, who can I count on, who can I trust, or who's there for me, I feel like even though I have a lot of friends and I know a lot of people, a lot of times I feel kind of alone, like I don't have anybody who's really there, like below the surface. A lot of the friendships are really shallow and I struggle to know which ones are deep and which ones are not but seem that way. I just don't feel like I have anybody who's there for me or that I can talk to when I need a friend* [Interview 4A].

Katie's feeling of social isolation, at least in terms of her friends, is obvious. Moreover, she is questioning what really makes a friend, especially a good friend—one she can count on. This is an important question to answer and one that has not been adequately addressed by sociologists despite the long-standing interest in social disorganization.

Society relies on social bonds between individuals for its overall cohesiveness. In my past research (Vela-McConnell 1999), I sought to capture the underlying components of social cohesion with the concept of social affinity, which represents the empathy and identification between individuals and/or groups. Social affinity includes three elements: social consciousness, sentiment, and action. In other words, it is based on having an awareness and understanding of others, a sense of identification with those others, and an internal transformation in one's self that may also result in taking action on behalf of others (1999, 37-39). Together, these components foster the social bonds between individuals and even groups that lie at the heart of the classic notion of social cohesion.

The challenge we face today is to strengthen the cohesiveness of society by establishing social affinity between even diverse groups of people. This is no small challenge given how the world—through technological development and globalization—is becoming a much smaller place, a place where diverse people are brought closer together. At the most fundamental level the test of modernity is symbolized by the tension between proximity and distance: in a modern world, we are simultaneously close and removed—attached and detached from one another. And the question is, "How do we reconcile the two?" Ultimately, that which undermines social affinity also undermines social cohesion (Vela-McConnell 1999). While those taking the social disorganizational perspective point to large-scale social processes like the technological, demographic, and cultural changes noted above, it is possible to examine the breakdown of social cohesion at an even more fundamental level. Much of what divides society and jeopardizes the cohesiveness of society can be understood through the lens of proximity and distance, specifically spatial and social distance.[11]

## Spatial Distance and Structured Segregation

In his essay on "The Stranger," Simmel speaks specifically to the role of spatial relations on social relationships:

> [S]patial relations not only are determining conditions of relationships among men [and women], but are also symbolic of those relationships. . . . The spatial relations of proximity and distance are symbolic of the relative attachment and detachment between individuals, and one who is a stranger is "not bound up organically, through established ties . . . with any single [person] (1971, 143 & 145).

In both the literal and symbolic sense, the stranger is the person we encounter who comes from another place and who is therefore "foreign" to us. Being from another place, there are no "natural" connections or ties between strangers. In other words, being removed from us spatially, the stranger is also removed from us socially. While the stranger may be standing right in front of us, she or he is both near and far at the same time because the stranger is socially distant. Simmel points out that intimacy is based on the similarity of those involved in the relationship, so those whom we see as different from ourselves are socially distant. By implication, those who have different ascribed attributes—such as race, gender, sexual orientation, and so on—and even different achieved attributes—such as level of education, occupation, and social position—are strangers to us and thus socially distant (Vela-McConnell 1999).

Spatial proximity has been the subject of much research in the field of social psychology, particularly as it applies to the subject of attraction: physical proximity plays a central role in the establishment of relationships (Hipp and Perrin 2009; Segal, 1974; Festinger, Schachter, and Back, 1950). It is also particularly relevant for our understanding of why friends tend to be similar to one another in terms of the ascribed and achieved attributes mentioned above—what is known as "homophily" (Lazarsfeld and Merton 1954) or more specifically as "status homophily" (McPherson, Smith-Lovin, and Cook 2001).[12] Making friends with others is not simply a matter of choice. Instead, the options available to us when making decisions are first determined by our social context: circumstances present us with opportunities or withhold certain opportunities from us and only then can we make a choice among the options available. Individual choice as an explanation for friendship homophily is overemphasized in the sociological literature (Feld 1982). Instead, individuals can only make what Feld calls "focused choices," meaning their choices are constrained by the diversity of the groups in which they participate. The structural reasons for patterns of friendship homophily actually start with the arrangement of our physical environments and the opportunities (or lack thereof) for interacting with diverse others with which they present us. Indeed, this is a key tenant in the Chicago School of sociology (de Souza Briggs 2002).[13]

The line of research focusing on the physical separation of subgroups from one another goes all the way back to a classic sociological study by Festinger, Schachter, and Back published in 1959. Their study examined the spatial ecology of friendship formation, focusing on the formation of friendships between those residents of a neighborhood who first met each other in brief encounters as the individuals went about their daily routines of coming and going through the neighborhood. Meeting people simply by running into them on a consistent basis is what they termed "passive contacts" because they are more circumstantial and not actively sought out by the individuals.

The researchers found that there was a strong relationship between different elements of the spatial arrangement of the neighborhood and the establishment of friendships through passive contact, particularly the physical distance separating the residences of the individuals and the functional distance separating the residents (for example, they may be physically close, but separated by a stairway or other "obstruction" that minimizes passive contact). In other words, the *opportunity* to meet is a primary determinant in friendship formation.[14] Moreover, they point out that their research was in homogeneous communities and they speculate about the impact of a heterogeneous population on their findings, saying, "It seems likely that in such communities ecological factors will play some part, though a less important one, in determining sociometric structure" (Festinger, Schachter, and Back 1959, 59).

Clearly, our total population is anything but homogeneous. In spite of this, we live in notably segregated neighborhoods and this pattern is true not only in the United States but abroad as well (Johnston, Poulsen, and Forrest 2007). This is most evident with regard to class (Dwyer 2010) and race (Korgen 2002). For example, an analysis of census tract data indicates that class segregation in the U.S. has increased between 1970 and 2000, rising 50 percent between 1970 and 1990 and then going down slightly in the following decade (Massey and Fischer 2003). While the rate of racial segregation continues to fall, particularly in the Northeast and the Midwest, such segregation is still prevalent. As noted by de Souza Briggs, "Those rates remain incredibly high in absolute terms" and "the rate of decline is minimal in a number of large and hyper-segregated metros" (2002, 12). The result is that, when it comes to race, there are few opportunities to meet and interact with those of a different race within one's own neighborhood, particularly for whites (84 percent of whites live in predominantly white neighborhoods). While other races tend to be more experienced with integrated neighborhoods, they tend to be integrated with other racial minorities, not whites (2002, 13). The result is that many people, particularly whites, do not have as many opportunities to meet and befriend people of other races. While class and race present clear examples of spatial segregation, many urban areas are also segregated by sexual orientation, age, and even religion. As we will see later in this chapter, friendship patterns reflect those patterns of segregation. Given how common the spatial segregation of diverse groups really is in our society, friendship homophily comes as no surprise.

Spatial arrangements are important but not sufficient in producing opportunities for friendship. Regular interaction is also required (de Souza Briggs 2002). The environments in which regular activities organize our interaction include our institutions and group affiliations. After the impact of geography, our institutions also shape our opportunities for meeting people who are different from ourselves, and these institutions are often segregated in such a way that minimizes our contact with diverse populations. Take the institution of education as an example. Like the neighborhoods in which they are found, schools can also be rather homogeneous, reflecting the demographics of their area. In fact, public schools are increasingly segregated (Orfield 2001). If the neighborhood is dominated by one race, so are its public schools. Our work environments also serve to segregate us, further constricting our opportunities to meet and interact with diverse populations. This is particularly true with regard to gender and level of education (an element of socio-economic status), though it is less evident for race and religion (McPherson, Smith-Lovin, and Cook 2001, 432).[15] This trend of segregation even extends into our voluntary organizations (2001, 432).

As with our institutions, organizations, and neighborhoods, those who come together in social groups are also disproportionately homogeneous. Most friendships are established through regular contact and such contact is most typical ingroup activities. So the composition of those groups is of critical importance. As noted by Feld, "People tend to choose their friends from among those with whom they have regular contact in one or another of their focused activities; the set of people who are available through these foci tends to direct their choices to individuals with particular personal characteristics" (1982, 797). When comparing the relative impact of individual choice—or "choice homophily"—and prior group composition—also known as "induced homophily"—on friendship patterns, it is evident that group diversity is the strongest predictor of friendship homophily. In other words, the heterogeneity of the group results in greater heterogeneity in the composition of friendships within the group. A more homogeneous group results in increased homophily in the friendships within that group (McPherson and Smith-Lovin 1987). Individual choice is secondary to group composition in terms of relevance for friendship homophily. In fact, the homogeneity of social networks is self-reinforcing in that individuals are more likely to welcome as friends others who are similar to them (Blieszner and Adams 1992). This is where the combined and reinforcing impact of social

1992). This is where the combined and reinforcing impact of social context and opportunity structures on the one hand and individual choice on the other is most apparent: our social context shapes our opportunities to meet and befriend other people, and then the choices we make further shape and reinforce our social context and future opportunities.

## Social Distance and the Construction of Social Boundaries

While individual choice is pre-empted by the role of spatial proximity and distance, individuals still do make a choice and these choices are very much influenced by their own attitudes, values, and beliefs. In a sense, a cognitive barrier is built up between those of different races, genders, sexual orientations, classes, and so on—what I am terming a "socially constructed boundary." Such boundaries are based on "assumptions of difference" between those who identify with different racial, gender, and sexual orientation categories even when they "share the same physical space" (Korgen 2002, 21). It is important to keep in mind that these boundaries are socially constructed, but many people experience them as quite real in their impact because they are built right into the larger structures of society (Wittig 1992). As observed by Audre Lorde, "Too often, we pour the energy needed for recognizing and exploring differences into pretending those differences are insurmountable barriers. . . . This results in voluntary isolation." (1984, 533). Hence, while spatial arrangements within society have a primary impact on friendship formation, some of the established pattern of friendship homogeneity is a direct result of choices individuals make based on the social boundaries created by their own prejudices toward and stereotypes of those who are different from themselves.

While physical proximity is important in the initial development of friendships, this is later superseded by other similarities, such as in the beliefs and values that are at the core of culture (Newcomb 1963). Returning to Simmel, because the stranger comes to us from a place that is spatially removed from ourselves, she or he is also removed from us socially, making social distance key to understanding friendship homophily and the challenges to social cohesion in our diverse world. Interacting with those who are similar to ourselves helps us to avoid cognitive dissonance—those inconsistencies that produce psychological tension—and validates our sense of who we are (Vela-McConnell 1999; Newcomb 1963, 1961, 1956; Byrne, 1971). The more similar people are, the more likely they are to understand each other (Simmel 1988). It should come as no surprise then that we are much more likely to socialize with those who are similar to ourselves (Gonzales, *et al.* 1983). However, insofar as individuals come from different cultures, they are socially distant from one another because of these dissimilarities and as a result they have a tendency to feel uncomfortable and be less understanding of the other. This lack of understanding and comfort can easily give rise to prejudice, which further distances the strangers from one another.

It is the separation of groups, and the socially constructed boundaries between different groups that allows for the emergence of prejudice and social distance. Gordon Allport first described this separation of groups in his classic book *The Nature of Prejudice* (1954). In this book, he described how in-groups and out-groups are created and with what effect. In-groups are characterized by a sense of "we-ness" and identification with the other members of the group. Because members of the group share a common identity based on their similarity to one another, a strong sense of social cohesion emerges within the group. In-groups are characterized by "feelings of loyalty, solidarity, attraction, and cooperation" (Vander Zanden 1987, 404; see also Shibutani and Kwan 1965). Ironically, this social cohesion is strengthened when the group is able to separate from those who are different and who do not belong within the group, what Allport calls the out-group (see also Lauderdale *et al.* 1984; Wilder and Shapiro 1984). As described by Shibutani and Kwan (1965), "The other . . . is seen as representative of a *different* category. We feel apprehensive before a creature unlike ourselves, for we are not sure of what he [or she] will do. Even after acquaintance there remains a residue of *uncertainty*—a vague apprehension, especially if the stranger maintains his [or her] reserve." Given the uncertainty and apprehension, it is easy to perceive them as a threat because the identity of the out-group undermines the legitimacy of the in-group identity and this feeling of threat opens the door for prejudice, stigmatization, discrimination, and even hostility (Baumann 2007; Moreland 1985; Blumer 1958; Speier 1941). These differences between the in-group and the out-group, as well as the prejudice and stigmatization that go with them, are a matter of in-group definition, authority, and power (Reicher 2007), and they are easily reified, taking on a reality of the group's own making. By implication, the in-group also begins to *create* differences between themselves and the out-group, differences that were not there before (Sherif *et al.*, 1961; Markides and Cohn, 1982); and once the boundaries between groups are drawn, the members of the in-group will see the other group through the lens of those socially constructed boundaries and with an ethnocentric bias that favors the in-group over the out-group (Tajfel *et al.* 1971). All of this creates social distance between the two groups, "a subjective sense of being set apart from (as opposed to being near to) certain people" (Vander Zanden 1987, 408).

There are a number of consequences of the social distance that is created through the separation between in-groups and out-groups. While it is acknowledged that close social ties between members of different groups are a challenge, social distance also reduces the likelihood of even weak ties (Hipp and Perrin 2009). Social distance leads to greater social exclusion on the part of one group toward another. Moreover, such exclusion escalates as each group further excludes the other (Jasínska-Kania 2009). As a result, the social boundaries between groups have the potential to get larger over time. In addition, there is a direct connection between the social distance discussed here and the segregation discussed above. Neighborhood segregation patterns not only increase social distance between groups (White, Kim *et al.* 2005), but it appears that social distance may also *produce* these same neighborhood segregation patterns even in the absence of housing discrimination (Fossett 2006a, 2006b). Finally, and of most direct relevance to the research presented in this book, those who have a strong in-group connection and sense of identity are less likely to establish friendships with those who are members of an out-group (Levin 2003).

In sum, social and spatial distance create a situation in which it is difficult for those from diverse backgrounds to meet and establish friendships with those who are different. Because of the segregation of our neighborhoods and institutions such as schools, churches, and work environments along the lines of class, race, sexual orientation, and so on, we have fewer opportunities to meet anyone other than those who are already similar to ourselves in these ways. Consequently, much of our freedom to choose our friends is removed without our noticing it. In addition, such segregation is tied to the emergence of socially constructed boundaries that give rise to prejudice, stigmatization, and discrimination toward those who are different. These attitudes and behaviors then shape the choices we do make when selecting our friends. They also shape our decisions in terms of where we live, which may further the segregation between diverse groups of people. Ultimately, social and spatial distance are mutually reinforcing and together they chip away at the empathy and identification required to create the social ties that are so important for society. In other words, as social and spatial distance increases, the possibility of establishing social affinity with diverse others becomes increasingly difficult, thus jeopardizing the basic cohesiveness of society (Vela-McConnell 1999). We will now turn our attention to the evidence for these divisions within our society as reflected in the existing patterns of friendship segregation.

## Patterns of Friendship Segregation

[F]riendship is . . . fundamentally egalitarian, and one of the strongest barriers to pure friendship is structurally conditioned inequality (Pahl 2000, 162).

By interacting only with others who are like ourselves, anything that we experience as a result of our position gets reinforced. It comes to typify "people like us" (McPherson, Smith-Lovin, and Cook 2001, 415-416).

As we learned in identifying what characterizes close friendships, these relationships are based on strong social bonds between two people. Accordingly, these and all intimate relationships establish the social cohesion that is the foundation of society: the social ties upon which all our institutions rest. Given our friendship patterns, however, it can be argued that the foundation of society is fractured along the lines of race, gender, sexual orientation, and so on. Our close, intimate ties do not extend to everybody. Instead, we are highly selective when it comes to establishing such friendships. So our bonds can be strong within groups of people, even when the only connection between them may be a demographic similarity, but may in fact be tenuous between different groups of people. Not surprisingly, friendships are based on shared interests, values, and good chemistry, but this simply reflects the choices we make *after* we have had the opportunity to meet people. With this principle in mind, it is important to examine the general friendship patterns that exist and dominate our society in more detail—patterns that reflect the very real divisions within our society.

It comes as no surprise that the friendships of the past were segregated along racial lines, or along other social boundaries such as gender, sexual orientation, class, religion, and so on. After all, society itself was much more segregated in these ways in the past. Nevertheless, much sociological research indicates that those same patterns of friendship segregation persist, reflecting the patterns of social stratification that exist in today's society (Rawlins 2009). Again, this tendency to befriend individuals who are similar to oneself in terms of different social status dimensions—such as race, gender, age, religion, education, and so on—is known as "homophily." Without necessarily intending to, we generally prefer to make friends with those who are similar to ourselves, and not just in attitudes, interests, and values, but similar in demographics as well.

The choice of friends with a similar social status is quite common and the trend is so strong that it cannot be considered a random occurrence (Verbrugge 1977). Such bias toward homophily in friendship is most pronounced for those who may be considered "best" friends. Not only are we more likely to befriend those who are demographically similar to ourselves—those who are socially proximate—but the few diverse friendships we do establish also appear to dissolve at a higher rate, especially cross-gender and cross-racial friendships (McPherson, Smith-Lovin, and Cook 2001). We are more likely to maintain friendships with those who are demographically similar to ourselves.

Homophilous friendship patterns do, however, vary among different social groups. Race and ethnicity remain the strongest divisions within our intimate relationships to this day.[16] Even so, such homogeneity is not equally distributed among all races. Whites tend to have the most homogeneous social networks. African Americans and Hispanics fall in the middle, while smaller racial and ethnic groups have the most heterogeneous social networks. On the other hand, while racial and ethnic homophily is the most pervasive, it appears that the trend is decreasing over time. Current research indicates that, as the racial diversity of the U.S. population has increased, the homogeneity of social networks has decreased (McPherson, Smith-Lovin, and Brashears 2006, 361).[17]

After race, homophily in terms of age is the strongest because much of our society is segregated by age (McPherson, Smith-Lovin, and Cook 2001). Age is followed by gender. What makes gender homophily particularly interesting is that, unlike with race and other demographic variables, men and women represent roughly equal portions of the population. The fact that homophily nevertheless is present in our gender relations indicates that much of the homogeneity in our friendship patterns with regard to gender is by selective choice rather than due to the lack of opportunities available. For example, our families tend to be diverse in terms of gender, so we have no lack of opportunity to learn how to interact with those of different genders. Even so, families demonstrate a rudimentary form of gendered divisions, such as in chores (Lorber 1994). It is when we move outside of the family that gender segregation really begins to take hold, particularly in the labor force and in our voluntary associations. Be that as it may, there are still opportunities available to befriend both men and women. The fact that we don't take advantage of those opportunities indicates that we self-segregate in terms of gender as a matter of choice, not just circumstance. As with race, gender homophily is not equally distributed throughout our population. Relationships tend to be more heterogeneous in terms of gender among young people and the highly educated. Gender homophily is also less common among whites and more common among African Americans and Hispanics (McPherson, Smith-Lovin, and Cook 2001; see also Rawlins 2009). Unlike race, though, current research indicates that gender homophily has remained stable over time (McPherson, Smith-Lovin, and Brashears 2006).

Religious homophily is also apparent, although it is not as strong as it is for race. Then again, this pattern varies for different religions and denominations as well as between metropolitan and small-town environments.[18] For example, there tends to be less religious homophily in small towns where residents are more likely to be exposed to those of different denominations whereas in larger cities, it is easier to surround one's self with those who share one's religion (McPherson, Smith-Lovin, and Cook 2001). On the other hand, there is typically less religious diversity in small towns than in larger cities where members of many of the world's religions—Christianity, Judaism, Islam, Buddhism, and so on—come together in the urban environment. Most such research on religious homophily, however, focuses on different denominations within the Christian faith. There is little data on homophily patterns in friendship in which the religious differences are in terms of faith, not denomination; for example, how likely are Christians to befriend Muslims and Muslims to befriend Jews or Buddhists? It is not difficult to imagine that a faith-differentiated pattern of religious homophily would be stronger than it is for different denominations within the Christian faith.

Class or socio-economic status (SES) can be thought of in terms of different dimensions: education, occupation (reflecting different levels of prestige), and wealth/income. The evidence suggests that homophily based on education and occupation is just as strong as homophilous patterns for gender and religion. When looking at property as a sign of wealth, the homophilous pattern is even stronger (McPherson, Smith-Lovin, and Cook 2001), especially at the very top and the very bottom ends of the class system (Simkus 1995). Class represents a status that can change over the course of one's lifetime, raising the question, "What happens to the pattern of class homophily as one's class status changes?" Research indicates that, as one's class status changes, one's friendship network also changes. Suitor and Keeton (1997) focused on this question in their longitudinal study of women who went back to college as adults. They found that, after ten years, the women would seek support for school and work from those with similar educational levels. Accordingly, as their status changed, their support network changed with it, but only in terms of support in those areas relevant to that status change: school and work.

There is very little research on the friendship demographic patterns of gays, lesbians, and bisexuals, which represents a major gap in our knowledge of homophily. It also betrays a research bias in favor of heterosexuals, even among social scientists whom one might expect would be more interested in diversity in all its forms. In the little research available, it was found that at least three quarters of gays and lesbians identify their best friend as also gay or lesbian. Among the 161 gay men included in this study, 82 percent identified their best friend as being either gay or bisexual, implying that only 18 percent have a best friend who is straight or whose sexual identity is unknown. Of the 122 lesbians studied, 76 percent identified their best friend as lesbian or bisexual, leaving 24 percent who are straight or unknown (Nardi 1992a, 114; see also Nardi 1992b and Price 1999). There was no comparable data for straight people indicating what percentage of these individuals had a best friend who is gay, lesbian, or bisexual. Given the fact that sexual minorities are much more likely to encounter the heterosexual majority than that majority is to encounter the gay, lesbian, or bisexual minority, it is easy to predict that the percentages are far smaller. Nevertheless, this is an empirical question that remains to be answered. In addition, anecdotal evidence suggests that gender makes a difference in the pattern of homophily when it comes to sexual minorities. For example, gay men may be more likely to befriend straight women than straight men, although this pattern may be less evident among lesbians. Still, all of this is conjecture based on the challenges I faced in finding gay/straight friendship pairs to interview for this study.

I found no research on the friendship demographic patterns with respect to differences in ability, which represents yet another major gap in our knowledge of homophily. It also betrays a bias in favor of the able-bodied. While it may be assumed that a similar pattern of homophily exists, this too is an empirical question that requires study. Even if such an assumption is accurate, we have no idea how strong the homophilous pattern might be.

The overall pattern of homophilous friendships is well established by past social research: we tend to maintain highly homogenous circles of friends in terms of race, age, gender, religion, class, and sexual orientation (Rawlins 1992; White 2006). And while there isn't any direct research on homophily in terms of ability, if the trend holds true, similar friendship patterns can be expected. Rawlins concludes that "friendships are statistically more likely to reproduce macrolevel, palpable social differences than to transcend them" (2009, 138; see also DeMott 1995 and Rawlins 1992). The fracture lines that run through the basic cohesiveness of society, lines that follow the course of social differences and inequality, are reflected in our friendship patterns. In turn, friendship homophily reinforces these divisions and socially constructed boundaries that are a very real part of our society.

## Friendships and Bridging Ties

Anthropologists have long acknowledged the importance and relevance of friendships and friendship networks in creating social cohesion (Eve 2002). Friendships and other informal relationships serve to bring people together into larger and larger networks, ultimately weaving together the fabric of society. Friendships also have the potential to help heal the rifts in our society created by the socially constructed boundaries of race, gender, sexual orientation, class, religion, age, and ability. A strong social fabric requires the inclusion of all its diverse peoples. And while inequality and discrimination are built right into the structure of our society and must be addressed at the institutional level, friendships that breach these social boundaries can have an important role to play in creating that "truly friendly society" described by Pahl (2000).

As understood by Tönnies and later by Wolfe, social cohesion—as a macro manifestation of micro-level social bonds—entails a sense of mutual or moral obligation. In discussing the idea of social capital, a contemporary concept that is of central importance in discussions of social cohesion given its recognition of the value of "mutual support, cooperation, [and] trust" (Putnam 2000, 22), Putnam argues that these mutual obligations are best captured within "networks of community engagement" because such networks "foster sturdy norms of reciprocity" (2000, 20). In contrast with the "specific" reciprocity between individuals, he assigns particular importance to norms of "generalized reciprocity," or the idea of doing something for another without expecting anything particular in return, because it fosters a sense of trust that "lubricates social life." This is especially true when there is "frequent interaction among a *diverse set of people*" (2000, 21; emphasis mine). Consequently, there are both individual and collective aspects of social capital; and at the macro level, social capital benefits from diversity of people.

At the same time, social capital varies along multiple dimensions, one of which is the "distinction between *bridging* (or inclusive) and *bonding* (or exclusive)" social capital (Putnam 2000, 22). Bonding social capital is of particular importance at the more micro level of fostering a sense of solidarity among individuals and the specific reciprocity that promotes trust and micro-level social bonds. It also creates a strong sense of group loyalty, the same loyalty that characterizes the in-groups identified by Allport (1954). Like in-groups, bonding social capital is thus a double-edged sword, strengthening group ties and the sense of "we-ness" within the group, though this is done at the expense of the out-group that is viewed with suspicion and even outright antagonism. For this reason, Putnam recognizes that bonding social capital must be balanced with the bridging social capital that fosters a more generalized sense of reciprocity and fashions the broader connections between diverse groups that are necessary for social cohesion at the macro level of society. In this way, bridging social capital has much potential for strengthening the social fabric of society.

As already discussed, however, the problem is that there is a plethora of evidence, much of which Putnam presents, indicating that social capital and civic engagement—the hallmarks of social cohesion—are deteriorating. Friendship is just one of many examples he presents. For Putnam, friendships represent an informal social connection, one that is of central importance in American life given its function in connecting individuals into much larger social networks. In fact, he points out how we are "five to ten times" more likely to spend time at home with our friends than we are to go "to the theater or a ball game" (2000, 96). On the other hand, if one takes a longitudinal view of spending time with one's friends, we are much less likely to do so today than in the past thirty to forty years. He concludes that "visits with friends are now on the social capital endangered species list" (2000, 100). This decline in friendship is but one indicator of the erosion of the social cohesion of society. Given the importance of these relationships in fostering the voluntary social bonds that hold society together, this decline is admittedly a critical indicator of the erosion of social cohesion. Recognizing the breakdown in civic participation and social engagement goes all the way back to Alexis de Tocqueville (1889).[19]

While we might not associate through organizations such as the bowling leagues idealized by Putnam as much as we did in the past, we are still associating with people and friendships are a primary source of social bonds in contemporary society. To assume that one-on-one associations are less valuable than organizational associations is a result of a bias that holds up some nostalgic view of the "good old days" as the epitome of a healthy society (Spencer and Pahl 2006). Friendships represent a primary example of continuing social bonds within the modern world. Moreover, *diverse* friendships—friendships in which each party is enmeshed within different sides of a socially constructed boundary such as race, gender, or sexual orientation—provide a key source of the bridging social capital that is crucial to the sense of generalized reciprocity and macro-level social cohesion idealized by Putnam. In fact, while friendship patterns suggest the prevalence of segregation along the lines of social demographics as described in the previous section, there is reason to believe that such friendship segregation may be decreasing. For example, the rate of interracial marriage has more than doubled between 1980 and 2008, jumping from 6.7 percent to 14.6 percent of all new marriages. For blacks, rates of interracial marriage nearly tripled (Passel, Wang, and Taylor 2010). Of course, marriage is not the same as friendship. Among the many differences, we tend to be much more conservative in our marriage choices than in our choice of friends such that diverse friendships outpace diverse marriages: if the rates of interracial marriage are going up, it is possible to be optimistic about the rates of interracial and other diverse friendships. Hence, friendships that cross these socially constructed boundaries of race, gender, sexual orientation and so on have much potential to counteract the trend of social disintegration.

In order to realize the potential of friendships—especially diverse friendships—to strengthen social affinity and bring different groups of people together, forging the micro-level social bonds necessary for macro-level social cohesion, and in order to strengthen the bridging social capital prized by Putnam, two conditions must be met: (1) the opportunity to meet diverse others must be maximized by promoting diversity and integration within the structures of society, particularly social institutions and (2) individuals must be able to bridge or tear down the socially constructed boundaries that exist in society, setting aside or reevaluating any prejudice, anxiety, or fear they have toward those who are different from themselves.

With regard to the latter of these two conditions, there is an underlying question of whether contact between diverse groups, contact that would increase if the first condition is met, actually serves to alleviate the fear and anxiety that comes with social distance and that results in prejudice and individual acts of discrimination. Within social psychology, much research examining this question has been done in hopes that the answer is "yes." In his research on in-groups and out-groups, Allport (1954) not only described the factors contributing to social distance between diverse peoples and the prejudice that characterizes it, he also laid out the parameters for what has become known in social psychology as contact theory. In order to reduce this prejudice, Allport concludes that we must promote "equal status contact" between diverse groups of people. In addition, diverse groups should work together "in the pursuit of common goals." The reduction of prejudice is more likely to occur when "this contact is sanctioned by institutional supports (i.e., by law, custom or local atmosphere)." Moreover, such group contact should be "of a sort that leads to the perception of common interests and common humanity between members of the [diverse] groups" (1954, 281). Thomas Pettigrew subsequently updated Allport's work, adding a fifth condition for reducing the prejudice and social distance between groups: friendship potential (Pettigrew 1997; Pettigrew 1998). The idea of friendship potential, while not explicitly identified by Allport as one of his conditions was prefigured in his work when he observed that housing integration "creates a condition where *friendly* contacts and accurate social perceptions can occur" (1954, 272; emphasis mine).

Allport's effort in laying out what has become contact theory inspired much research on integration between diverse groups, including and perhaps especially research on diverse friendships, particularly interracial friendships, since friendships embody the idea of "friendship potential." Unlike the more fleeting encounters we may have with diverse peoples in integrated settings such as neighborhoods, friendships achieve a much greater depth of connection. Such friendships demonstrate the positive effects of intergroup contact on reducing prejudice (Barlow, Louis, and Hewstone 2009).[20] In fact, these positive results extend beyond intergroup contact between friends (Bousfield and Hutchison 2010).[21] Even imagining intergroup contact (Turner and Crisp 2010) and viewing diverse groups on television (Ortiz and Harwood 2007) can reduce prejudice toward out-groups. Moreover, intergroup contact has the potential to reduce intercommunity conflict because of its ameliorating effect on the feeling of threat and fear toward the out-group (Hughes *et al.* 2008), though not all would agree (Brown and Hewstone 2005).[22]

Overall, there is strong support for the claim that intergroup contact reduces prejudice, especially contact that reflects the conditions identified by Allport; and such contact is effective not just for race but for other social boundaries as well. What is more, this effect tends to generalize to the entire out-group, not just individual members (Pettigrew and Tropp 2006). Intergroup contact "reduces prejudice by (1) enhancing knowledge about the out-group, (2) reducing anxiety about intergroup contact, and (3) increasing empathy and perspective taking" (Pettigrew and Tropp 2008, 922). While it has been repeatedly demonstrated that intergroup contact is effective in reducing prejudice, there are a number of additional mediating factors that have been identified, including intergroup anxiety (Bousfield and Hutchison 2010),[23] minority perceptions of discrimination (Tropp 2007), the length of contact (such that extended contact has more positive effects) (Cameron, Rutland, and Adam 2007; Cameron *et al.* 2006), the frequency and quality of contact (Harwood *et al.* 2005), the degree of intimacy (Trail, Shelton, and West 2009), and perceived social norms about intergroup friendship relations (Feddes, Noack, and Rutland 2009).

All of this research is a source of optimism with regard to the positive effects of increasing contact between diverse groups of people, particularly contact in the context of friendship: in the global sense, and acknowledging the multiple mediating factors and conditions, intergroup contact appears to reduce the sense of anxiety and fear between in-group and out-group members, reducing the social distance between them and the prejudice and discriminatory behavior that often go with it. Thus, the second of the two conditions identified above can be met. Nevertheless, there is still the first condition: increasing the opportunity to meet and interact with diverse groups of people. This is largely an issue of social structure, though there are definite connections between this social structure and micro-level of social interactions. For example, while there is much support for intergroup contact and its effects at reducing prejudice and social distance, the positive effects of such contact may be confined to the individual level rather than the group level (Brown and Hewstone 2005). Moreover, while contact reduces prejudice and social distance, such prejudice results in an avoidance of contact (Binder 2009).[24] Consequently, the intergroup anxiety and prejudice that already exists encourages self-segregation on the part of in-group and out-group members, further entrenching the structural patterns of segregation and institutional discrimination. It is the structural divisions within society, reflected in the segregation of diverse groups in neighborhoods, schools, churches, work environments, and even within our families and social circles, that are the more daunting hurdle we face in realizing the potential of diverse friendships to cultivate the social cohesion we require in our society. It is to the impact of social structure that we turn in the following chapter.

## Studying the Exceptions Rather Than the Rule

We have seen that those friendships that involve people of different races, genders, sexual orientations, classes, religions, and so on—in other words, those friendships that cross these socially constructed boundaries—are far less common than those friendships where the friends are similar to one another in terms of these demographic characteristics. There is a body of sociological and psychological research that attempts to answer the question of *why* such a pattern exists; however, this is not the question that interests me here. Instead, I'm more intrigued by those friendships that go against the norm, the friendships that are more rare, the unlikely friendships where the socially constructed boundary apparently has not posed an impediment to the development of a close relationship. While these friendships are exceptional, I believe we have a lot to learn from them. They embody the ideals of a world in which a diverse population can live and work together not just in spite of their differences, but actually drawing inspiration and strength from those differences when forging the social bonds that are essential to a healthy community and society.[25] In other words, these friendships that cross social boundaries have the potential to decrease the misunderstandings between diverse groups of people and significantly move us along the path toward healing the corresponding divisions within society that shape our attitudes and behavior with regard to those who are different from ourselves.

Friendship—particularly friendships that bridge diverse populations—is but one example of how people can be brought together, fostering a sense of closeness, connectedness, and kinship. In my past research (Vela-McConnell 1999), I distinguished between those who compartmentalize themselves from others—in other words, creating and upholding divisions based on race, gender, and sexual orientation—and those who break the down the socially constructed boundaries between themselves and others. This pattern is also evident among friendships: many friendships uphold the divisions within our society. Then again, there are those exceptional friendships, those studied for this current project, that break down and challenge such boundaries. These unlikely friendships present us with an exciting opportunity to understand how people can overcome the differences that separate them, bringing diverse individuals together and increasing the overall social cohesion within society.

Some social scientists and even journalists have written books about friendships that cross these social boundaries (see, for example, Rawlins 2009; Rude 2009; Gee 2004; Korgen 2002; Raybon 1997; Fisher and Galler 1988; Rubin 1985; Bell 1981).[26] The efforts of these authors to understand the possibilities for friendships that cross social boundaries in our society have made important contributions to our understanding of diversity, the role it plays in personal relationships, and the ability we have to bridge the gap between ourselves and those who are different from us. Yet, all of them have one common shortcoming: each focuses on a single social boundary at a time. Some focus on race, others on gender, still others on sexual orientation. From some, we learn about friendships that cross gender lines, but we have no idea how this compares to friendships that cross racial lines, sexual orientation, or any other socially constructed boundary. The same can be said about all of these sources: by focusing on a single social boundary, we fail to understand how different social boundaries and establishing friendships and social bonds across those boundaries compare. Even when multiple social boundaries are included in the same book, such as Rawlins' (2009) inclusion of both gender and race, they are treated entirely separately. While gender and race are obviously quite different in their details, they are both socially constructed category systems and thus they may actually have much in common in terms of the dynamics of bridging socially constructed boundaries.

It is my hope that the research presented here will be a significant step in filling that gap. What I chose to do was compare a variety of socially constructed boundaries (race, class, gender, sexual orientation, religion, ability, and age). Such an approach allows direct comparisons between these social boundaries. The research question guiding this project was, "How do those who are different in terms of race, gender, sexual orientation, and so on establish and maintain a close friendship?" In answering this question, it is important to look at both the similarities and differences between social boundaries. For example, how do friendships crossing racial lines differ from those crossing the lines of gender, or sexual orientation, or some other socially constructed boundary? What does that tell us about race in our society? What can we learn about gender from such comparisons? Or sexual orientation? Or class? While it is important to examine these similarities and differences between socially constructed boundaries, it is equally if not more important to understand what crossing social boundaries entails *regardless of the specifics of each boundary in question.* In other words, what is *similar* in crossing the racial, gender, and sexual orientation divides? What holds true regardless of the unique qualities of race, gender, and sexual orientation? In order to answer questions like these, a single study must include different socially constructed boundaries so that the same data is collected in the same way and analyzed using the same process. Only then is it possible to draw such comparisons, looking for both the similarities and the differences. This was the approach used in conducting the research for this book. With this approach in mind, it is now possible to begin addressing the questions noted above. In so doing, we can examine the positive effects—as well as the challenges—of intergroup contact more closely and thus gain a deeper appreciation for how these friendships strengthen the fabric of society.

## Notes

1. While Liz Spencer and Ray Pahl do not offer an actual definition of friend or friendship, they do an extensive job of mapping the topic, presenting us with the most up-to-date glimpse into the nature of friendship. Through an inductive research process, they set out to define friendship relations along several sociologically relevant dimensions. For example, to distinguish friends from kin (those with a blood tie or bond through marriage) and close versus more distant relationships, they distinguish different types of relationships along two dimensions: the "degree to which relationships are . . . *given* [such as kin] or *chosen* [such as friends]" and the "strength of the bond" between two persons—high or low commitment (2006, 41). For the purposes of the following research, my focus was on chosen relationships with a higher level of commitment: what I have termed "close friends." As already noted, Spencer and Pahl also distinguish between simple and complex friendships as well as between historical, latent, and active friendships.

2. These characteristics confirm what Spencer and Pahl described and they note that the qualities they identified "confirmed the findings of many other studies in this field" (2006, 59). (See also Rubin 1985; Fischer 1982; Weiss and Lowenthal 1975; and Argyle and Henderson 1984.)

3. Spencer and Pahl distinguish between historical friendships (friendships that no longer exist but that are a part of a person's biography), latent friendships (where there is infrequent contact between the friends, but they still have some sense of presence in each other's lives), and active friends (where there is regular contact between the friends and a strong sense of presence in each other's lives) (2006, 74-75). These are useful distinctions to make in mapping out the territory of friendship from a sociological perspective; however, for the purposes of the current study, my focus was exclusively on active friendships. Of course, since the interview process captured the friendships under study in a relatively brief time period and did not extend for years, we have only a snapshot view of the friendships. Given that friendships change over the life course (see Spencer and Pahl 2006; Pahl and Pevalin 2005; and Pahl 2000), it is to be expected that some portion of the friendships studied will eventually move from active to latent or historical friendships. And while research participants were asked about the history of their friendship in great detail, such accounts are inevitably shaped through selective memories and might not represent a complete or wholly accurate account of the friendship's past.

4. The idea of relating to one another in a variety of ways alludes to Spencer and Pahl's (2006) distinction between what they term "simple" and "complex" friendships—a distinction that reflects the type and degree of attachment between the friends. What characterizes simple friendships is that "the relationship is limited to one main form of interaction," whether the friend is a useful contact, someone who can do a favor for us, or someone with whom we can just have fun (2006, 61). Complex friendships are multifaceted in that the friends can relate to one another in a variety of ways. For example, they can have fun together (as in simple friendships), but they can also provide help when needed, be a confidant, or even a soul mate (2006, 65). While the friendships in my study

did vary in terms of the degree of attachment between the two individuals, those included were what Spencer and Pahl would call "complex friendships."

5. For this reason, the research presented in this book excludes friendships that occur within other legally recognized relationships or their equivalents. For example, spouses or partners who are also close friends were not included in order to isolate those friendships for study that do not have the rationalized/bureaucratized recognition (and therefore legal/contractual support) that such kin relationships have. In other words, it was my choice to focus on those relationships that were purely voluntary in nature.

6. This is also not to say that those of a different status (Rawlins 1992) or unequals cannot be true friends, but they are friends of a different sort when power differences are present within the friendship—thus the problems with nepotism, *quid pro quo* favoritism (or harassment), and fraternization.

7. As Pahl notes, "Individuals [who] make their commitment to each other without reference to group-derived status, norms and values . . . are likely to withhold information about the internal structure of their relationship in terms of its guiding norms and values from the outside world. Seen in these terms, as one observer put it, 'every friendship is thus a potential culture in miniature and also a potential counter-culture'" (2000, 163).

8. Here is what they say: "[T]he amount of social stratification in a society can be defined usefully as the variable degree to which persons of approximately equal social status choose one another for intimate relationships such as marriage and friendship, beyond what would be expected on the basis of chance factors alone" (1976, 1307).

9. Michael Eve is highly critical of the fact that the focus of much of the research in the area of friendship has been restricted to such dyadic relationships. He argues that "intimate friendship is, of course, an interesting area, but when it . . . [is] conceived in social psychological terms and as a dyadic relationship based on the exchange of 'emotional support' and on pure individuality, it inevitably becomes difficult to make connections with other sociological themes; hence the topic seems very much apart—not really part of the social structure or even governed by fully social criteria (2002, 387). Eve's point is well taken: it is very important to recognize that friendship is very much a part of the larger social structure of society. His criticism, however, seems to be aimed more at the psychological approach to social psychology rather than the sociological one.

10. As noted by Allan and Adams, "Like all personal relationships, even when they appear to those involved to be dyadic constructions—an expression of their own personalities, interests, and creativity—[friendships] are none the less shaped by contextual factors that lie outside the direct control of particular individuals" (1998, 183).

11. Temporal distance is the third social location variable I originally identified as affecting the development of social affinity (Vela-McConnell 1999). I do not include it here because it is not relevant to the subject matter of this book. While friends might be from different generations—a situation of age difference that is included in this book—they are certainly contemporaries. Thus, temporal distance between friends is minimal.

12. Homophily based on demographics is called "status homophily" in order to distinguish it from similarity in values or "value homophily" (McPherson, Smith-Lovin, and Cook 2001, 419).

13. Sociologist Xavier de Souza Briggs observes, "There is nothing new in the notion that the *physical* separation of sub-groups in human settlements goes hand in hand with segregated social relationships, lifestyles, economic success, and even social and political attitudes. Indeed, this idea, and the linked notion that segregation levels reflected a group's relative level of assimilation in the wider society, are foundations of the Chi-

cago School's conception of the city and therefore of modern society" (Briggs 2002, 9-10).

14. In summarizing their findings, they observe that "obviously, there are other methods of making friends. The men of the project undoubtedly meet one another in class and school activities. People probably meet at parties, and so on. However, the relationships between ecological and sociometric structures is so very marked that there can be little doubt that in these communities passive contacts are a major determinant of friendship and group formation" (Festinger, Schachter, and Back 1959, 58).

15. This varies according to the type of group. Voluntary groups for women tend to result in "relationships that are highly homophilous on age, education, religion, marital status, and work status" (2001, 432). Hobby groups seem to be the most heterogeneous in their membership, integrating people from diverse backgrounds, particularly those with different levels of occupational prestige (2001, 433).

16. Again, McPherson, Smith-Lovin, and Cook note, "In a national probability sample, only 8 percent of adults with networks of size two or more mention having a person of another race with whom they 'discuss important matters' less than one seventh the heterogeneity that we would observe if people chose randomly from the population" (2001, 420). Of course, this applies to a person's entire social network, not just close friends. If the question had been restricted to close friends, the percentage, in all likelihood, would have been even smaller.

17. While this data refers to entire social networks rather than just friends, the pattern may still hold true even if to a lesser extent.

18. For the purposes of this research, religious differences were restricted to differences in religion, not in Christian denomination.

19. Such a view into the disintegration of society is described by Spencer and Pahl as "apocalyptic," and they further state that "the chorus of gloom has indeed become so deafening we can hardly hear" (2006:17).

20. See also Feddes, Noack, and Rutland 2009; Heinze and Horn 2009; Crystal, Killen, and Ruck 2008; Kawabata and Crick 2008; Vonofakou et al. 2008; Vonofakou, Hewstone, and Voci 2007; Tropp 2007; and Aboud, Mendelson, and Purdy 2003.

21. See also Binder et al. 2009; Crystal, Killen, and Ruck 2008; Prestwich et al. 2008; de Souza Briggs 2007; Saenz, Ngai, and Hurtado 2007; and Cover 1995.

22. Some studies on intergroup contact have demonstrated mixed results (Trail, Shelton, and West 2009; Shook and Fazio 2008; Stolle, Soroka, and Johnston 2008; Hughes 2007; Dixon 2006; Hamm, Brown, and Heck 2005; Goldsmith 2004; and Yancey 1999) or even negative results (McGlothlin and Killen 2006 and Towles-Schwen and Fazio 2006), but these studies are far outnumbered by those that support the intergroup contact hypothesis first proposed by Allport. See, for example the two meta-analyses completed by Pettigrew and Tropp (2008 and 2006).

23. See also Barlow, Louis, and Hewstone 2009; Binder et al. 2009; Prestwich et al. 2008; Turner et al. 2007; Finchilescu 2005; Harwood et al. 2005; Levin, Van Laar, and Sidanius 2003; and Voci and Hewstone 2003.

24. Blumer's (1958) group position theory stands in contrast to Allport's intergroup contact theory by highlighting the sense of threat experienced by members of the in-group toward the out-group (see also Blumer 1955; Goldsmith 2004; and Bobo 1999).

25. For example, in her study of interracial contact and perceived discrimination, social psychologist Linda Tropp found that "having a friend in the racial out-group corresponded with greater reports of interracial closeness among both black and white respon-

dents. . . . [T]hese findings suggest that . . . friendships across racial boundaries may diminish the extent to which black Americans would rely on perceptions of discrimination in forming their intergroup attitudes" (2007, 79).

26. For example, Lisa Gee published a book titled *Friends: Why Men and Women Are from the Same Planet* (2004) in which she draws on interviews and historical research on friendships between men and women. In her book, she attempts to dispel the myth that "men are from Mars, and women are from Venus" and the corresponding message from the popular movie *When Harry Met Sally* that tells us that men and women cannot ever really be friends. Lillian Rubin, in her extensive research that resulted in the book *Just Friends,* also found that men and women can be friends, but that the question of sex had to be overcome first: "when I asked about their friendships with the opposite sex, most people's thoughts turned quickly to the ways in which sex, whether acted on or not, both gives the relationship a special charge and also creates difficulties that are not easily overcome" (1985, 149). As a result of that "special charge," Rubin found that such cross-gender friendships were more rare among couples as compared to those who are single. Robert Bell included cross-sex friendships in his book *Worlds of Friendship* (1981) and highlighted how expectations for a sexual relationship have significantly restricted the possibility for cross-gender friendships. However, the reasons for the relative lack of such friendships aren't always so obvious. Other, equally important reasons have to do with friendships within the larger context of marriage, the fact that friendship is predicated on equality (something that is still far from universal with regard to gender), the relative lack of social contexts that bring men and women together in the first place, and so on.

These examples focus just on gender. There are other, equally compelling examples of research and writing on interracial friendships. Journalist Patricia Raybon examines her experiences with interracial friendship in the book *My First White Friend* (1997). Sociologist Kathleen Odell Korgen (2002) provides an engaging description of the dynamics of crossing the racial divide in her book by that title. Social psychologist Linda Tropp examined interracial contact, including within the context of friendship, and its impact on perceived discrimination. She found that "contact in the form of interracial friendships may help to counteract the detrimental effects of perceiving discrimination" (2007, 79).

# Chapter 2

# Structuring Friendship Opportunities

[F]riendship is typically not defined as a tie which is grounded in circumstance but instead as one which emerges through the actions of each individual and the assessments they make of each other's personal qualities. Yet, clearly friendships are social constructions as well as personal ones. Their contexts do influence the manner in which they are formed and the exchanges they come to involve (Allan and Adams 1998, 190).

What is the context that allows for the emergence and development of friendships that cross the socially constructed boundaries of race, gender, sexual orientation, and so on? When talking to those I interviewed, I found that the research participants oftentimes took even the possibility of their friendship for granted: it was so much a part of their daily experience that they didn't even think about it. Many were surprised by all of the questions that I asked, not because the questions themselves were surprising but because they simply had never considered such questions to be important or relevant. They were just friends, nothing special. For example, Bao (who is Hmong) and Irene (who is Black) both grew up with friends of other races and this paved the way for their future friendships. Now they can be friends despite racial differences without even thinking about it. For this reason, they are in a position of taking such cross-racial friendships for granted. In the wrap-up to each interview, I asked the participants to sum up how they have broken down the barrier (in this case based on race) and bridged the (racial) gap between them through their friendship. Here is what they said:

> IRENE: I don't know. I mean it's so hard for me to answer just because I've always had friendships with different races, and I've never thought of it as this like tremendous thing, you know, like this big deal.
> BAO: Yeah, I agree. And I think for me, if you would have asked me this ten years ago, I think I would have a different answer than I would today, just because in today's world you do see a lot more people of different colors being friends and, like Irene said, I grew up where it was so normal for me to have

> *friends of different colors. It wasn't something that was a life-changing experi-*
> *ence or whatever. But I think if Irene and I were friends ten or even twenty*
> *years ago, then not that many people of different colors were friends or it*
> *wasn't as common. Today it's just so common that I don't think . . . you know,*
> *yeah* [Interview 19C].

Ironically, taking something for granted really is a luxury afforded by those in a position of privilege. They don't have to think about it; they don't have to worry about it. It just comes "naturally;" it is second nature to them given their past experience. So, in this sense, both Bao and Irene were raised in "privileged" environments characterized by the presence of members of more than one race.

A sociologist, however, cannot afford to take such relationships for granted no matter how mundane those in the friendships believe them to be. It is the job of sociologists to question the world around them, particularly what people take for granted about their everyday lives (Berger 1963). When the taken-for-granted-reality is questioned, one will often find something surprising. For example, while friendships such as those studied here feel mundane and common to those I interviewed, they aren't really that common (as discussed in chapter 1); and as uncommon as they are now, they were much less so in the past. In fact, the emergence and development of these friendships is highly dependent on the social structure of the historical time period and context in which they are located.

For this reason, it is important to engage what sociologist C. Wright Mills (1959) called the sociological imagination. For Mills, it is vital for the sociologist to recognize the connection between an individual's everyday life experiences—what he calls "personal troubles"—and the larger social structure and cultural climate—what he calls "public issues." While our personal troubles are experienced privately and in an entirely individual way, a good sociologist will recognize that they actually fit within a larger social pattern. For example, while each of our friendships is unique in its specific details, all friendships fit within certain predictable social patterns at a more abstract level. We've already seen the patterns of homophily within friendship. In the next chapter, we will also see how these diverse friendships follow some general stages of development regardless of the idiosyncrasies of each individual friendship. These represent larger social patterns with regard to our individual experiences of friendship. The point that Mills makes is that our unique biographies are "caught up" within the larger social structure and historical time frame in which we live our lives. In order to more fully understand our biographies from a sociological perspective, we must also understand that larger social structure. Observing our individual friendships without taking that larger perspective into account makes it all the more likely that we take those experiences for granted. Given this perspective, the fact that those I interviewed did just that comes as no surprise.

In this chapter, I am going to focus our attention on the social context in which friendships that bridge the various socially constructed categories emerge, develop, and are sustained. Sociologists Rebecca Adams and Graham Allan argue that understanding the social context of friendships has been sadly neglected in past research and that it needs to be given our full attention.

> [I]ndividuals do not generate their relationships in a social or economic vacuum, any more than they do in a personal vacuum. Relationships have a broader basis than the dyad alone; they develop and endure within a wider complex of interacting influences which help to give each relationship its shape and structure (1998, 2).

The temptation in a culture such as our own—a culture defined in part by the value it places on individualism—is to explain all human behavior in individual terms, as if there are no factors beyond the individual or, if there are outside factors, to minimize their relevance in shaping individual behavior. In the case of friendships crossing the socially constructed boundaries of race, gender, sexual orientation, and so on, the temptation is to look at the individual—his or her values, attitudes, beliefs, interests, experiences, prejudices, stereotypes, personality type, perceptions, and so on—independently of social structure and outside of the larger social context; but to do so would be to neglect the sociological imagination. While it is very important to look at the individual and all of his or her own personal qualities, it is equally if not more important to consider the social context in which we find that individual—the cultural and institutional context as well as the group context. Adams and Allan understand context to mean, "the conditions external to the development, maintenance, and dissolutions of specific friendships. In other words, we are referring to those elements which do 'surround' friendships, but are not directly inherent in them, the extrinsic rather than the intrinsic" (1998, 4). In many important ways, it is this larger social context that shapes the individual in terms of his or her values, beliefs, interests, experiences, prejudices, stereotypes, perceptions, and so on. While this point may seem obvious upon hearing it, it bears mentioning because it is so often overlooked within our culture of individualism.

The social structure of society—how society and the groups and institutions that comprise it is organized—is what provides us with opportunities to forge such friendships, opening and closing doors to us depending on our position within that social structure. By starting here, we can better appreciate what these friendships reveal about our social world and the impact it has on our daily lives. We'll begin with the most broad dimensions of those public issues Mills highlighted: our socio-cultural context, including history, our cultural values and normative expectations, and the larger aspects of our social structure. We will then begin to narrow our focus by moving on to the institutional context in which these friendships emerge, such as the workplace, educational and religious settings. Narrowing our focus even further, the group context will prove to be just as important to the emergence and development of these friendships. Social networks are an important factor in meeting people from diverse backgrounds. More importantly, the groups to which we belong—and especially our primary relationships with a spouse, partner, boyfriend, or girlfriend—have a direct impact on the acceptance of friends from diverse backgrounds.[1] Finally, it is important to consider how these larger social contexts impact and shape individual experiences and perceptions.

## Socio-Cultural Context

The socio-cultural context in which these friendships crossing social categories actually emerge is caught up with the worldview, values, and normative expectations that dominate our culture. For example, we have fully developed belief systems (i.e. cognitive culture) about race, gender, sexual orientation, and so on—beliefs that shape our values and corresponding norms (i.e. normative culture). Moreover, to the extent we perform our gender or race or orientation (or what have you) through the clothes we wear—the products and brands we buy—we are demonstrating the material dimension of our culture (Ogburn 1950). In this way, our culture provides the broadest context through which our friendships develop. Again, thinking at this abstract level does not come easily to those of us inhabiting a culture that is much more individualistic. It is important to recognize the significance of such a broad context: "[F]riendship and similar ties of informal sociability do not lie outside the influence of macro-level structures, but instead are moulded by them in myriad ways, few of which are consciously recognized by those involved" (Allan and Adams 1998, 188). Nevertheless, much of the research on social networks, such as friendship networks, fails to take the socio-cultural context into account (Hsin-Chun Tsai 2006), a significant oversight. To fully understand these friendships, it is imperative that we examine the larger cultural context in which they can be found. To do so, we will focus on gender as our primary example, keeping in mind that the same principles apply to other socially constructed categories.

Ideas about gender, gender norms, and expectations for interactions between genders were freely expressed throughout the interviews. While no one voiced anything about limitations or expectations for interracial interaction, they felt very free to express such limitations and expectations for cross-gendered interaction. This doesn't mean that we are "over" racism. Indeed, in order to succeed in bridging the racial divide, even in the context of friendship, it is necessary to overcome a long history of racial injustices and current disparities (Rawlins 2009). Instead, our lack of hesitation for cross-race friendships implies that people have learned that it is unacceptable to express such views with regard to race. Also, keep in mind that this was a highly unrepresentative sample of the U.S. population—a group of people who are anything but "average" when it comes to dealing with social categories. So then, why all the commentary about gender from those I interviewed? This seems to indicate how entrenched our views of gender are, even among such an open-minded and outside-the-norm group of people. While the separation of races is no longer acceptable, at least in an ideal sense, the separation of genders is still quite common. Moreover, while a few had things to say about their own gender biases, most focused on the reactions they received from other people who couldn't understand or accept that people of opposite genders could simply be friends. Let's take a close look at the experience of my interviewees with regard to cross-gendered friendships and see how the socio-cultural context plays a powerful role even for those who successfully crossed between the social categories of gender.

It is helpful to begin by asking how we perceive and understand gender. What are our values and beliefs about gender? At its core, sex is something we view in dualistic terms: there is only male and female and they are complete and utter opposites. While there is nothing natural about separating people into these opposite categories (Butler 1990), this assumption is deeply embedded within our culture. Naturally, such a view leads to all kinds of preconceptions about how we express our sex through gender, stereotypes that even those inter-viewed—who are presumably much more open-minded about these things given that they are crossing such socially constructed categories as gender—voiced on a consistent basis. A cognitive culture characterized by such dualism gives rise to a normative culture that sets expectations for each gender—normative expec-tations that emphasize the differences between men and women—and a material culture of separation between the two genders. We have very strong precon-ceived ideas about how men and women complement each other not just bio-logically, but emotionally and interpersonally as well, leading many to assume that the "natural" relation between a man and a woman is a romantic and sexual one (Rawlins 2009). Such a socio-cultural context creates normative pressure to avoid interactions that are not understood in this way (Rude 2009).

As an example of the interplay between the cognitive, normative, and mate-rial dimensions of our culture and their relevance for gender, consider Caroline's experience when I asked her about straight men and women simply being friends.

*I had that conversation with a guy that I went out with, and he said, "I have several close female friends" and I thought, "Hmm, I wonder if we would stay friends if this [dating relationship] didn't work out?" And I just thought, "No, I don't think so." So yes, I've always had a prejudice against having friendships with straight men, always.*

*I think this prejudice is based on a combination of culture and upbringing. I was raised a Catholic, and while I'm sure my father never said to me outright, "All guys want to do is get in your pants," but that was kind of the type of up-bringing that I had. We were never allowed to have boys, whether they were our boyfriends or not, upstairs in our bedroom area. In our bedroom, of course not; but not even upstairs. So, from the very beginning there was this automatic distrust. You can't trust boys, so there shouldn't be this connection.*

*And I never really thought about it, but that's probably where my preju-dice against friendships with straight men started. And my mom, as liberal as*

*she is, was even more adamant than my father about that rule. So, you know,*
*from the very beginning there was this sort of prudish raising kind of philoso-*
*phy in my household, and I guess I didn't ever really move beyond my upbring-*
*ing. I didn't get into a serious relationship with a guy until I was sixteen or*
*seventeen years old. And I've never experienced a breakup with a boyfriend*
*where it was possible to be friends* [Interview 39A].

The scenario Caroline describes highlights how all three dimensions of culture
interrelate with one another, shaping her experience of gender and gender relations to the point where she finds it impossible to simply be friends with a
straight man. That is why our interview focused on her friendship with a gay
man, who is believed to be a "safe" alternative for a straight woman (Rawlins
2009). Her parents had a very strong set of beliefs about boys and girls, a set of
beliefs shaped by the Catholic faith. This belief system then gave rise to certain
norms—rules for Caroline to follow when relating to young men. These rules
even took on a physical manifestation through the separation between the se-
cluded privacy upstairs where boys could not go and the downstairs of the home,
which was much more of a public setting and therefore subject to observation by
the parents. Within Caroline's cultural context—as embodied within her faith
and family—she was socialized to believe that straight men and women could
not simply be friends, especially if they had a previous dating relationship. Instead, her friendships with men are relegated to family—father and brothers—
one mentor, and one gay man.

Similar experiences and views were expressed among many of those I questioned about gender and friendship. As another example, Bao has no friends who
are male. She doesn't really think that it is possible for men and women to be
just friends.

*In terms of gender, if you become like close friends with someone and you con-*
*fide in them, then it's like you've taken it to the next level where you could*
*cross over and make it into more of a romantic relationship. I'm not saying that*
*it hasn't been done, but for me I just always feel like it's just one of those things*
*that's a gamble. You know what I'm saying? So it's either you're dating and*
*you're more than friends, or you're just acquaintances. You can't just have a*
*guy friend that you'd confide in like you would with a girlfriend, you know* [In-
terview 19A].

From this commonly held point of view, as soon as a man and a woman get to
know each other better, the level of intimacy increases and for many of us there
is an expectation that such intimacy between men and women must lead to
something much more than friendship (Rawlins 2009). Again, the exception, of
course, would be gay/straight friendships where they are also different in terms
of gender because the possibility of a sexual relationship has been removed.

These sorts of cultural expectations, that straight men and women can't be
friends without it leading to something more than friendship, have created chal-

lenges for those individuals who attempt to do so. For example, Hugo—a married man—describes a point of tension in his friendship with Debbie, who is single. He started as her mentor in school, but they have become friends and their friendship has lasted well beyond her graduation.

*Gender did create some problems a while back, two years ago or so. I asked her, "Where is this friendship going to go?" But the question was misunderstood to be a sort of proposition. Obviously, we've fixed up the misunderstanding because we're still talking to each other. But I felt terrible about it. As a matter of fact, when it happened that day—I can't remember if she came into my office or she just caught me in the hallway—and oh she was really mad at me. I mean, she said, "I'm so mad at you, Hugo." And I said, "Well I can understand." She says, "Well no, because I can't talk to you anymore." I said, "Yeah, you can," and we did talk about it and got it all figured out. We figured out what our friendship is and isn't and we got our friendship back on track* [Interview 33A].

From these examples, it is apparent how influential our socio-cultural context is in determining who our friends can be or in determining whom we allow to befriend us. Our belief systems—in this case about gender and gender relations— give rise to normative expectations that regulate our interactions with people who are different from us.

This preconceived notion that men and women can't be friends without being more than friends seems to set up a self-fulfilling prophesy in which men and women are prevented from becoming friends before they even really give it a try. Consequently, there are comparatively few successful male/female friendships where both individuals are straight to point to as examples. This was noticeable when trying to identify friendship pairs for interviews. It was much easier to find interracial friendships than it was to find cross-gender friendships. Then people notice how few straight male/female friendships there are and in their eyes this only serves to "prove" that such friendships are not possible. This is a classic example of circular reasoning: we construct a reality (i.e. "There aren't any straight, cross-gender friendships that are just that—friendships") based on a belief in something that isn't inherently true (i.e. "Straight men and women simply can't be just friends"). This is true *only* because people—guided by their socio-cultural context—believe it to be true and act on that belief. In sociology, this is known as the Thomas Theorem: "If you define something as real, it will be real in its consequences" (Thomas 1928).

In a similar act of faulty and inherently heterosexist reasoning, many in our society tend to believe that, because men and women *can* have sex that it is therefore "natural" and even inevitable that they do have sex. So, having the ability for sexual relations is conflated with what is perceived as "natural." Furthermore, what is "natural" is also believed to be "preordained" and inescapable. As observed by Rawlins, many believe that "since people are supposed to reproduce, basic primal attraction can get in the way of friendship. It is natural to express cross-sex closeness sexually." Those who believe this then place great pressure on cross-sex friends to "recognize 'the true nature' of their relationship" (2009, 113). As a result, even among those who establish successful, cross-gender friendships, there is pressure placed on them from others in their social circle. Guided by the belief system regarding gender relations into which they were socialized, family and friends will often find it difficult to believe that a man and woman can simply be friends. Many tease the friends, asking when they're just going to admit they're in love and hook up. For example, while the focus of our interviews was on race, both Colin and Kelly (he's black, she's white) mentioned how gender became an issue for them due to the reactions of others. In fact, Colin felt that their gender difference was more of an issue than race, not because it's an issue for them, but because other people make it an issue in terms of assuming that, because they are friends, they must be sleeping together.

> *Well, a lot of my old friends had a hard time with the fact I'm friends with Kelly. They say, "You must be sleeping with her." They always say that. But you can't tell me it's impossible to be friends with a girl until you've tried a few times. If you can talk about it, it's possible. I think my friends have gotten used to it* [Interview 1B].

This was also the experience of Kris with regard to his friendship with Kim. He and Kim met through a group of friends who get together and go skiing about once a year. These aren't just ski trips; they're party trips as well and so include a lot of drinking and the occasional "hook-up" among those who aren't already seeing someone else. While on these trips, both Kris and Kim (separately or together) have been questioned and teased by other friends asking them why they don't just hook up since they get along so well anyway. As Kris tells it,

> *There was a certain amount of hooking up that happened on these ski trips within our group of friends, and there were multiple times when people would ask, "Why aren't you two hooking up?" With all the hooking up that's going on, it was as much to poke fun. These trips were about having a wild time, and that we did. But, as I described earlier, I liked her as a friend and didn't want to screw that up. And sometimes I would have a girlfriend back home. It was never my style anyway* [Interview 37A].

In Kim's experience, it wasn't joking around by her friends. It was a serious question, and the question came from friends who weren't a part of the skiing group.

> *I had one girlfriend who wasn't part of the ski group and who, when she met him, she's like, "Oh, my gosh!" I'm like, "No, he's just a friend." She's like, "You've got to be kidding." I'm like, "No, really. He's just a friend. There's*

*nothing there." "Oh, okay." I mean, when you're just friends, you're just friends. You can't explain it. You just have to be adamant about it. "No, really, we're just friends"* [Interview 37B].

Kris and Kim's friends good-naturedly point out the apparent deviance from the norm of hooking up between two people who, at the time, were both single. It is a common experience for those who are straight and in cross-gender friendships for their wider circle of family and friends to enforce the normative expectations we have regarding gender relations in our culture. The teasing serves as a negative sanction—a reaction from others that, intentionally or not, reflects disapproval for breaking a norm. Such teasing highlights how the two friends are stepping outside the norm and serves the function of signaling the friends that they should "get with the (gender) program" and "fall back into step" with everyone else. It reflects the strong socio-cultural belief we have that "men and women can't be close friends indefinitely; underlying sexual tensions within the friendship will eventually ruin the idea of permanent platonic friendship" (Rawlins 2009, 119). Just because sex is possible does not mean that it is inevitable. Otherwise, and setting the inherent heterosexism of the above argument aside, it would be impossible for *anyone* to be platonic friends given that sex between those of the same sex is possible even if not desirable by one or both parties involved. Assuming that sex is inevitable robs us of any sense of self-determination and presumes that we are ruled exclusively by biology and instinctual drives. Moreover, this assumption fails to take the impact of the socio-cultural context into account. The possibilities for platonic, cross-sex friendships vary "according to historical and sociocultural circumstances" (Rawlins 2009, 109). Hence, it is not always and everywhere assumed that men and women cannot simply be friends. In fact, our culture here and now seems to be changing in this regard. Rawlins points out that television shows such as *Friends* and *Seinfeld* are increasingly likely to portray cross-sex friendships.

> It depends on one's culture; times are changing and cross-sex friendships are seen as okay now. From kindergarten on, students describe participating in youth coed sports, for example. In the college environment, they may have many more relationships that are cross-sex friendships than they do sexual relationships, and they perceive such relationships as the best thing for them to do (2009, 121).

From these examples focusing on cross-gender friendships, it is easy to see how our socio-cultural context shapes the opportunities we have or don't have to establish and maintain diverse friendships. Many of us are raised with the belief that such friendships are difficult at best, if not impossible. Men and women are commonly viewed as complete and utter opposites and therefore cannot come together for anything but romantic or purely sexual relationships (cognitive culture). In order to prevent unwarranted romantic or sexual relationships, we physically separate men from women as much as possible even in our daily lives (material culture). Moreover, we enforce this separation by establishing norms to guide us in what is considered to be appropriate behavior (normative culture). Those around us enforce these norms, in both subtle (as in teasing) and not-so-subtle (as in punishment for a boy entering a girl's room) ways.

While the examples provided focus on gender, the socio-cultural context for friendships crossing race, sexual orientation, religion, age, class, and so on is just as influential. For example, in the interest of being open-minded and equal, we're often taught not to talk about our differences in terms of race, sexual orientation, class, ability, and so on, for fear that such talk would lead to increased tension. Many believe that Christians and Jews cannot befriend Muslims because their religious beliefs are "diametrically opposed" to one another, or that people of different racial groups cannot truly be friends because, culturally speaking, they are so different they could never really understand each other. These misleading beliefs set up our culture and values as if they are insurmountable obstructions—an objective reality that is beyond an individual's ability to alter and overcome. Such beliefs (cognitive culture) lead to actual avoidance and separation (material culture) and rules governing what is and is not appropriate for conversation (normative culture.) We then have a socially constructed "reality" that divides one group from another (Berger and Luckmann 1967).

## Institutional Context

It is oftentimes within institutional settings that diverse people come together—people who might otherwise have never met. Whether it is the workplace, school, or church, such settings are crucial to making friendships that cross social categories of race, gender, sexual orientation, and so on possible in the first place. The more diverse these settings are, the more opportunities people have to develop relationships and deeper friendships, particularly since these settings often not only bring people together but provide them with opportunities to work together toward common goals, one of the criteria identified by Allport (1954) as leading to successful intergroup contact. Simply bringing different groups together is not enough to create positive social bonds between them. On the other hand, if such contact is supplemented by working together toward a common goal, positive social bonds are much more likely to develop (Sherif 1956). It is within institutional settings that we move from simple contact toward the achievement of common goals, a point that highlights the importance of fully integrated schools, churches, workplaces, and so on.

In the past, segregation (based on race, gender, or whatever socially constructed category) meant that there were fewer opportunities to meet people from other social categories, much less work with them with some level of parity in status. Race-based segregation would be the obvious example here. Under the Jim Crow system, contact between white and black was minimized and the contact that existed was not between equals. Blacks always had lower status vis-à-vis whites no matter how low the status of the white person in question. They lived in separate neighborhoods, went to separate churches, and had separate social circles. If they happened to work in the same place, blacks always held subservient positions.

While we no longer live in a world where there is legal segregation, social segregation is still very much a part of our lives. The long history of educational and economic inequality is still felt today, choking off "the structural possibilities for [those of different races] meeting and choosing each other as friends" (Rawlins 2009, 172). Instead of legally segregated neighborhoods, we have evidence of red-lining—where banks and real estate agents funnel people of different races into different areas—and "white flight"—where whites, who used to live in the cities and faced sending their children to the same schools as black families, have moved to the suburbs where most people are the same race and send their children to the suburban schools to be with others just like them. We've already discussed the physical and social separation of the genders, but we also tend to self-segregate in terms of religion and ability.

Class is perhaps one of the most prominent ways in which society has divided one group from another. As seen in the previous chapter, class segregation is actually increasing in our society (Massey and Fischer 2003). Housing costs and the lack of mixed housing are but one explanation for such segregation. Moreover, this class segregation often will be the root of racial segregation as the successful and affluent (who are more likely to be white) secede from more economically (and therefore racially) diverse areas (Vanderpool 1995). In collecting data for this book, I came to a renewed appreciation for how class-segregated we are as a society. Class was the single most difficult category in which to find friendship pairs. There were very few people who had friends from a different class standing, whether I looked at class in terms of money, status, or power. Again, while this study was not based on a representative sample of the U.S. population, it does indicate that we do not generally "come across" people from significantly different class backgrounds in our daily lives and when we do, we are not typically interacting as equals. Instead, it is usually from an impersonal distance where the development of a friendship is extremely unlikely to occur.

Quinn and Mike were among those very rare individuals who were willing to be interviewed who come from different class backgrounds. Quinn is in his late twenties and comes from a working-class background. He is the first member of his family to have gone to college, which he had just completed when I interviewed him. He helped his mother clean homes in order to earn money for school. Mike, who is in his late forties and has teenagers of his own, comes from a mid- to upper-middle class background. He currently works as a strategic relations manager for a large corporation. They met on an interfaith trip to Eastern

Europe and Italy where they visited former concentration camps. In their paired
interview, Quinn pointed out that, except for the trip, he and Mike might never
have met because their lives and life circles are so different given their current
class statuses. Mike echoed this point, saying,

> There are so many differences between us that we wouldn't have naturally met
> if it wasn't for the trip, because you [Quinn] live in the city and I don't. And for
> a chunk of your life you were going to school and I don't. And while you were
> in school and working, I was just working in a different community. And the
> combination of having an opportunity to meet on that trip—together with the
> fact that, for our own individual reasons, class didn't matter to us—there were
> none of the obstacles that would commonly present themselves [Interview 15C].

Mike goes on to describe his experience with a class-segregated society.

> We live within neighborhoods of people who are somewhat similar to our-
> selves; we work with people who are somewhat similar to ourselves. Where I
> work, there's lots of different kinds of positions that pay a wide range of sala-
> ries, and at one point, you know, the business was small enough that we were
> all kind of in one building. As the business grew, we went into different build-
> ings. And I miss it because it's less of a rich experience. There's just fewer dif-
> ferent kinds of people [Interview 15C].

In much of our social world, class segregation for the most part does not allow
people from different classes to meet. For Quinn and Mike, circumstances had to
allow them to meet in the first place. In this case, their opportunity came from
their religious institutions. Both men noted how their churches were much more
economically diverse than their neighborhoods or workplaces. When presented
with the opportunity, they took it, although, as Quinn describes, it required him
to move out of his element.

> I was open to becoming friends with people on the trip, but I felt a little bit un-
> comfortable doing so because I didn't know anybody really, and you know,
> there was kind of an age gap with most of the people and kind of a class gap,
> too. I didn't quite know if I related to everybody on the trip, but Mike and his
> wife were very comfortable people to talk to and kind of went out of their way
> to include me and things like that. I just felt comfortable in befriending them;
> or they almost kind of befriended me it felt like [Interview 15C].

It is apparent that Quinn had to move out of his comfort zone in befriending
Mike. Even so, they have to make an effort to connect with one another now that
the trip is long since past. Quinn describes their experience of staying in touch.

> You know, it requires effort and we have to go out of our way to call each other
> rather than just bumping into each other at the golf course or something. We
> don't see each other as often as people who go to school together or work to-

*gether or something like that, but there's definitely a certain rhythm that I feel like, you know, it does feel strange if we haven't done something in a while. One of us will call the other and so it requires some sort of initiative on our part, but it's not that difficult to maintain even if the contact isn't as frequent* [Interview 15C].

Despite the initiative required to maintain their friendship beyond the context of the trip and the challenge of moving out of one's comfort zone in order to establish a friendship in the first place, the trip provided them with an opportunity they'd never have otherwise given how class-segregated our society is. Given the relevance of the institutional context, I imagine that many people who would be open to friendships across socially constructed boundaries never get to make friends like Mike and Quinn because such segregation is not conducive to meeting and interacting with diverse others on an equal-status basis. Rude's research on cross-racial friendships notes three characteristics of institutional contexts that are conducive to the formation of diverse friendships: (1) the institutional setting must be an integrated one,[2] (2) it must provide an opportunity for personalized interaction, and (3) it must allow the individuals to discover a common, superordinate identity—"an identity common to both that cross-cut their more visible . . . differences" (2009, 92-94). It is apparent that, in the case of Mike and Quinn, these conditions were met in the context of their interfaith trip to Europe and they were able to establish a cross-class friendship that otherwise would not have been possible.

Class segregation is obviously a prominent feature of the social and institutional structure of our society. But it is by no means the only contemporary source of segregation. We even self-segregate by age and ageism is a common phenomenon despite or perhaps because of the ageing of society (Bousfield and Hutchinson 2010; Harwood *et al.* 2005; and McPherson, Smith-Lovin, and Cook 2001). In their paired interview focusing on the age difference between them, Bob (who is the older of the two and retired) and Jerry (who is close to twenty-five years Bob's junior) talked about the separation of the generations. Bob made the good point that there is less contact between generations today than in the past when you might have three generations in the same household.

*BOB: I don't think the kids are exposed that much to older people.*
*JERRY: I would agree with this.*
*BOB: Especially in older families where the extended family was all living together, you had more generations, aunts and uncles and family friends intermingling more.*
*JERRY: Yeah, there was a lot more interaction between different generations. Even when I was growing up, my parents had me young so I had great-grandparents and grandparents. And now my sister just had her first baby and there's only one set of grandparents left. Because people are waiting longer to have children, they [the children] aren't exposed to as many grandparents or great-grandparents as you were at one time, you know.*

*BOB: I can also see, at least in small towns and neighborhoods where you tended to know everyone, older people would be friends to kids. Kids would do chores for them and they'd become friends. And the families, they also were closer together. Now your folks retire and move to some retirement community or eventually end up in an old-folks home* [Interview 11C].

While contact between the generations is still very much a part of our lives, Bob and Jerry notice how it is declining over time. Kids still see their surviving grandparents, but it's more likely to be a visit than sharing a household. Older people are more likely to separate themselves into retirement communities and we are more likely to place our elderly family members in rest homes. In the classic one-room schoolhouse, children of all ages were together. Now they are separated by grade level and between primary and secondary schools. In other words, we basically have a situation where the segregation between the generations is increasing. This again demonstrates the importance of the institutional context in either bringing diverse populations together or keeping them apart. So, while Bob and Jerry feel they haven't actually *done* anything to bridge the age gap in their friendship, the emergence of their friendship first depended on an institutional context (they are neighbors within the same condo building) that allowed them to meet in the first place. Without this context providing the opportunity, such a friendship would be much less likely to occur. Without institutional support for such friendships, individuals aren't even given the option to overcome ageism, sexism, racism, homophobia, and so on. The choice to live by prejudice or reject it is taken away from them.

A remaining question to consider is why we engage in so much self-segregation according to race, gender, sexual orientation, class, religion, ability, or age. Deborah (who is a convert to Judaism) spoke to this question in the context of her interfaith friendship with Fatima (who is Muslim).

*I think friendships between Muslims and Jews are rare for the same reason that we have racial prejudice or any other sort of prejudice. It's because people don't understand each other on a personal level; they look at the group or the label that you're associated with, and don't get past that. I think it's important for people with similar backgrounds or whatever to have that sense of community, but you got to step out of it sometimes and I think that's the problem. People don't step out of their own communities often enough . . . I think fear has a lot to do with it. And I think the more frightened people get of world events and the economy or whatever, the more they cling to what's known and familiar, not the unknown devil. They're least likely to go exploring if they're concerned for their safety, whether it's real or imagined. There's also something safe and comfortable about being with people who are just like you and think like you and look like you. So, I think those are the barriers. And some people have difficulty perspective taking, getting into somebody else's shoes* [Interview 17A].

A great point that Deborah brought up is that many people don't leave the comfort of their circle. In the context of religion, it's almost as if people fear that by finding a different religion interesting they then have to believe it. So they are less likely to even try to understand such a difference. We can better understand this by looking at it in terms of identity. An appreciation for a different culture, religion, race, or what have you may become a part of who we are, but we don't have to become a part of that culture or let that culture take possession of us. We can if we want to, but there's no automatic, involuntary "possession" there. I found this very interesting, especially when placed in the context of the other social boundaries. Perhaps we fear that by sympathizing or empathizing with the other, we will become the other or become like the other. For example, someone might think, "I'm going to turn gay if I associate with gay people." Or, "I'm going to become a sissy or a wimp if I associate with women too closely." Or, " I'm going to be less white if I associate with too many blacks."

These thoughts are indicative of an awareness of what, in social psychology, is known as a "courtesy stigma" (Goffman 1963, 30). In other words, we can be "guilty by association." This isn't so much that one will turn gay by associating with gay people, although some may feel that way. Instead, it is more a question of how we believe others will *perceive* us. They might perceive us to be gay if we associate with too many gay people. This isn't simply a groundless fear. Research indicates, for example, that those straight male college students who roomed voluntarily with a gay student were more likely to suffer a courtesy stigma than those who involuntarily roomed with a gay student (Sigelman *et al.* 1991). We see that the other is a target of prejudice and we fear becoming the targets of the same prejudice.

Deborah also highlights some classic points that sociologists understand to be integral to the dynamics of in-groups and out-groups as discussed in the previous chapter (see Allport 1954). We can get so caught up with the differences between ourselves and the members of a different group that we lose sight of our commonalities. It is easy to fear those others because of their differences. It is the classic fear of the unknown. As a result, we are less motivated to roletake and see the world from their perspective. Instead of an accurate understanding of the other group, we take a distorted view of them characterized by stereotypes and labels. Ultimately, we avoid contact with the other group and self-segregate among those who are similar to ourselves (Tredoux and Finchilescu 2007; Finchilescu 2005).

To the extent that such social segregation exists, we live in a society where the possibilities for friendships crossing social categories are not as wide as we might think. We like to imagine we live in a world in which there is egalitarianism and greater parity in status; nevertheless, given the evidence described above, we are deluding ourselves as to its extent. Even so, it is true that our workplaces, schools, churches, and sometimes even neighborhoods are more socially integrated today than in the past, for these are the contexts in which the vast majority (33 out of 40—82.5 percent—of the friendship pairs) of those interviewed met and established their friendship.

In terms of the data gathered for this study, and keeping in mind that the data is not representative of the entire U.S. population, simply taking a look at where the friends met is informative and suggestive of the larger social patterns at work. The largest proportion of those I interviewed met in the workplace (14 of 40, or 35 percent of the friendships included in the study).[3] Twenty percent (8 of 40) of the friendships began in a school setting (mostly college—only one friendship began in elementary school). Churches and religious organizations accounted for 7.5 percent (3 of 40) of the settings in which the friends met. The same figure holds true for those who befriended a neighbor or roommate (outside of the college setting)—7.5 percent—as well as those who met through a club or group (such as Alcoholics Anonymous, the Kiwanas, or a gym)—again 7.5 percent. Two of the friendship pairs (5 percent) depended upon an institutional context other than the ones already mentioned—one a bar setting, another at a day camp for children.

Given that 82.5 percent (again, 33 out of 40) of these friends met in such institutional contexts, it is apparent that it is our work environments (Putnam 2000), our schools (Rawlins 2009 and Fischer 2008), our churches (Rude 2009 and Yancey 1999), and so on that provide us with our primary opportunity to cross paths and interact as equals with those who are different from ourselves in terms of race, gender, sexual orientation, and so on. This is why the integration of these institutions has played a crucial role in shaping the demographic diversity of many people's friends. To the extent that these institutional settings are more fully integrated across the lines of race, class, sexual orientation, gender, religion, age, and ability, we are presented with more opportunities to meet people from diverse backgrounds and perhaps establish lasting friendships with them. Even so, as it became evident above, we are required to step outside of our own comfort zone and overcome any fear of differences that we may have. On the other hand, to the extent that we continue to self-segregate within our schools, churches, clubs, bars, workplaces, and so on, we limit our opportunities to establish such friendships regardless of how integrated these institutions are. While this means we never have to step outside of our comfort zone, it also means a life that is closed off and isolated from an increasingly diverse world around us.

So, we now know that the majority of those studied—82.5 percent—met within integrated institutional contexts. The remaining seven friendships (17.5 percent) were established outside of an institutional context and instead emerged out of a larger social network of friends. This pattern seems somewhat counterintuitive. We generally think that we make friends through our other friends. However, that was not the case for the majority of these unlikely friendships that bring together people from different social categories. And while it is possible that this is an idiosyncrasy of the sample, I think there is more going on here.

Given what we have learned with regard to self-segregation and our homophilous relationship patterns in which we are more likely to establish friendships with those who are similar to ourselves, it seems more probable that the people we meet through our existing social network are not that likely to be as diverse a group as those we meet within other institutional settings. Recognizing this point further emphasizes the importance of the institutional context to the emergence of these friendships. Outside of the workplace, our schools, and our churches, we are not as likely to meet people from diverse backgrounds, much less establish significant friendships with them. Even so, while our existing social networks might not be the most fruitful in terms of meeting people from diverse backgrounds, they are—as will be seen in the next section—absolutely crucial to developing and sustaining these friendships.

## Group Context

The group context is perhaps the most readily apparent to all of us in terms of the friendships we develop. While the socio-cultural and institutional contexts are of great importance, it is the influence of our friends, partners/spouses, and family that exert the most direct influence on our relationships. If this group context is inclusive and accepting (Crystal, Killen, and Ruck 2008), then it is much easier to pursue diverse friendships. In her research on intimate partners, Felmlee argues that "couples do not exist in isolation; rather, they are embedded in social networks that influence them in a variety of ways" (2001, 1259). While the friends studied here are not intimate couples, these dyadic relationships are also embedded in influential social networks. They too are shaped by the approval or disapproval of the members of the social network. As Felmlee observes, positive reactions are likely to strengthen the dyadic relationship while a lack of support or actual disapproval may undermine it.

While only a minority of those friendships studied actually emerged within this group context, it is nevertheless quite clear that a supportive social network of family, friends, and partners/spouses are crucial to the long-term maintenance of these friendships that cross social categories. Among those I interviewed, and as will be described below, there was only one friendship in which there was an adverse reaction to the friend of a different social category among the closest members of the friends' social network. In this particular friendship, the level of intimacy and closeness has noticeably decreased, although the friendship has survived. Beyond that, while some family, friends, or partners/spouses may have expressed initial surprise and may have taken time to warm up to the friendship, all of those I interviewed expressed how the members of their social networks were largely supportive of their friendship. Keep in mind, though, that those studied represent the success cases; so it comes as no surprise that the vast majority of them report supportive social networks. Not surprisingly, the reactions of some members of our social network are much more influential than the reactions of others; but, as will be seen below, it is the response of the partner or spouse which seems to exert the most influence in maintaining these friendships. Balancing one's obligations to one's partner or spouse with the outside friendship can be a challenge for the individual. So, how is this balance achieved? We will also consider the question of how the individual who reaches out to someone outside of her or his social category is subsequently accepted by members of her or his own social category.

## Extended Family and Other Friends

The vast majority of those interviewed experienced positive reactions from the others who are closest to them. When there are negative reactions from others, one has to consider the salience of those reactions and the salience of the connection between those reacting negatively and the individuals in the friendship. So, for example, Kelly (who is white) describes some negativity on the part of her grandparents to her friendship with Colin (who is black):

> There's still the family pressure from my grandparents of, "You're not dating him, are you?" That causes some strain for Colin. If he were to go to a family event, he doesn't want to hear what they have to say when it's like that. And it's really hard to change someone who's really that set in their ways . . . they kind of have the mindset of, "It's okay to be friends with [blacks], just don't date them." I suppose what makes the difference for them is the possibility of multiracial grandchildren. That, and just their own stereotypes of what type of relationship an African-American male has with a Caucasian female [Interview 1A].

While Kelly has experienced this negativity on the part of her grandparents, how much does she care that they have a negative reaction—especially since she and Colin are not dating (while her sister is dating him)? Is it relevant to her? Are their opinions important to her as she makes her own decisions? In this case, it is apparent that the reactions of her grandparents, while they exert some pressure upon her, are not salient enough for Kelly to change her mind about her friendship with Colin.

Nicole (who is straight) has had a close friendship with Eva (who is lesbian) for the past twenty-two years. They met in college and, while they live in different states, they keep in touch regularly and visit one another at least once a year. The majority of Nicole's friends are very accepting of Eva. Still, there are a few with a more conservative outlook who are not open to their friendship. She noted that she has a full spectrum of friends with regard to attitudes toward gays and lesbians, which makes Nicole one of the few interviewed who has indicated that any of her friends are less open about such diversity. At the same time, her friends with differing views on the issue know not to say anything too offensive to her; but it does sound like she talks about the issues with them. In fact, there are times when she will challenge some of her less accepting friends.

> *I have friends who are in different stages of homophobia. I definitely have friends who don't understand people being gay. They sort of see it as a choice rather than as who a person is intrinsically. And I have friends who are completely fine with it and have their own gay friends, and I have friends who are trying. They're sort of in the middle—stuck and struggling with it: "I think it's fine and it's none of my business, but marriage is still between a man and a woman," you know. So, I've had those sorts of conversations with some of my straight friends.*
>
> *From my end, I just find it baffling. And I'm like "Well, what does marriage mean? Marriage stands for a commitment. It's about love. It's about two people wanting to share their lives together." So, I actually question my friends . . . "Help me understand this. I don't understand what you're saying." I also try to influence people when there are measures on the ballot and things like that. I try to get them to vote, you know, to honor those relationships even if, from a religious standpoint, they don't think that marriage can be possible between two people of the same sex. I just try to get them on the sort of more philosophical angle of rights and legal privileges. . . .*
>
> *I think people who don't get how I can be good friends with a lesbian, you know, I think they know me well enough not to say that because that would just shut me down. Like, "Okay, I can't talk to you anymore." If somebody were to try to say anything bad about Eva to me or try to interfere with our being friends because of the fact that we're different in that way, I mean neither Eva nor I would respond to that in any sort of a way that other person could get any satisfaction out of* [Interview 36B].

Nicole is not afraid to challenge some of her less accepting friends. Moreover, it is apparent in this passage that her friendship with Eva is much more salient to her and has a much higher priority, given that she is willing to no longer speak to those who would actually vocalize whatever problem they had with her friendship. This attitude and experience is very much like all those I interviewed. When they faced negative reactions from others, which were rare, it was from those whose relationship was less salient to them than the friendship that was the focus of the interview. Their friendship was more important to them.

The idea of terminating a relationship with a person who was not accepting of one's friend actually came up several times over the course of my interviews, even if the unaccepting person was a boy/girlfriend or partner/spouse. For example, Hugo sent an e-mail (with his friend Debbie's permission) to me describing how Debbie's boyfriend was jealous of Hugo and could not understand or believe that their friendship wasn't actually an under-cover sexual relationship. *"Three weeks ago he told Debbie she had to 'pick him or me. There is not enough room for me in the relationship.' Debbie picked me! I cannot believe this even today. She said, 'I would be crazy to give up a friend like you. You're fam-*

*ily. You're always there for me.'"* In the same vein, Eric was adamant that anyone who didn't accept the fact that Brad was gay wouldn't be his friend. Speaking directly to Brad, he said, *"If someone were not to accept you or mistreat you
because they knew you were gay, they wouldn't be my friend anymore. And if my
wife would have reacted differently, I might not be married today. I mean that.
I'm serious"* [Interview 7C]. In his one-on-one interview, which occurred prior
to this paired interview, Eric explained this same point to me, saying, *"If my
wife objected, that might put our relationship together in jeopardy because I
would wonder, 'Who is this person I made some commitments to'"* [Interview
7A]. Statements and actions such as these not only indicate the strength and importance of these friendships crossing social categories for those who enjoy
them, they also highlight how important it is for them to have friends,
boy/girlfriends, and partners/spouses who share their same values with regard to
diversity within their social circle. It is out of those shared values that the supportive group context is created.

Again, however, the vast majority of those interviewed had no negative reactions from those around them.[4] These friendships exist and thrive in a group
context that is, by and large, highly supportive of diversity within their social
circle. For example, Sarah (who is bisexual) notes that most of her circle of
friends wouldn't be upset by the sexual orientation difference between herself
and her friend Matt (who is straight) because she hangs out with people whom
she describes as already open-minded [Interview 2C]. This is typical: the circle
of people around the two friends, because of a similarity in attitudes and values,
are already pretty supportive. Adding to this point, Laura explains that, from her
experience, her friends are just as likely to have other friends who are from different social categories. Given that her friends also have a diverse friendship
network, the fact that one of her closest friends is male elicits no reaction at all.
In fact, she noted how homogenous her circle of friends is in terms of values
supporting diversity, highlighting how we tend to insulate ourselves among like-
minded people.

> *I have friends who are similar in that they have had some long-term friendships
> with the opposite gender. So, it's like you start to realize how much you insu-
> late yourself among like-minded people sometimes—very diverse people, but
> very like-minded in terms of values. That's interesting* [Interview 9B].

In fact, given how common this supportive group context is, one might argue
that it is group contexts such as this that make these friendships possible in the
first place, although research on those who were not successful in creating and
maintaining these friendships would be required to validate that conclusion.

## A Partner or Spouse

Perhaps the most salient of relationships within the group context would be one's spouse or partner. It is here that the impact of the group context was most apparent and required the greatest effort on the part of the individual interviewed—and sometimes the effort of his or her friend as well—to navigate through the relational dynamics. Moreover, within our socio-cultural context, couple relationships are typically given priority over friendships (Rawlins 2009 and Brain 1976), which makes maintaining friendships that go against the wishes of one's partner all the more challenging. It is a common experience for a friendship to change when one member enters a love relationship with a third individual. When introducing a third person, the dynamics are much more complicated and there is the possibility that one or another individual may feel left out—in this case, the spouse/partner or the outside friend (see Simmel 1950). Therefore, it requires more work to make sure that the spouse/partner's desires and needs are met while simultaneously trying to maintain one's friendship in such a way that the friend doesn't feel abandoned or neglected.

The complications arising from such a triad are familiar to most people. Here, though, we are going to focus on how the difference in social category from one's friend can (but does not have to) further complicate this dynamic. There were several friendships in which the reaction of the spouse or partner was problematic for outside friendships; although in only one of these instances did the reaction have negative consequences for the friendship.[5] As might be expected, those instances of a negative reaction from a spouse or partner were often a result of the possibility of a sexual attraction between the two friends. Managing the issue of attraction within the friendship itself will be covered in chapter 4. Here the focus will be on the impact of the spouse or partner on the overall group dynamics. Keep in mind, however, that these cases were not typical of those studied. In the vast majority of cases, the partner or spouse was supportive of the friendship, again highlighting how a supportive social network helps these diverse friendships succeed.

The first example of a friendship in which a partner is less supportive involves Jordan, a bisexual man[6] who is in a long-term relationship with another man, and his straight friend Shawn. Jordan, for much of his life, has lived within a largely heterosexual world. As a result, the vast majority of his friends are straight. Only since he began his relationship with his partner has he begun to move within social circles of gay men and lesbians. In contrast, his partner Nate is very connected to the gay community and this difference between them has been a source of some tension in their relationship. For example, Nate is not comfortable with Jordan's straight friends even though they are all accepting of Jordan and ask how Nate is doing, showing their interest. According to Jordan, Nate's reaction is all about his comfort level in a straight environment as opposed to a gay environment.

*Nate's gone through so much . . . perhaps abuse or simply not being accepted. And he carries that with him, so if he gets upset about something, he turns a cheek and walks away and his smile's back on. He's gotten to the point where he's chosen not to attend or partake in functions with my straight friends or even around my family. I've called him on it and, you know, that's something we need to work on. All my friends have been receptive to him, always asking where he's at if he's not there, and the boys have been very social and go up and talk with him. You know, the guys for the most part, are totally fine with him* [Interview 38A].

Nate apparently struggled while growing up and coming out and was in a lot of conflict with straight individuals; hence it is understandable that he is uncomfortable in an environment he sees as "straight," even if the individual straight people we're talking about here have no problems with his sexual orientation. The irony is that, while Jordan's friends—especially Shawn and his wife—are comfortable with and accepting of Nate, Nate's gay friends are not all that accepting of Jordan, due in large part to his "strait-laced" ways—what they perceive as closeted. In other words, they seem to be intolerant of what Nate is willing to put up with, even if it annoys him at times.

*. . . [I]t's the same with his friends. They aren't all that accommodating. Actually my friends have been much, much more receptive than his friends while his friends have been much more judgmental of me. And it's hard for me not to be judgmental based on some of the things that were said and some of the things that are done by his friends* [Interview 38A].

While Nate's reaction to Jordan's straight friends has been a cause of some consternation, Jordan tolerates it and dismisses it as somewhat comical. As a result of this unconcerned attitude on his part, Jordan's friendship with Shawn has endured. In fact, the two couples will occasionally get together for dinner.

When you introduce the issue of attraction, however, the group dynamics can change dramatically. Jealousy is perhaps the most significant hurdle in these situations (Rawlins 2009). Brian's partner Corey has no problem with his friendship with Caroline because she is a woman and is therefore not threatening to him or their relationship. Sexual attraction is irrelevant as an issue. This apparently is not the case with Brian's gay male friends, at least those whom he actually dated, even if only for a couple weeks.

*When I met Corey, I had two male friends in my life that I had dated in the past, although the dating portion was very, very short. It was sort of like we went out a couple of times and I decided right away this was not working for me, but I really like the person and so chose to pursue a friendship with them. And we became good friends. These two guys have totally moved on. I moved on. They have partners and houses and dogs and whatever, and I have the same, so it's not like there's any chance of going back to dating. I just really enjoyed their company; but when Corey and I began our relationship, the fact that I had friends that I used to date really bothered him a lot. From my perspective, Corey shouldn't have any problem with that, but he had a big problem with it. Caroline and I talked about it when I asked her, "Would that make you uncomfortable?" She had a difficult time understanding the context given that all those involved are men and we're talking about gay culture, not straight culture. But she said, "Well I know that, back when I was married, if my husband had an old girlfriend who was a friend, it would have bothered me." But she's like, "This may be different for two guys and I don't understand the gay world in that way"* [Interview 39B].

Brian was put in the position of having to terminate those friendships because of Corey's strong negative feelings based on the past attraction and what he sees as a potential threat to his relationship with Brian. Since then, Brian has been wary in his friendships with other gay men simply because of the possibility of attraction and a jealous reaction on Corey's part.

*Given that Corey was super upset about the friendships I had with people I dated before, I'm very sensitive to making him uncomfortable with any male friends I might have. So, in the back of my mind when I'm interacting with friends of mine that are men, it's just something I worry about. I just would never want it to be a problem* [Interview 39B].

This jealousy actually became a significant problem in their relationship and, in a subsequent communication from Brian, I learned that he had ended his relationship with Corey. Corey's envious and controlling attitude was one reason for the breakup, but was certainly not the primary cause.

This issue falls into that broader pattern of a partner's view being crucial in cases where there may be or has been a physical attraction with an outside friend. It is extremely important for a partner to not feel threatened by a friendship. Accordingly, people have to deal with it in basically one of two ways: make the effort to increase the comfort level of the partner (a technique that will be covered in depth in chapter 4) or terminate the friendship—or at least demonstrably ease up on its intensity. Brian's situation exemplifies the termination of an outside friendship. The cross-gender friendship between Pam (who is single) and Tim (who is now married) illustrates a situation in which the intensity of their friendship has noticeably waned.

Pam and Tim have been good friends since Pam was a little girl. Tim was a friend of her older brother and they used to spend time together while waiting for her brother to come home from work. This provided them with the opportunity to engage in long conversations. Their friendship has survived life's complications, such as Tim moving to another part of the country and later returning, Pam going off to college, and so on. While able to preserve their friendship through those transitions, they struggle to maintain that same level of intimacy now that Tim is married to Becky. Pam, while friends with Becky, describes her as someone who gets jealous easily when it comes to Tim. She did not take kindly to Pam and Tim spending time alone together and actually confronted Pam about it.

> *Tim is married now and his wife Becky is a friend of mine. I think Becky's a really jealous person and had a really hard time with our friendship, and that's really affected it. She tends to be jealous of anybody—especially women—who's cool with Tim. You know what I mean? She's an awesome person, but that's just how she is, you know. She actually had a very big problem with me at first and I was totally oblivious to it. We had to go and sit down and talk. She's like, "I'm really bothered by this." And she kind of accused me of a lot of things and it was really, really weird. I was very sad, you know. And she straight out said, "Don't touch Tim." Tim and I are so relaxed, it was nothing for me to put my arm around him, or have his arm around me, which is really nothing to me. So I felt really uncomfortable after that conversation. Probably a year later or even less, she's totally apologized. She's like, "I was mean, insecure. I was jealous and blah, blah, blah." And I was like, "Well, do you feel better? Because you know that that isn't how it was . . . or do you feel better because Tim and I don't hang out anymore." And she basically said, "Well, I think if you were still hanging out a lot, I'd have a problem again"* [Interview 26A].

This passage exemplifies a point made by Rawlins when he says that, "it is difficult for a partner to understand and allow much time and affection for a perceived competitor." Such jealousy "drives a wedge between cross-sex friends" (2009, 123). As discussed earlier in this chapter, Becky is someone who does not think it is possible for men and women to be merely friends: if a woman is friendly with a man, she must have designs upon him. This is a point of view that is very foreign to Pam, but Pam has had to accommodate it. Today, she is much more understanding of Becky's position, especially given that Becky's relationship with Tim was so recent compared to her own.

> *I'm much more understanding now. It really bothered me at the time. I was a little annoyed with her because I thought it was unfair. I thought it was very possessive, you know. And I was annoyed with Tim because he never even mentioned it to me, and I know that he had talked about it with her. And I thought that he was showing that he didn't really value our friendship much if he was going to let her dictate something like that, you know. And now I think differently about it. It wasn't about me at all. And I understand that now; but at the time, it really bothered me. I was mad. I really stayed away from Tim for a long time because I felt like when we were together, I was under a microscope. You know what I mean? My natural way of behaving was not okay, you know. So that sucked* [Interview 26A].

As a result, Pam rarely sees Tim alone anymore. This prevents them from having the more intimate conversations that characterized the previous stage of their friendship.

*Tim and I still hang out, but certainly not every day like we used to. So, I'm still very cool with him and, you know, I would never not be cool with him, but we're not at all in the place that we had been for so long where we just saw each other all the time and hung out. Now when we see each other, it's usually in large groups for a barbeque or something because Becky made it very clear that she didn't feel at all comfortable with Tim and I hanging out by ourselves. They play volleyball on Friday nights and invite me every week, but I never go. So, I could see more of him, but I couldn't see more of just Tim. I'd have to say Tim and Becky . . . and I love them and I'm cool with that . . . but it's changed the dynamic of our friendship a lot. It's limited, you know. It doesn't have to be like that, you know, but it is. And like I say, our relationship is totally depend-ent on our communication and now that that's been compromised, it's nothing like it used to be as far as the way that we can talk and learn from each other. Those opportunities to talk are just gone. I expect that we'll always be friends, and I'm sure that as Becky maybe gets more comfortable with whatever, I imagine I'll be able to have that again one day. It's not something that I'm really bothered by like on a day-to-day basis, but . . . [Interview 26A].*

What is interesting about this situation is the difference in gender is not a prob-lem or hurdle between Pam and Tim. The fact that Pam is a woman rather than a man is a problem for Tim's wife Becky and it is her *reaction* that *makes* gender a factor that prevents them from maintaining as close a friendship as they once had (Felmlee 2001). In other words, the group context involving a spouse or partner can have a direct and negative impact on a friendship—a relationship without any institutional recognition as in marriage and therefore without any officially recognized legitimacy in society.

Both Pam and Tim are highly committed to their friendship, although Tim's commitment to his wife and kids is necessarily higher in terms of priorities. So, in terms of the relevance of the reactions of others for the friendship itself, it really depends on how committed the friend is to that outside relationship *as compared to* how committed the friends are to each other. It is a question of the priority of commitments: which relationship has higher priority? And when one relationship involves a partner or spouse, it is that relationship that is most likely to be given precedence (Rawlins 2009).

This issue of priorities does not have to involve attraction at all, as in the friendship between Barbara and Janice. They met at their workplace and have been friends for close to ten years, although their friendship developed only gradually. The focus of their interviews was on sexual orientation—Janice is lesbian and Barbara is straight. In their case, the fact that each of them is in a committed relationship with a partner or spouse adds an interesting complicating factor to their friendship—a complication that has nothing to do with posses-siveness or feeling threatened. Barbara describes her husband, saying:

*He's not one of these possessive people. I mean, we do not have a possessive relationship. He goes out. Some of his best friends or most of his friends are*

*women, and he'll go out to lunch with them alone. I don't give a shit. You*
*know, that's fine. You go out and do what you want. I trust him completely and*
*he can do that. So, we often have separate things that we do with separate peo-*
*ple. Mine are usually with women. His are usually with women, so there we go*
[Interview 22B].

Possessiveness is not the issue here. Instead, it is a matter of couple dynamics.
While Barbara spends a lot of time with her gay and lesbian friends like Janice,
she doesn't spend that much "couple time" with them. She wants her husband
Gene to enjoy going out on a double date with gay and lesbian friends, but if
he's not clicking with the other couple and doesn't have a good time, Barbara is
conscious of that. So they're less likely to do that in the future.

*You know, there's always one person in the couple who drives the friendship.*
*That's just kind of the way it works. I think that when you've got couple friends,*
*if you're not connecting with both pairs of the couple, the friendship doesn't*
*work very well. So if Gene can't connect with both of them or at least one of*
*them on some level, or I can't do the same thing, then the friendship doesn't*
*really work, because it's a twosome, and it's kind of hard to make it work. Be-*
*cause of this, I think that Gene and I—as a couple—feel closer to the hetero-*
*sexual couples than the gay couples, only because I think that Gene is the one*
*who has a harder time connecting. If he doesn't connect, then he's not happy.*
*And if he's not happy, then I'm not happy. And so if he's sitting there the whole*
*night being bored to tears thinking, "Why the fuck can't we get out of here?"*
*then I'm not happy. But I don't have to worry about him when it's a solo sort of*
*thing and I'm hanging out with my friend when he's not there* [Interview 22B].

While Gene is comfortable with gays and lesbians, he doesn't feel he has
enough in common to bond with them, particularly in the case of gay men. *"He*
*doesn't feel uncomfortable with the gay guys. He doesn't have any prejudice,*
*but he just doesn't know what to talk about, because the interests are so very*
*different. That's what it stems from"* [Interview 22B]. What Barbara describes is
far more subtle than Gene having a prejudiced attitude that interferes with his
wife's friendships. This is more about establishing connections. If he sees fewer
similarities, there's less opportunity for a connection to emerge. Note that this is
a matter of perception, not necessarily fact. In fact, individuals from diverse
backgrounds can have a lot in common, as seen in many of my interviews. Still,
if a person doesn't even see the possibility of commonality, then the opportunity
to establish connections may be forfeited because he or she doesn't even look
for such commonalities. I imagine this is why so few cross-category friendships
develop even as individuals become more tolerant of differences. In this case, it
hinders his wife's own friendships. Not that Barbara doesn't have and maintain
such friendships, but she's more likely to do this on her own. At the same time,
Gene receives a much higher priority in her life, which means that Barbara
won't be spending as much quality time in the evenings with friends like Janice.

*Gene has much higher priority. I mean my commitment is mainly him. He's my forever, you know, and he's the person that no matter what will always be there till the day I die, unless he dies first. He'll always be there. But, friends do come and go. Life changes, people move; but he's the one that's there and so yes, he's the higher priority in the friendship than anyone else. He's my best friend. So he's the number one priority.*

*I would like to be able to do more [with Janice and her partner], but I understand that sometimes it just doesn't work. And like I said, I'm not sure how much Gene connects and so sometimes that's hard. You know, we have limited time and so we might have to choose who we're going to do things with as a couple. Sometimes you got to say, "Okay, well who can Gene connect with?" because he tends to be an unhappy person. I don't know why. We couldn't have kids. Sometimes that makes him very sad. But our couple friends have kids and so I think that brings him a lot of joy to spend time with their children. And so I like to do that for him. Children are a really important thing for him. And so in our couple relationships, the children become very important. And so that's who we mostly do things with, because that's something that Gene needs in his life. And it's like I said: he's a priority. So if we do fewer things with other people as couples, that's fine [Interview 22B].*

So, Barbara and Janice became friends and even good friends, but there's still a larger group context that interferes with further potential development of the friendship. As many others note, Barbara's least favorite thing about her friendship with Janice is that they don't have as much time to spend together as she would like because they're both so busy; and part of what makes Barbara busy is her marriage, not just work.

This experience of trying to do "couple things" with one's friends and it not actually working was actually rather common among those I interviewed who were coupled. Jenna (who is lesbian) and Emily (who is straight) experienced the same thing, although they've known each other long enough that their friendship had to change when each one got partnered/married and had children. The hurdles that exist in their friendship are caused by devotion to their respective families, which consumes a lot of their time. This has caused them to lose some of their spontaneity and ability to get together as often. Emily admits that it makes her sad that they do not get together as often but realizes there has been a change in their lives. Again, sexual orientation makes no direct difference in their friendship. On the other hand, Emily confesses that getting together as couples with her friend Jenna and Jenna's husband is sometimes an uncomfortable event. Jenna explains that it is hard for Emily's husband to be around so many women. It is not that he does not like Jenna and her partner, but that there is no male for him to relate to. She thinks it is his lack of self-esteem and frustration because his wife "attaches on to other women" so easily.

*The only difference that my being a lesbian has had on our friendship has to do with Emily's husband Dan. Dan doesn't have trouble with me being gay. Instead, I think he has a lack of self-esteem and maybe self-confidence that makes*

*him uneasy when Emily is attached to other women, 'cause I think it's out of his*
*realm, something that he can't touch. I've heard him say in the past that he is*
*uncomfortable when he's in a big group. There are many times when we're at*
*parties together and Dan's the only guy there. And I think that's hard on Emily.*
*That's really hard on Emily, and I think that's affected our friendship in that I*
*think we would spend more time together otherwise. I think if I was in a rela-*
*tionship with a man, that we would probably spend more time together, be-*
*cause then Dan would have someone to hang out with who wasn't a girl. She*
*talks about them having more couple friends to hang out with, and I know she*
*means a man and a woman together, not two women or not two men. So I think*
*that would have made it easier for us to spend more time together* [Interview
24A].

In the cases of both Jenna and Emily and Barbara and Janice, the husband of the
straight person in the friendship has a hard time identifying with the lesbians and
therefore prefers not to spend time with his spouse's lesbian friend and her partner. In other words, a common couple dynamic is here combined with the added
effect of sexual orientation: the husband feels that he has even less chance to
identify with his wife's friend. This really highlights that, in those friendships
where one or both friends are partnered, the attitudes and comfort level of three
or four people must be taken into account, not simply two people. This multi-
plied effect of attitudes makes such friendships even more challenging. As
we've seen, in both of these cases they have been at least somewhat successful
at maintaining the friendship despite spouse/partner challenges. The case of Pam
and Tim indicates that there are times when the spouse "wins out" and the intensity of the friendship diminishes or even dies entirely. If the friendship died entirely, then they wouldn't even have been included in this research project; so
that outcome may actually be much more common than indicated here. At the
very least, the couple dynamic does add a challenge to the friendship because
they do not end up seeing as much of each other as they might want to if one or
the other (or both) of their respective partners are not willing to join in, because,
when partnered, the emphasis seems to be on doing things as a couple. For this
reason, partners are given higher priority when there is a lack of connection with
the friend.

Because group dynamics are so dramatically affected by the presence of or
addition of one or two partners/spouses, friends will often make a demonstrable
effort to connect with their friend's partner/spouse or encourage their own part-
ner/spouse to connect. Such "common friends" are particularly effective in managing the larger group dynamics (Rawlins 2009, 122). This is due to the fact that
the friendship and the couple relationship become embedded with one another,
increasing the overall stability of these relationships (Felmlee 2001; see also
Hallinan 1974 and Simmel 1950). This is exactly how the friendship between
Kris and Kim has developed over time as first one got married and then the
other got engaged. Both are straight and the focus of their interviews was on
gender. The reader will recall that they met through a group of friends who regu-

larly get together for a ski trip. When Kris later got married, Kim didn't set out to become friends with his wife Brianna in order to maintain her friendship with him. From her perspective, it just happened. *"I wanted to be friends with her, but I was never so intentional about it. I had a lot of other stuff going on at the time while dating Kris's friend. So actually, Brianna and I are friends because we're friends, because we like each other"* [Interview 37C]. Kris, on the other hand, was very intentional about encouraging Brianna and Kim to become friends by providing them with opportunities. At one point, he and Brianna had a conversation about their approach to having opposite-sex friendships.

> *A guy friend of mine was married but still maintained relationships with other women that he'd dated. So, his wife sort of felt like he was keeping them in reserve. That's where it becomes so important that those friendships be out in the open. In his particular case, he would sometimes get together with those ex-girlfriends for lunch and basically he had relationships with these people independent from his wife. Well that isn't conducive to trust and mutuality and that's why I felt it was so important that Brianna, Kim, and I over time evolve a mutual friendship. And it was absolutely intentional on my part. I encouraged Brianna to chat with you [Kim] and encouraged you to chat with her.*
>
> *Early in our marriage, Brianna and I had a conversation about friends of the opposite sex and whether one could do that. We had a very explicit conversation about how the friendship needs to involve all three parties and that if it can't evolve to that, then that is probably a friendship that may not get as much time as other friendships. As a result, it would probably wither. They say that you should talk about money and children before you get married because those are such important things. But I would say that the subject of friends would certainly be another conversation worth having because if it turns out someone was of the opinion you can't be just friends with someone of the opposite sex, that can be a source of friction* [Interview 37C].

Kris and his wife Brianna came up with a common understanding of how to approach it, engaging in open dialogue and perhaps even negotiation. For her part, Kim is looking forward to getting married to her fiancé Eddie and believes that this will bring her and Kris closer together since they would now have the opportunity to do couples things together: something that's never been possible before. *"It might be easier for me when I'm married. We can do couple things together. I think Kris and Brianna really want me to get married so we can do double date stuff"* [Interview 37C]. What this attitude and Kris and Brianna's agreement about opposite-sex friendships have in common is the fact that partners are included in order to strengthen the friendship in question. Without that effort at inclusion, the friendship may suffer.

## Accepting Those Who Have Crossed Category Lines

Finally, for these friendships to emerge and succeed over time, two questions must be addressed: (1) are they accepted within the group context and social category of their friend? And (2) are they accepted within the group context of their own social category when they return? Or do these individuals become "marginal men" and women in the sense of the term used by Robert Park (1937): "destined to live as strangers in two 'different' and 'antagonistic' cultures" (Korgen 2002, 72). This is an area that has been particularly neglected within sociological research (Allan and Adams 1998).[7] Individuals who establish these friendships that cross socially constructed categories, as will be seen in chapter 4, have to reach out and meet their friend halfway across the social boundary that separates them.

Much of what has already been covered in this section addresses the first question. Still, there is one point to add: often the person from outside the social category is viewed with curiosity and even suspicion within the circle of friends they enter. For example, in the gay/straight friendship between Dave and Tom, it was not until the paired interview that Tom learned for the first time that Dave's gay friends wondered if Tom were really straight or merely a closet case.

> DAVE: *Well, you know, there has been some reaction within my social circle quite frankly, and it's reflected poorly on them.*
> TOM: *Oh, really? You have people that have reacted . . .*
> DAVE: *Well, their reaction to you at first was, "Well, he's a closet case." I'm like, "No, he's not a closet case, he's straight." And they said, "No, he's a closet case." I said, "Okay, well if he's a closet case, then the line starts behind me because I met him first. But I'm telling you, he's not a closet case." Gay men all wish that straight men were open and accepting and above board like you are and could get along with them and accept them as they are, how they are, where they are and not give a shit; but when they meet a straight man who's like that, they immediately flip into the, "Well he's just a closet case" mode. Well, you can't have it both ways. It took about, oh I'd say six months after they kept meeting you and meeting you and meeting you. And you're very consistent and very much the same and finally they got it in their heads. Now, it's a non-event. "Oh, Tom's here. Tom is Dave's friend." It doesn't even come up. It's not even mentioned.*
>
> *I think there might have been a certain amount of, I'm going to use the word envy on their part because in some ways they wished they had a friendship like that . . . that deep down they wish they had a nice, straight friend they had lots in common with and they got along with. That's what our friendship has been. And I think that they were a little envious of that; but I think they showed their own bigotry and their own double standards and their own prejudices. I think those attitudes reared their ugly head, and I confronted them on those issues directly, and I really held their toes to the fire and made them accountable for what they said. I forced them to address what came out of their mouth. I told them, "You can't have it both ways." Basically, I very bluntly told*

*them to put up or shut up. And so I think they all shut up and then they all had to think about it, and like I say at this point it's not an issue.*
*TOM: I'm surprised. I wouldn't have thought that you would have the reaction from them that it sounds like you had. I'm surprised. It's interesting. I didn't realize that was going on at all. I didn't know that. I'm not sure what to think. I'm just surprised that it went on and I guess I'm surprised that your gay friends would have thought that.*
*DAVE: And I will say this: you are the exception compared to most people. I mean you are probably one percent of the heterosexual male population as far as, (a) it doesn't matter, but (b) having your whole life together and being very comfortable with who you are and where you are and how you are and what's going on in your world.*
*TOM: Thank you. You're being way too flattering, but I'm not sure that's . . . I think other people maybe just haven't had the opportunity to be in this situation* [Interview 6C].

Dave spent a lot of subsequent time during this interview engaging in "damage control" to make sure Tom knew it had nothing to do with him and how he behaved and had everything to do with how these gay men thought. For his part, Tom indicated that this was interesting and that he was surprised. I think this information was too new to him for Tom to feel much more than that: surprised and interested. And this isn't an isolated example. Like Dave, Brad also mentioned how other gay men react to comfortable straight men by assuming they must be closet cases [Interview 7B]. Within his circle of friends, however, no one has said that about his friend Eric because not many of Brad's gay friends have met him given that he lives in another part of the country. Both of these cases exemplify the courtesy stigma discussed earlier in the chapter: the sexuality of the straight friend is questioned simply because he is close friends with a gay man.

While these examples focus on gay and straight men, the phenomenon is not limited to them. Men who were good friends with women were perceived as being more in touch with their feminine side, and the women in these friendships were likewise perceived as being more in touch with their masculine side. Whites who befriended people of other races were perceived as "less white on the inside" and their counterparts were perceived as being more white on the inside. In other words, the perceptions of others tended to highlight how the friend from outside their own social category was actually more like themselves. We tend to assume that those with whom we interact must be similar to ourselves (Shibutani and Kwan 1965). As a result, the friend is perceived as more acceptable within their group context.

Then there is the second question posed above: What happens when the individual who has stepped outside of his or her own social category in order to establish a friendship returns to his or her own group context? Do members of their own group accept them? Actually, the exact same thing happens, only in reverse. The members of their own group potentially perceive the individual differently—as more feminine than most men or more masculine than most women, as less white or less Latino, and so on. Courtesy stigma yet again operates such that there may be "guilt by association" in the eyes of others, as if we are not "real" members of our own group. Those who step out of their own ingroup and establish friendships are subsequently marginalized within their own group (Castelli, De Amicis, and Sherman 2007). In-group members expect loyalty and they expect the other members of the in-group to be just like themselves in terms of who they will accept as friends (Shibutani and Kwan 1965). The fear of being perceived as disloyal to one's own group is potentially a major reason why these friendships that cross socially constructed boundaries are less common than one might expect. It prevents some people from even attempting to build such friendships. Others, as will be seen below, feel permanently disconnected from and unaccepted by members of their own social category and so they never really return to it.

Overall, what we have learned in this section is how critical the group context is for these friendships that cross social categories. In cases where there is a partner or spouse, that partner or spouse must be considered an integral part of the group dynamics. While, as in the case of Kris and Kim, this can work to strengthen their own friendship, it can also create special challenges to maintaining one's friendship (as we saw in the previous two cases involving Barbara and Janice as well as Jenna and Emily), or may even threaten the friendship, as we saw with Pam and Tim, whose friendship teetered on the brink for a while and has certainly diminished in intensity. Friendships "do not exist in isolation" (Felmlee 2001), so the larger social network in which these diverse friendships are embedded is a crucial factor in their emergence and survival. The group context must be supportive in order to encourage a diverse set of friends. Moreover, the members of the larger social network must be willing to accept into their fold the individual who has moved beyond his or her own social category in establishing friendships.

## Individual Context

While it is crucial for a sociologist to consider the cultural, institutional, and group context in which the individual resides, there are still some very important sociological points to consider at the level of individual experiences and how they might further shape the individual's opportunities to develop and maintain friendships that cross social categories of all kinds. For example, individuals often engage in "cognitive filtering" in which they attribute a host of additional differences upon those who are demographically different from them. In this way, they disregard potential friends on the basis of the socially constructed boundaries between them (Rude 2009; see also Tajfel *et al.* 1971). On the other hand, our focus here will be on how those studied selected in favor of those who were demographically different from them. We will consider the relevance of having similar personal qualities with one's friend. In order to go beyond the obvious, we will also look at how the individual has internalized the norms from our broader cultural context and the impact that has on their friendship patterns. Moreover, there were a number of those interviewed who expressed how disconnected they felt from the members of their own social category. The individual's personal experiences with members of other social categories are also highly influential in this process. Together, these factors shape the comfort level of the individual in moving outside of his or her own social category when establishing friendships. Finally, there is the issue of perception. Ultimately, one's individual perception of social categories and their relevance is shaped by all the previously mentioned factors. And it is that perception that creates so much openness to establishing friendship ties that cross over different social categories.

## Similar Personal Qualities

Perhaps the first individual-level factor to come to mind would be the personal qualities that the two friends have in common. Given how much is already known about the relevance of these similarities and our later attention to how the friends concentrate on their hidden commonalities (see chapter 4), I will focus less on this in favor of other individual-level factors. You will recall from chapter 1 that the research on homophily indicates that we tend to develop relationships with those who are similar to ourselves. The focus there was on "status homophily," which is based on demographics like race, gender, and sexual orientation. At the same time, we tend to develop relationships with those who share our same values, attitudes, beliefs, and interests. This is known as "value homophily" (McPherson, Smith-Lovin, and Cook 2001, 419). While the diverse friendships studied represent those crossing socially constructed boundaries and the pattern of status homophily discussed in the previous chapter, it appears that they still reflect the trend toward value homophily. These cases demonstrate that value homophily supersedes status homophily in the development of these relationships.

Our friends are people with whom we share our interests, whether for skiing as with Kris and Kim or good conversation over a cup of coffee as with Hugo and Debbie. While shared interests are important, it was apparent that shared values were much more influential even if they weren't specifically mentioned. For example, recall that Mike and Quinn met on an interfaith trip to Eastern Europe and Italy. While they are different in terms of their class backgrounds (the focus of their interviews) and also religions (Mike is Jewish while Quinn is Catholic), an important part of what keeps them together is their shared value system that was reflected in their both signing up for this particular trip. As Mike says,

> Our politics are similar, the way we perceive people in relationships and public behaviors between and among people I think are similar. I think we both value honesty and kindness. I think we both are concerned with the class issue. There's a saying from the Talmud, which is a book of writings that support the Torah, the first five books of the Old Testament, that says: "Act now while you can, while you have the chance, the means and the strength." So we're both driven to do that and to help those who need help. And he's actually been a role model for people. He's much better at this stuff than I am [Interview 15B].

While Mike highlights the fact that he and Quinn share the same values, Miriam highlights how the fact that she and her friend Dave have common values allows her to respect his input and opinions despite all the differences between them.

> We have a lot of shared interests, but there are some key differences where I could . . . wow, we're very different. But I think that, at the core of who we are and what makes us tick, we're probably more alike than we are different, you know. Things come up where you would rely on somebody who's really close if you needed to talk about something with them. For example, I can imagine a bunch of things that are going to come up with the kids where, even though he doesn't want kids and doesn't want to be around kids, I would still very much value his opinion on how to deal with a situation with the kids or something. You know, I definitely, definitely value his opinion on things, because I know that he's coming from the same belief system that I have. So, even though there's going to be some differences between us that probably get bigger, there would still be a situation where you'd say, "Gosh, I really want to talk to somebody who knows me really well and whose opinion I trust and I value on this, even if it's about something where we're very different. It's going to relate back to something where we're very much the same. Okay [Interview 8A]?

Miriam repeatedly returned to the idea that she and Dave share many if not most of their core values and how rare that is for a lesbian and a gay man. For her, that was very important and a key aspect of their friendship despite all the differences in their personalities and in gender.

While held by the individual, values are very much tied to the individual's larger social context. As we saw when covering the socio-cultural context, we are socialized into a particular worldview with all the values that go with it. The values we hold are largely shaped by the structure of society and, more importantly, our position within that social structure (Steinberg 2001). So, to the extent that these social boundaries place us in certain positions in the overall social structure, and to the extent that our values are shaped by those positions, there will be cultural differences and differences in values among the various strata in the hierarchy. At the same time, there will be cultural similarities within each stratum of society. Perhaps that is why it is not surprising that most of our close friends are from the same social category and share the same value system.

On the other hand, my data indicate that those from different strata who share a close friendship often have similar values. This leads me to two points. First, given that these friendships are statistically rare, those individuals who have such friendships may have certain values that vary from those in their same strata (which must be coupled with an opportunity to establish a friendship crossing social categories, as already discussed). While these differences in values between the individual and the others in his or her own social category may be small in most cases, there are some notable examples where they are actually quite large. This point will be taken up below when we look at how some of those who establish friendships across socially constructed boundaries feel disconnected from the members of their own social category. Second, as observed by sociologist Emile Durkheim (1984), shared values are a central means for uniting people. In fact, shared values may create a bond between people from different levels within the social hierarchy, which indicates that values may actually be able to cut through the stratification system and make links across different strata which might not otherwise be possible. Nevertheless, circumstances must allow people from different strata to meet and have the opportunity to discover their shared values, so there still must be structural opportunities; at that point, shared values take over and allow the establishment of a longer-term relationship—a relationship that may help blur the lines within the stratification system. In keeping with Steinberg, social structure gives rise to a particular value system; and that value system in turn further shapes (though often reinforces) the social structure.

## The Sense of Disconnection

As already noted, it is likely that those individuals who enter friendships that cross social categories have a set of values that may vary from those who share their social category. This ultimately results in a sense of disconnection from one's own group. It is notable that in 38 percent of the friendships studied[8] one or another or sometimes both friends expressed some degree of disconnection from their own group, although that varied as some of them expressed much more disconnection than others. This sense of disconnection usually arises from a lack of contact with members of one's own group *as compared to* the amount and quality of contact with members of another group. Such personal experiences create a sense of discomfort with one's own group and a greater sense of comfort with members of the other group. Both personal experiences and the sense of comfort are so important that they will be treated separately below. For now, we will simply look at the sense of disconnection itself.

The sense of disconnection that arises out of a lack of contact with members of one's own group was most often seen in the case of race. Recall the case of Bao and Irene from the introduction to this chapter. Both individuals feel a sense of disconnection from their own social categories, Bao because she is not following the cultural traditions of the group in which she grew up by completing college, working on a master's degree, and not getting married and having children yet, and Irene because she was adopted into a white family. This is how Irene describes her experience:

> I identify myself as an African-American woman, but I don't have any strong relationships with people of my race. I mean I know of people, and there's role models that I do have, but as far as like an intimate, personal relationship, I don't have any of those. Growing up, I never really had the option. There were no black families in Hayward. If there were black kids, it was from being adopted. Of course, I've since met people, but not an overwhelming number of people . . . just a few, you know. I don't really know why. I think maybe it's just my comfort zone or something. It's not like I try to avoid it, but I don't really reach out to it I guess. Or sometimes I feel like I have to sort of prove myself or be different than who I am. I mean, the black friends I do have will give me a hard time about like being from a small town and the way I talk and the way I . . . you know, just different things [Interview 19B].

Irene's parents made every effort to expose her to black culture, but Irene wasn't into it.

> My parents always tried to . . . I mean, for February we'd drive down to the city almost every weekend for Black History Month for different events and whatever. They really tried to instill in me . . . I mean, I have all black babies and Barbie dolls and all that kind of thing. And so it's not like I was excluded from black culture. It was just kind of something that I didn't want. We tried to celebrate Kwanza at my house one year. They even tried like soul food things and greens. I hated that. Like everything they tried, I hated. I just want some hot dish or a casserole or something! I felt like ignorance is bliss, you know. It was sad and it really disturbed my parents a lot when I went through that phase, and they were bothered by it because they felt like, "Oh, what could we have done differently?" and I'm just like, "You did everything you could have done. I just didn't want to do it and I didn't want to take the risk" [Interview 19B].

Irene feels that all this effort on the part of her parents wasn't really what was needed, although she felt it was important. What she was lacking was the everyday exposure to black role models and culture. Growing up, she didn't miss it; but looking back now she notices the gap that was there. Today she faces the problem that many blacks don't think she is black enough because of her dress, the way she talks, what she eats, and for the fact that she hasn't struggled—at least in the same way that they have. So, Irene is a person who is largely disconnected from her own race in terms of having close, intimate relationships, a recognized pattern in the study of diverse friendships (see Korgen 2002).[9] Nonetheless, she identifies as an African American woman, although this seems to be in the more abstract sense. Most of her friends have been white and a few other races besides black. And while she knows black people and will occasionally hang out with them, she doesn't have any close friendships with other blacks.

The same sense of disconnection from one's own race worked in reverse in the case of Melissa, who is white but who has very few white friends.

> *Honestly, it probably had something to do with the fact that before I got to college I didn't have any white friends ever . . . since when I was little. I've never had a close white friend and it's nothing against that. It's just who I've associated myself with and then my interests and the way I think and the way I am, you know. It's just like you're drawn to similar people. And I'm totally not biased because there's girls at college from my high school who are white who I've gotten closer to because we're here and I realize we do have things in common. But when I got to college, I was really shocked at how white it was. I was like, "Who are my friends going to be? There aren't any people who look like they listen to the same music or go to the same clubs or anything"* [Interview 5B].

What both of these cases tell us is that simply being a member of a particular social category is not sufficient to bond and identify with other members of that category. If there is no connection to the culture and experiences of the other members of that group, there will be a strong sense of disconnection and a much greater likelihood of establishing friendships with those who are outside of one's own social category.

Notice that this pattern really depends on how one understands the nature of a socially constructed category such as race, gender, or sexual orientation in the first place. An outside observer who simply looks at Irene will categorize her as black based on phenotypes and skin color and then, looking at Melissa, will categorize her as white; the observer assumes that skin color is an *objective* measure of one's race (Korgen 2002). What we've learned from Irene and Melissa, however, indicates that their *subjective* experience of race is actually quite different. While they might classify themselves as "technically" one race, that does not mean that they really feel a part of that social category on the inside. Social psychologists distinguish between one's *social identity* and one's *self identity* (Hewitt 2000). Social identity refers to how others perceive us and categorize and understand us as a result. In this way, Irene is perceived and categorized as black while Melissa is perceived and categorized as white by those who don't actually know them. Self identity, on the other hand, refers to the way in which we see, define, and understand ourselves. For both Irene and Melissa, there is a disconnect between their self identity and their social identity. The result is that they both experience a *subjective* sense of disconnection from the social category to which others have *objectively* classified them.

The same principles apply when looking at all socially constructed categories, not just race. For example, Sarah, who considers herself bisexual in terms of sexual behavior, does not really identify as bisexual in the sense of fitting into a category.

*I'm not a part of the gay community. I've never been to Pride. I'd really like to, but I just haven't ever been that involved. Besides, it seems like it all revolves around going dancing and drinking and I can't drink because I'm an alcoholic. So, there's not much there, it seems like—at least that's advertised openly. I know a lot of women who are bi, but I don't know if any of us really classify ourselves as bi. I mean, that's just the general attitude because it's frustrating for me to classify myself. I've talked to other women about it and a lot of them feel the same way* [Interview 2B].

Regardless of whether her perceptions of the gay community are accurate or not, her subjective experience is one of disconnection and even a hesitation in classifying herself as bisexual.

While not as common, I came across a similar example in the cross-gender friendship between Hugo and Debbie, whom we already met in the first section of this chapter. After asking me to turn off the tape recorder, Hugo took the opportunity to come out to me as a transgendered person. This was highly personal information and I was only the third or fourth person s/he told. Even his wife and children did not know. At the time of my individual interview with her, Debbie had not yet been told of Hugo's gender identity. As a result of gaining confidence in coming out to me, and knowing that this was relevant for the research process, not to mention that s/he felt close enough to trust Debbie, s/he did come out to her prior to our paired interview. While Debbie explained that she didn't fully understand it, she was completely supportive of Hugo and their friendship seems to be deepening as a result. This example highlights how complicated a simple, objective view of sex as a social category can be. In terms of sex, the differences between Hugo and Debbie are limited to what is biological in nature: Hugo occupies a biologically male body. Internally, emotionally, and subjectively Hugo feels very much like a woman and therefore feels rather disconnected from men as a social category. In this inner, subjective sense, Hugo is much more similar to Debbie than an objective view of biological sex would indicate. So, in the end, Hugo feels s/he has much more in common with Debbie. In fact, Hugo considers her/himself to be just "one of the girls" and so doesn't feel all that different from Debbie in that respect.

As indicated in all of these cases, the feeling of disconnection from the other members of one's own social category—as objectively defined by outsiders—opens the door for friendships that cross socially constructed categories. The individual who fails to identify with the members of one group will invariably identify with the members of another group, and it is with that other group that they will establish their personal relationships. As discussed in the section on group context, the problem here is whether these individuals will ever be fully accepted by the other members of either social category. Irene is not really accepted among blacks, but how well is she accepted among whites and other races besides her close friends? The same question could be asked of Melissa. She talks about how she's not really accepted by other whites, but many blacks look at her with distrust as well. And while this is purely speculation because it hasn't happened yet, consider Hugo: Hugo is still biologically male and looks male from the outside, but how many other men would accept her/him if s/he revealed that on the inside he is a woman? In the final assessment, it is important to consider the *pull* toward the other social category that the individual experiences, but also the *push* out of her own social category.

## Personal Experiences

The sense of disconnection from one's own social category goes hand in hand with one's personal experiences and life histories (Rude 2009). The experiences one has with the members of diverse groups of people, particularly early in life, enhances the likelihood of developing close friendships with diverse others later in life (Ellison and Powers 1994). As described in the previous section, Irene had very little experience associating with other black people while growing up. In fact, the few black people she knew were all adopted just as she was. As a result, her personal experiences were largely shaped by a white culture and context. While such feelings of disconnection are closely tied with these personal experiences, there are other forms of personal experience that can open one up to friendships with those from different social categories. The individual may simply have grown up in a context where there was an exposure to a diverse setting and thus would have much more experience with members of the other gender or racial group than other people might. In the case of sexual orientation, where a person's orientation is not immediately apparent, as it is—generally— with race and gender, the straight friends may actually have had prior experience with someone coming out to them and so they were more prepared when their friend came out. Still, our experiences with members of another social category are not always positive. When that is the case, it requires much conscious effort on the part of the individual to avoid generalizing that bad experience to other members of the group and assuming they are all the same.

Some of those interviewed recall growing up in a relatively diverse setting. Such exposure to diversity early on can shape the personal experiences of the individual in such a way that she or he is much more open and accepting of those who are different. As we saw, that was certainly the case for Melissa, who grew up in a neighborhood where whites were not the majority. Given her early friendships with black and Latino kids, she eventually came to prefer their company. Fatima also describes growing up in a comparatively diverse setting in

Pakistan. She grew up in a liberal Muslim context. Religious differences were not all that relevant in terms of developing friendships. She had friends who were Hindu, for example, and no one had a problem with that.

> *In Pakistan, we have people from other religions. Like the city I come from is very secular. It's got a lot of people from Christianity, Hindus, and Buddhists. The thing is, I never thought about religious differences when I was younger. I think the world has become more stressful now than when I was growing up even though Hindus and Muslims have always had problems, you know. But my father had wonderful Hindu friends, so I didn't grow up in that kind of . . . I mean, honestly, I never thought about it, because religion was not . . . I mean you didn't base your friendships or judge people according to their religion. You were just friends, you know. And you enjoyed their culture.*
>
> *Deborah was the first Jewish person I knew. Because of the conflicts in the world, I think people always kind of . . . It gets harder for Muslim people to know Jewish people because of the Palestine-Israel conflict. But with me and Deborah, it's been an interesting experience to learn about her religion. With my background and being the person I am, I just kind of enjoy meeting other people and learning about them* [Interview 17B].

For Americans who simply listen to the news, Fatima's personal experiences might be rather surprising since we hear so much about divisions between Pakistan (largely Muslim) and India (predominantly Hindu). Yet, Fatima took all this for granted. It simply was not an issue. She didn't have any Jewish friends while growing up, but that was because there weren't any Jewish people around her. If there had been, she doesn't think there would have been a problem befriending them. She attributes her openness to developing a close friendship with her Jewish friend Deborah to that diverse and open-minded context in which she grew up.

It is important to highlight that simple contact is not what Fatima focused upon; instead, it was actually associating with the members of other groups that made the difference for her. In other words, the opportunity to interact with and get to know—on a more personal level—members of other social categories is what largely shapes one's personal experience base, not simply seeing members of other groups from a distance. So, in the gay/straight friendship between Dave and Tom, Tom has had several gay friends in his life, going all the way back to high school. Even then, he doesn't remember it being a challenge for him to befriend a gay person [Interview 6B]. Eva's sexual orientation was never an issue for Nicole in large part, she believes, because she has known people who are gay or lesbian and has other current friends who fall into that category, although her friendship with Eva is the closest [Interview 36B].

In the case of a gay, lesbian, or bisexual individual, there may be a coming out process involved in the context of the friendship—a topic that will be covered in more depth in the next chapter. In other words, when the two individuals befriended one another, there was an assumption that both were straight and after the friendship developed, one person had to inform the other that this was not the case. If the straight individual within the friendship pair had prior experience with someone close to her coming out, she found that the news was not at all shocking and was able to quickly adjust. Long before Barbara met Janice, she had experienced her brother's coming out first hand. Seeing the process so close to her made Barbara really appreciate the personal struggle involved in coming out and how important the reactions of those around the gay or lesbian individual are in the coming out process.

> *My brother is gay and he came out when he first got to college. Since then, I've had to deal with his adjustment to that, his relationships, you know, sort of how those things have gone. I saw him going through all of that and watched him evolve more into acceptance of who he is. So I've certainly thought about sexual orientation before meeting Janice and the impact that has on other people and on the person themselves. My brother had tons of friends who, when they came out, were kicked out of their house, you know. And fathers wanted nothing to do with their sons. My father was an ideal father. I mean, he was sad about it because he knew that Peter's life would be harder. But he said, "I loved him yesterday. Why wouldn't I still love him today?" There was never an issue with my family and him being gay. I saw what impact coming out has on other people and so I became much more aware of and thought a lot about those issues* [Interview 22B].

While it is clear that Barbara accepts her gay brother for who he is and is deeply sympathetic toward those going through the coming out process, her journey was not necessarily an easy one. In fact, it involved much struggle.

> *It turns out that my brother's first encounter as a homosexual man was with a person that I was sort of involved with, and I didn't know that until he came out. So, it led to all kinds of problems and there was a lot of weirdness between Peter and I. I had to work through that. I didn't have a problem with him being gay, but I definitely had a problem with what happened. I mean, it would have just been like, you know, if it was a sister who did it. I mean it was not the fact that he was gay. It was the fact that it was a betrayal of me. And he, of course, doesn't see anything wrong with it—never has, never will. So, there were issues I had to deal with, but my parents raised me well. So I was able to deal with all of that and come to terms with it. But I am genuinely a pretty open-minded person* [Interview 22B].

While her personal experience was not entirely a positive one—in fact, it was a particular challenge for her—Barbara still learned a lot from her brother and his coming out process. It is important to point out how she separated his sexual orientation from his behavior with the young man she was seeing at the time. Many people make the mistake of linking an individual's behavior to the social category that individual belongs to as if all members of that group behave the same way. Such erroneous generalizations lead to all kinds of stereotypes and prejudiced attitudes toward the group. Nevertheless, Barbara did not make that generalization and so was ultimately much more accepting of her brother and his sexual orientation and has been very accepting of gays and lesbians ever since, particularly in her friendship with Janice.

Among those interviewed, there were very few individuals who had negative experiences with members of other social categories—experiences that would prohibit them from befriending individuals who belonged to such a group. Barbara was one, but we just saw how she separated the behavior of her brother from his sexual orientation, thus sidestepping feelings of prejudice toward other gays and lesbians. Out of the forty friendship pairs, there were only two people who had negative experiences with members of another social category and for whom that experience has posed a particular challenge to them because of a resulting prejudice on their part. In one of those cases, the person interviewed has been very intentional in trying to overcome such prejudice. In the other, the past negative experience has actually become debilitating in terms of befriending other members of that social category.

Unlike most people when asked about prejudice, Sam (who is white) acknowledged outside of the context of his interview that he had struggled with racism at times. His struggle was due to some bad experiences with members of two groups in particular: Jews and blacks. Growing up, there were a number of Jews at his school, most of whom he did not get along with at a personal level. They also fit a number of the stereotypes he's learned about the group. In addition, several black men assaulted Sam while he was in college. This was a more challenging situation for him. Intellectually, he knows that just because a few members of a group behave this way that not all members of the group are the same; but he still has a visceral reaction, particularly when he's on the street. In fact, he won't go to the area where he was attacked. So, Sam is struggling to avoid generalizing that experience to the entire group. At the same time, though, he doesn't think that these experiences would prevent him from befriending a member of such a group. He has befriended members of other racial groups: the focus of his interview was on his friendship with Rodney, who is American Indian.

Based on her personal experiences, Lisa (who is also American Indian) strongly feels that whites just don't "get it" when it comes to understanding her feelings about racial oppression. This struggle that she has experienced with white people has resulted in a strong lack of trust for whites in general. In fact, most of her friends are not white—whether Asian, Latino, black, or American Indian. Lisa knows a few white people, but they're more like acquaintances than anything else. Accordingly, while my interview with her focused on race, her friend Hugo was not white but Latino. She sees them both as not white, what she terms "brown people," and that one commonality overshadows everything else, allowing her to establish a close friendship that, for her, is quite rare.

*I still don't have a lot of trust for white people. Some of my acquaintances are white, but they just don't get things the way that—what I call—"brown people" do. Among brown people, there's always been that understanding.*

*Like I heard this advertisement the other day and it was about how the white buffalo was sacred to the Native American people, and this was an advertisement for a used car lot! And they were saying how they were going to treat their customers sacred like Native Americans treated the white buffalo sacred. And I was like, "Oh, my God; that is so wrong."*

*And when I tell white people about my life, they're like, "So?" They just don't get it. I mean, I don't know why they don't, but they don't get it. There's this girl who I grew up with who's white—we lived next door to each other—and, I mean, I would honestly rather hang out with an acquaintance who is not white than hang out with her because there's just nothing that she can possibly understand. I've been over it with her before, but she has the same attitude as the other people: "Well, why don't you guys just get over it? That happened to you guys generations ago." And I said, "Well, it would be easier for us to get over if it wasn't still happening on the day-to-day basis. But she'll never understand that because she's not brown skinned, you know. She'll never have to deal with that.*

*But that's a lot of what I look for in my friends. I'm more drawn to people who are from a variety of cultures. Like even the girls at work, you know. A lot of them are from Africa and are refugees and stuff, and it's just been easier for me to relate to them or just easier for me to talk to them. Another one of my friends is Asian, and I've never had an Asian friend before; but we have so much in common, it's unbelievable* [Interview 35B].

For Lisa, race seems to be about separating all that is white from all that is not white. This is understandable given all her experiences with white people. The downside, however, is that she has generalized her feelings toward most white people. The result is that, while she has friends of other races, none of them are white; instead, they are all "brown people." She has a polarized understanding of in-group and out-group characteristics (Shibutani and Kwan 1965). This makes her rather exceptional among those I interviewed given that most of them had positive experiences with the members of other socially constructed categories and, of those who had negative experiences, they did not generalize those negative feelings to all members of that group.

These last two examples are exceptional among those interviewed. The more common tendency was for those who now enjoy friendships across socially constructed boundaries to have had more positive experiences with members of other groups and, if they had negative experiences, they avoided generalizing them and assuming that all members of that particular group were the same. Moreover, they were much more likely to have experienced more diverse social settings over the course of their lives and therefore have had positive experiences associating with members of other groups. Such experiences help to open up the possibility of establishing a friendship that bridges different socially constructed categories.

## Comfort and Familiarity

When there is a sense of disconnection from the other members of one's social category, the issue boils down to one of comfort: with whom does one feel comfortable? In addition, having more positive experiences with members of other groups will contribute to a sense of comfort and familiarity with them, opening the door for a friendship to emerge. This is where the members of marginalized groups have an advantage over those in privileged groups: they will oftentimes have much more experience in dealing with and relating to those in a position of privilege than the privileged have with the marginalized, resulting in what Du-Bois (1961) describes as "double consciousness:" an awareness of the culture of both the marginalized and the privileged.

This difference in experience is the function of privilege as defined and explained by Peggy MacIntosh (1988; see also Rothenberg 2002) in her work on white privilege. MacIntosh understands white privilege to be "an invisible package of unearned assets that I can count on cashing in each day, but about which I was meant to remain oblivious. White privilege is like an invisible weightless knapsack of special provisions, maps, passports, codebooks, visas, clothes, tools, and blank checks" (MacIntosh 1988). In her article, she then goes on to list twenty-six examples of white privilege. Topping the list is: "I can, if I wish, arrange to be in the company of people of my race most of the time." Privilege number sixteen reads as follows: "I can remain oblivious of the language and customs of persons of color, who constitute the world's majority, without feeling in my culture any penalty for such oblivion." In other words, those in a position of privilege can choose to live their lives apart from marginalized groups and are even in a position to completely disregard the culture of those groups without fear of recrimination. While MacIntosh writes about the privilege associated with the white race, the same principles apply to other socially constructed categories. Hence, it is possible to speak of male privilege, heterosexual privilege, Christian privilege, and so on. So, straight people never really have to interact with gays or lesbians and, if they do, they are oftentimes oblivious to that fact. Men can choose to completely disregard and discount the experiences of women if they so choose. Christians interact with others simply assuming they are also Christian or, if it is visibly apparent that they aren't, Christians don't have to take the time to look at the world from their point of view.

On the other hand, those who belong to marginalized groups have no choice but to deal with those in a position of privilege because those are the people who are "in charge" and dominant within the culture. Blacks, Asians, Latinos, American Indians, and so forth cannot go about their daily lives without exposure to white culture and influence and they cannot afford to disregard it. Success in a white-dominated world means familiarity with and adherence to that white culture and, more often than not, subsuming one's own culture in the effort. This is what assimilation is all about (Steinberg 2001). And again, the same applies to other forms of marginalization. Women *must* take men's perspectives and influence into account in order to succeed in a largely "man's world." Gays and lesbians have no choice but to deal with straight people on a regular basis, meeting them on their own terms and often "playing straight" in order to succeed. Muslims, Jews, Hindus, Buddhists, and atheists—among a host of others—have to tolerate well-meaning strangers saying "Merry Christmas" or "Happy Easter."

The members of all marginalized groups often have a lot more experience dealing with the privileged than the other way around. And so they are more likely to be familiar with the members of the privileged class. This difference in levels of experience and familiarity was even evident in my data collection process. It was far easier to identify research participants by approaching members of marginalized groups rather than the members of privileged groups. The marginalized were far more likely to have friends from other social categories than the privileged. For example, it was much more productive to ask a gay or lesbian person if he or she had any straight friends than to ask a straight person if she or he had any gay or lesbian friends. I found far more contacts taking that approach. The evidence suggests that the members of marginalized groups have more experience in dealing with the privileged and are likely to be more familiar with the culture of the privileged group; as a result, they are more likely to have developed friendships across those social boundaries (see also Korgen 2002). For many in a position of privilege, there has been very little exposure to—and little opportunity to familiarize themselves with—the members and culture of marginalized groups. The consequence is that they are less likely to have friends across socially constructed categories and, when they do establish such friendships, there is often more learning involved, as will be seen in chapter 4.

While the members of marginalized groups often have much more experience in dealing with those in a position of privilege, it does not mean that those experiences have been positive. In many instances, they are not. Consequently, familiarity does not automatically lead to feelings of comfort. As seen in the previous section, Lisa had many bad experiences with whites—so many, in fact, that she has no friends who are white. While that is an exceptional case among those I interviewed, similar negative experiences have led other members of marginalized groups to approach those in a position of privilege in a tentative manner until they can ascertain whether those privileged individuals will be open and accepting of them. For example, Lenora's first impression of Melissa (whom we've already met above) was shaped by the fact that Melissa was white, but Lenora, who is black and Cuban, quickly discovered that Melissa spoke like she did in terms of slang, and so on. She later learned that she and Melissa come from similar backgrounds: urban areas with a large number of racial minorities. This familiarity and similarity made Lenora much more comfortable with Melissa.

*When I first met Melissa, I thought she was an average white girl. I thought she
was just like crazy; but as she talked to me, I realized she was not like all the
other white girls I've met. She's more urbanized because she lived in the city itself while everybody else is from the suburbs or something. And I realized that
she's just different. She just had a lot of things in common with me* [Interview
5A].

Despite her initial skepticism, once Lenora felt comfortable with Melissa, she
was able to open up and become friends with her.

For her part, Melissa was aware of the fact that, when they first met, what
Lenora would see is a white girl and that she would possibly have a precon-
ceived notion of all that entailed. So Melissa took it upon herself to let Lenora
know that she was cool with their racial difference. In other words, she started
dropping hints that were intended to make Lenora feel comfortable with her.

*I remember saying something to let her know that we listen to the same kind of
music. Like, "Do you have that new CD?" Sometimes I have to do that because, you know, otherwise I'm just one of so many white girls here. And that's
fine; it's just sometimes if you don't, people don't understand that you have a
lot of similarities if they just take you for what they see. I could also ask, "Did
you see the new Denzel Washington movie?" and then she's like, "All right,
she likes Denzel, too." So one thing after another led her to realize that we had
a lot in common* [Interview 5B].

Melissa's approach indicates that she is aware of the fact that she's in a position
of privilege and is therefore likely to be perceived as someone who is unable to
identify with Lenora and her culture. She took intentional steps to make sure that
the impression she gave was of a white girl who was anything but "typical."

The dynamic between Lenora and Melissa is very similar to the experience
of Dave (who is gay) in his friendship with Tom (who is straight), although it
took much longer for him and they were already developing a friendship. The
question for Dave was, "how close a friend is Tom going to be?" This question
was particularly important to him given that they work for the same company—
a company he considers to be homophobic—and he didn't want to jeopardize a
working relationship. If he felt comfortable with Tom, he could come out and
their friendship could grow from there. If he weren't comfortable, they would
not become that close as friends. So Dave had to spend some time figuring out
whether Tom would be okay with him.

*Our friendship progressed very slowly at first because we were colleagues.
There was too much to lose and not a lot to gain. I needed friends, but I didn't
need a problem at work, so this took a little bit more tiptoeing around and
dancing. I needed to know if he was going to have a problem with me being gay
and me being a colleague and me being a friend. If there was going to be a
minefield in there, it was going to be easier to just cut the corner and walk
away because I didn't need the potential conflict. I didn't need to pour gasoline*

*on the fire. So, yes, I would characterize our friendship as a slow burn, and it is kind of like climbing stairs in a stairwell. You know, you put a little bit of weight on, you start to shift the weight and as the stair takes the weight maybe it creaks a little bit; then you put more weight on it. Once you're safely established on the first step, then you pick the other foot up off the floor and you put it on the next step and you slowly climb little by little. And as time progresses, as you put weight on each step and you feel comfortable on that step, you move on to the next step on that stairwell. Pretty soon you've climbed the stairwell* [Interview 6A].

So again, Dave was very tentative at first, testing the waters to see if it would be okay for him to come out to Tom and continue with their friendship. He needed to feel comfortable first.

In the same way that Melissa dropped hints for Lenora, Tom did his best to make Dave feel comfortable. The trick for him, given that one's sexual orientation is not a visible difference in the same way that race is, was to avoid implying that Dave was gay if he were actually straight and might take offense at the implication. So, he had to avoid the direct approach that Melissa took. Instead, he just made an effort to convey his openness.

*I thought Dave may be gay early on, but I never said anything. It didn't bother me, but I guess Dave was probably concerned about it . . . that he was gay and he didn't want me to know. He probably thought that would affect our relationship if I knew he was gay. He thought that maybe I wouldn't want to be friends with him. But I didn't say anything. I thought if he wanted to bring it up, if he felt uncomfortable with it, you know . . . I didn't want to make him feel more uncomfortable. And I was thinking, "Well, what if he's not gay and then he takes offense?" I just thought it didn't bother me and if he wants to bring it up, you know.*

 *Then it came to a point where it was blatantly clear that I knew and he must have realized that I had to have known and nothing had changed. Maybe it was a bigger deal for him because maybe he was more paranoid about losing our friendship than I was, because I knew and I was comfortable with it. Maybe he was wondering how I was going to react, so maybe it was a bigger deal for him than it was for me* [Interview 6B].

Tom had to be careful in making sure Dave felt comfortable enough to eventually come out to him, so he had to take a much less direct approach than Melissa did. Nonetheless, both cases indicate that they were concerned about the comfort level of their friend and were simultaneously demonstrating that they were comfortable with the fact that their friend was different from them. In both of these instances, and in many others, the result was a much closer relationship.

It is these feelings of comfort and familiarity that are so important in establishing friendships that cross social categories. At the same time, while these individuals are obviously comfortable enough to have established such friendships, this does not mean that they might actually feel even more comfortable in the company of those in the same group as themselves. While this is not true for all those interviewed (as we saw with Melissa, who actually felt more comfortable in the company of blacks and Latinos because of her personal experiences growing up), some indicated that they felt more comfortable among members of their own group. For example, in his interview, Brad mentioned that, despite his close friendship with Eric, he still feels more comfortable in the company of other gay men. This is due in large part to the familiarity and the shared experience of being gay, coming out, and so on.

> *I think overall I enjoy being around gay men more, just because of that sense of, you know, the common experience. But that's not discriminatory in terms of, you know, "I'm not going to be your friend just because you're not gay," . . . that kind of thing. There's just a difference in that comfort zone or whatever. In a perfect world, orientation wouldn't even be an issue, you know. But we're not in a perfect world. Earlier in my life, I wanted gay and straight to be the same and equal so that, if I was at a straight cocktail party, I would feel just as comfortable as I do at a gay cocktail party. There are times that you color your language in a certain way, you know. I mean, I can't imagine myself being at a straight cocktail party and saying, "Hey, girlfriend!" like you might at a gay party. Not that I say that much, but I would never do that at a straight party. So, I mean, that's all about your comfort level* [Interview 7B].

It is simply uncomfortable or awkward when one is in the minority—the odd one out. Still, Brad has been in such situations much more than his friend Eric has and is thus more practiced at it. So, while he prefers the company of other gay men, he doesn't avoid associating with and befriending straight people. Such feelings do not prohibit developing friendships outside of one's own group. The differences in comfort level have to do with each group as a whole as opposed to any specific individual within the group. In other words, Brad feels quite comfortable with Eric, but is *less* comfortable with straights as a whole without being *un*comfortable with straights.

Overall, it is clear the importance that familiarity and comfort have in establishing friendships across social categories. This is where the promise of intergroup contact theory lies (Allport 1954): the more positive experiences we have connecting with members of diverse groups of people, the more open we will be to establishing friendships and multiplying the bridging ties across these socially constructed boundaries. Such comfort opens the door for establishing these friendships in the first place. And while the members of marginalized groups have much more experience interacting with the members of privileged groups than vice versa because of the nature of privilege, such familiarity does not mean that they are completely comfortable when befriending members of the privileged group for the first time. Instead, there is a period of testing the waters to see how open-minded the privileged individual really is. If the privileged individual is sufficiently astute and able to recognize this, then she or he will make every effort to directly or indirectly send signals to the marginalized individual indicating that they are "cool" with the difference between them, thus maximizing the level of comfort.

## Perception

Ultimately, the similarity in personal qualities (interests and values), the sense of disconnection from one's own social category, one's personal experiences with members of other social categories, and the sense of familiarity and comfort one has with members of other social categories all play a role in shaping one's perception of the other group and one's perception of the gap—if any—between the two socially constructed categories. How do the individuals perceive the social category difference between them? How might the relevance of that difference change over time?

The relevance of perception is very well represented in a particular scene in the popular movie *The Matrix* (1999). In this scene, the main character—Neo—is watching a boy sitting cross-legged on the floor and gazing intently at the spoon he holds in his hand. As the boy focuses on the spoon, it dips, bends, twists, and then snaps back into place when the boy turns his attention to Neo. He then holds out the spoon for Neo to take. Neo accepts the spoon and examines it, as if to see if it is a "normal" spoon. As Neo inspects it, the boy says, "Do not try and bend the spoon. That's impossible. Instead, only try to realize the truth." Neo, looking the boy in the eyes, asks, "What truth?" "There is no spoon." Neo looks back at the spoon. "There is no spoon?" The boy replies, "Then you'll see that it is not the spoon that bends. It is only yourself." Neo holds out the spoon and tries to focus, tilting his head slightly as he does so. He sees his reflection on the surface of the spoon. A moment later, the spoon dips and bends in the same direction as his head, his reflection bending as well. When his concentration is interrupted, the spoon snaps back and he returns the spoon to the boy. This scene brilliantly captures the idea that the way we look at an object (whether a spoon or a socially constructed boundary such as race, gender, or sexual orientation)—how we see and perceive it—is largely dependent on our own cognitive understanding of it. The relevance of social categories has nothing to do with our ability to objectively measure the differences. Instead, it is our own inner, subjective perception of it that matters (see also Rude 2009).

Still, there is a danger in looking beyond those socially constructed differences between diverse groups of people. In the last chapter, I noted an observation by Audre Lorde about spending too much time looking at the differences between groups of people. That was only part of what she said, however. Here is the entire passage: "Too often, we pour the energy needed for recognizing and exploring differences into pretending those differences are insurmountable barriers, *or that they do not exist at all*. This results in voluntary isolation, *or false and treacherous connections*" (1984, 533; emphasis mine). Clearly, this is a question of balance. It is possible to go too far in either direction, assuming that differences between groups are dominant, resulting in a situation in which those from different groups are seen as nothing more than a member of that group, or assuming that there are no differences in individual experience whatsoever arising out of membership within a particular other group (Rawlins 2009). The latter extreme, where important experiential differences between groups are wiped out and ignored as if they are not relevant results in a harmful form of "color blindness" (when applied to racial categories). The idea of "color blindness" reflects the neo-conservative belief that, if we could simply "not see" race, we could recognize our sameness and the problems associated with racism would disappear. Some liberals have also begun to feel this way, believing that "if we act as if race does not matter, it will not matter" (Korgen 2002, 5). This position, however, ignores the very real impact of race in privileging some and marginalizing others.

> Research indicates that race, while a social construction, is still a powerful force at all levels of U.S. society—and not a force to be ignored. Colorblind attitudes may help some individuals develop and maintain friendships across the racial divide, yet they do nothing to diminish the divide itself. In order to reduce the racial divide, we must first be able to see it clearly" (Korgen 2002, 103-104).

Race—and all demographic categories—is very much like the spoon in *The Matrix*. We need to recognize that it is a social construction that is still manifest in our social world with very real consequences for everyone, regardless of one's racial identity. At the same time, how we see and perceive it is dependent on our understanding of it. It is a mistake to be overly concerned with differences between groups just as it is a mistake to be dismissive of any differences. In other words, it is best to recognize the very "historical differences and opportunities" that exist between groups (Rawlins 2009, 173) but to not let them get in the way of establishing close relational ties with diverse others. This is a very delicate and difficult balance to maintain.

The focus of the interviews required that I bring the socially constructed boundary each pair of friends is bridging front and center. Nevertheless, this is admittedly an artificial situation. For many of those I interviewed, there is no social boundary, indicating that social boundaries are largely a matter of perception. As a result, I found myself caught within a paradox: I was focusing on social boundaries that, for many of my interviewees, did not exist in the first place. The relevance of perception serves to highlight the point that the boundaries between different categories of people are socially constructed and that they are meaningful only for those who give them meaning. By inference, those who refuse to cross social categories are those who create the boundaries between them in the first place and thus limit the potential options for their behavior. If social boundaries are simply a matter of perception, then they are important only to the extent we make them important (Thomas 1928).

By directing my research topic and questions to the subject of bridging the gap between different social categories, I was *making* it an issue for those I interviewed—calling their attention to something that many didn't even have to think about. This does not mean that the research topic and interview questions were the wrong approach. As discussed at the beginning of this chapter, it is very important to engage the sociological imagination and ask questions about what we take for granted. Thankfully, the research participants were strong-willed enough that they didn't feel obligated to accept the reality I presented to them: the reality of a social *boundary*. For example, in the wrap-up to their paired interview regarding the gender difference between them, Laura and Chad were not afraid to simply say there was no gap there.

> LAURA: *I don't think there's been a barrier between the two of us. I would say that, at some point, we made individual decisions about not adopting gender role stereotypes and not judging people by those.*
> CHAD: *And be supportive of each other in choosing . . .*
> LAURA: *Choosing what's best for that individual.*
> CHAD: *Right. I feel like there isn't a gender gap between us.*
> LAURA: *Well, that's how I answered before. It's like there isn't a gap between us.*
> CHAD: *Because we've chosen alternative, you know . . . you're still going to be a woman and I'm still going to be a man, but just communication.*
> LAURA: *Hm mmm.*
> CHAD: *Being real intentional about our actions and not assuming, you know . . . being intentional about how we act and not just assuming what society says. That kind of breaks it down a little bit. It's like, "Okay, I can do this because I want to do this, not because it's a role . . . an expectation"* [Interview 9C].

Ultimately, this may be a major part of what distinguishes the people I interviewed: the guts to disagree with what society hands them as "reality" and the backbone needed to step outside of the mainstream and create their own reality—a reality where gender, race, sexual orientation, and so on do not have to divide people.

Notice that it is the idea that race, gender, or sexual orientation represents a *boundary*—a barrier of sorts arising merely out of the existence of that difference—that is the focus of this perception. This is not to say that the differences in race, gender, or sexual orientation are *invisible* to the individuals involved. They are certainly visible. It is the *relevance* of the difference that is at stake. So, the perspective that these individuals take is very different from the idea of "color blindness," or any other form of blindness for that matter. They recognize that individual experiences are fundamentally shaped by the social identity of their friend, but that the social identity does not represent the entire person: they are still individuals who are unique and different from their group affiliation. For example, Christina (who is Philippino) and Ellen (who is white) frame the relevance of race in their friendship in terms of "background" and "foreground." For them, race is always apparent and respected, but it is largely in the background because there is so much to the other person that becomes more important. Those other dimensions of the individual are much more in the foreground. In their paired interview, Christina and Ellen speculate as to what might bring the racial difference between them from the background into the foreground. Notice how they use "foreground" as a verb, indicating that bringing race into the foreground requires a departure from their norm in which race is a part of the background.

> CHRISTINA: You know, for me, I don't think we've ever had a situation where race would have come out as a difference; but then I wonder whether, depending on the social situation, it would. I always wonder like, if I ever get married or have some sort of thing and my Philippino friends come and my so-called academic friends, what would that mixing look like? But then I feel like, "Oh, it'll be fine. It's fine with me and it's fine with my family."
> ELLEN: Or it would get foregrounded because we wanted to talk about it at some point and really think through it. And so we use that as something to, you know, spark a conversation—especially in the context of our academic work on diversity. So, I think that's the kind of stuff that will foreground the conversation for us. "Help me understand this." So, those kinds of things.
> CHRISTINA: Yeah, I think for Ellen it would work from a more personal level whereas I've already lived it, you know. I've had white boyfriends that I've had to bring into the house. It's something that I'm just used to.
> ELLEN: Yeah, we really foreground it when talking about teaching.
> CHRISTINA: Right, it's been very much there; but personally, race hasn't felt there. I think, yeah . . . it's the thing that's there but not there, you know. And until some situation comes along, we won't know [Interview 34C].

The distinction Christina and Ellen make between background and foreground highlights their mutual views on color blindness: you can't pretend that the other person has no race because that does them a disservice, ignoring an important part of who they are. But at the same time, race isn't everything they are either. People are multi-dimensional and should be perceived as such. In fact, when asked what made her friendship with a person of another race so successful, Ellen noted that you just have to "go there," you have to go to the place that many people choose to avoid and be willing to talk about the difference between them [Interview 34A]. Such an exchange of storytelling serves an important purpose for the friendship. It allows the individuals to discover the differences as well as the similarities between them, a process that actually nurtures the friendship (Rawlins 2009).

Not all those I interviewed were so intentional. Jerry's friend Bob is decades older than himself and, when describing the fact that they are friends despite such a wide age difference, says that they are "thoughtlessly friends," meaning that, while they know it is present, they don't dwell on the age difference between them.

> *People are so conscious about these differences and all separate from each other. I think it should be different. I think it should be just like, you know . . . People should be thoughtless in choosing their friends. It's sort of like Bob and me; it's sort of like, it's nothing . . . I guess the friendship I ultimately wouldn't have consciously chosen. I wouldn't have said, "Bob, I think I'd like to be your friend," you know. It's just like it happened and I went with it and I really enjoy it. And if more people just did that and allowed themselves to sort of like explore different things, you know . . . Just be different. I think people should be thoughtless in choosing their friends* [Interview 11B].

From Jerry's perspective, people put too much thought into choosing their friends, as if you don't want to be seen with certain kinds of people. In his young crowd, it might be perceived as weird to be hanging out with a guy who is much older than him, but he doesn't let that bother him. In fact, he hasn't put much thought into it at all. While there is a significant age difference between them, Jerry and Bob are "thoughtlessly friends."

The examples provided so far are ones in which neither member of the friendship perceived a social boundary as existing between them. Yet, this is not always the case. In some friendships, one or both members experience a *change* in perception such that the social boundary, while prominent in the beginning, recedes into the background. This point will be discussed at length in the next chapter when covering the stages of friendship. In such cases where there is a change in the perception of the social boundary, the individuals have to set aside any assumptions they may have had initially when befriending someone different from him or herself. This shift in perception was already alluded to when we looked at the cross-racial friendship between Lenora and Melissa. When Lenora first saw Melissa, what she saw was "just another white girl." Even so, her impression of Melissa and the relevance of race changed as they got to know one another. In their paired interview, they recapped this shift in perception.

> *MELISSA: I don't notice things like that* [race] *really anymore. It's really nothing to me, but that's just me.*
> *LENORA: Yeah, I don't see it anymore. I did earlier, you know . . . like the differences in her family life. I noticed that; but now I just love her family to death and it's like there is really no difference. They're crazy just like my family is. Just a normal family. Like I said before, I didn't have that many white friends before, so it did make a difference early on; but then I got to know about who she is and the color just went away* [Interview 5C].

So, the color difference between Lenora and Melissa was rather prominent when they first met, but it receded into the background as the friendship developed. Now what they notice is what they have in common.

We've also seen this change in perception operate in the friendship between Dave and Tom. Sexual orientation was a big deal for Dave in the early stages of their friendship largely because he hadn't come out to Tom and was trying to assess how open Tom would be to his being gay.

> *I think initially sexual orientation was an issue and I think at this point it's a to-*
> *tal non-issue. And I think initially it was more my issue with our friendship*
> *starting out. I think it was a big deal to me because I didn't know what his com-*
> *fort level was. As I got to know him more and have seen what his comfort level*
> *is, I don't think it was really ever an issue with him. I think it was an issue with*
> *me, and I was the one who was kind of slow to adapt. But once I realized that*
> *he wasn't going to have a problem, it became a non-issue to me* [Interview 6A].

As in the friendship between Lenora and Melissa, once Dave got "over the hump" where sexual orientation was prominent in his mind, its relevance receded into the background and they could move on with their friendship. And again, the commonalities between them became much more relevant to their friendship. Finding and focusing on such commonalities was a prominent theme among those I interviewed and this will be taken up in chapter 4.

Overall, the perception of each friend was that the difference between him or her was ultimately irrelevant to the friendship. For some, this realization came after the friendship began to develop. For others, the difference never was an issue. Regardless of the particulars, the prominence of the difference between the two friends is minimized, an observation that goes all the way back to Allport (1954) who noted that closer contact with diverse others results in individuals perceiving fewer differences. The irony is that, while many of those interviewed claimed and truly believed that the difference between them was no issue or became less of an issue over time, in actuality these differences did have a major impact on the friendship overall. This impact varied depending on the socially constructed boundary in question, the nature of that boundary, and—as alluded to already—on the stage of the friendship (in terms of its development). This topic will be the focus of the next chapter. Moreover, the vast majority of those interviewed relied on certain interpersonal techniques in order to manage and therefore minimize the relevance of the difference. In other words, by using these interpersonal techniques (which are the focus of chapter 4), their perception of the relevance of the difference between them was altered in such a way that it receded in its importance.

Together with similarities in interests and values, the sense of disconnection from their own group that some individuals feel, the personal experiences they have with members of other social categories, and the sense of familiarity and comfort with the members of other groups, the question of perception is an important part of the individual context in which friendships crossing social categories emerge. At the same time, not all of these will be present in all cases and to the same degree. While the vast majority of friends described having common interests and values, not all mentioned the other elements of the individual context. For some, past personal experience played a prominent role while for others it was their first time closely interacting with a member of that particular group. In other friendships, it was clear that one or both parties felt disconnected from the members of their own group; but this was not true in all cases. Taken together, however, these elements of the individual context allow us to see where the individual may be coming from when they approach a friendship such as this: what is it that she is bringing with her when she meets someone from a different social category and establishing a friendship? While this is very much a question concerning the individual, a sociologist who is utilizing the sociological imagination will recognize how this individual-level biography is caught up in a much larger social milieu that includes the group, the institutional, and the socio-cultural contexts. These friendships do not exist in a vacuum and cannot be studied as if they are independent of the world around them. In order to fully understand these unlikely friendships, it is of vital importance to take all levels of context and social structure into account. Once we have fully understood the contexts in which these friendships emerge and develop, it is possible to look at the friendships themselves, the overall impact of the social boundaries on the friendship, and the interpersonal dynamics involved in bridging the differences between them.

## Notes

1. For detailed, analytical discussions of levels of context, see Adams and Allan 1998.

2. Interestingly, Korgen's (2002) research on cross-racial friendships resulted in a different conclusion from that of Rude (2009) with regard to the integration of institutional settings in which these friendships emerge. Her findings in this regard also diverge from my own. While Rude and I both found that these friendships were established in the context of integrated settings, Korgen found that the cross-racial friendships she studied typically emerged within a predominantly white setting (92.5 percent of the 40 friendships studied). She attributes this to racial segregation (2002, 61 and 77). While I agree that segregation is still a major impediment to the emergence of diverse friendships, I wonder if her sampling strategy (advertisements in college and local newspapers coupled with snowballing) inflated the significance of this segregation. For example, if the colleges were largely white and if the local newspapers were in largely white areas, that could easily skew the sample in favor of segregated settings. On the other hand, the reverse criticism could be leveled against Rude and myself: perhaps our sampling methods favored integrated settings.

3. This breakdown of where the friends I interviewed met does not take overlapping institutions and contexts into account. For example, some of those who met in college

were able to be more specific and say that they met through athletics or campus ministry. In these overlapping cases, I identified the primary affiliation and gave it priority in calculating these numbers. So, if they met in a school setting I counted that as primary, regardless of whether they got more specific and said school athletics or campus ministry.

4. A contrasting point made by one of those I interviewed (and hinted at in other interviews where dating might have been a possibility) was that, while friends might be very supportive of a diverse friendship circle, they might not be supportive of someone who dates outside of their own social category, in this case race. Irene (who is black) notes that people (both black and white) do indeed take notice of men and women who are of different races and who appear to be together, even if they are not romantically involved. There's something about the male/female interracial combination that is different [Interview 19B]. This point goes right back to what was described with regard to the reactions of Kelly's grandparents to her friendship with Colin described above.

5. This represents only 2.5 percent of those friendships studied, indicating that in 97.5 percent of the cases studied there were no negative consequences for the friendship.

6. It is important to note that Jordan prefers not to offer any particular label for his sexual orientation. For ease in telling his story, I use the term bisexual because it best captures his sexual behavior and attraction.

7. As observed by Allan and Adams, "It would certainly be useful to have more studies which explored in detail how the networks in which particular friendships, and particular sets of friendships, are embedded influence the character of the solidarities" (1998, 187).

8. Fifteen of the 40 cases.

9. Korgen describes the case of Steven, whose "middle-class status and his proximity to white, middle-class peers in both his school and his neighborhood have made him culturally, in many ways, more similar to his white friends than his black classmates. In addition to his taste in clothes and manner of speech, the activities that Steven was interested in were also popular among the white children with whom he grew up" (2002, 25).

# Chapter 3

# Social Boundaries in the Context of Friendship

*QUINN: I know I've never really expressed this to you, and it's not a problem in the relationship; it more or less just came up with the last interview and thinking about class. I'm the first one in my family to graduate from college . . . higher education just hasn't been very emphasized. I guess I feel this kind of self-consciousness—that is self-imposed, I think, but nonetheless—about educational achievement and then the subsequent job opportunity type of achievement. Am I doing enough? I always want to sound like I kind of got things together and that I'm working towards some sort of admirable goal. That's one of those sticky things . . . it's not necessarily an economic class kind of difference, but it has played into the friendship. It's kind of like the "socio" part of socioeconomic class: coming from a strong educational background and experiencing, maybe correctly or maybe incorrectly, that self-consciousness in my achieving. I want to sound like I got my act together and really I don't. That's just one of those subtleties, and it hasn't been a barrier or a problem, and it's not something that you've imposed on me. It's something that I impose on myself.*

*MIKE: No, it makes sense. A couple of things: I'm surprised. I'll start with the last one. What you find to be self-conscious strikes me as self-confident. I don't know how smart anyone is. I find, for example, even as recently as the last film we saw, that you had more important things to say than most everyone else there. You have the confidence to say what's on your mind, which is something that a lot of people struggle with. That's probably why I value you and value our friendship* [Interview 15C].

A distinct advantage to including multiple socially constructed boundaries within the same study is the ability to achieve two goals that have not been achieved in past research. In the first place, it allows us to see what all such social boundaries have in common in terms of the interpersonal dynamics required to bridge them. In other words, what do race, gender, sexual orientation, and so on have in common when it comes to two friends bridging that difference between them regardless of the idiosyncrasies of each socially constructed boundary? This topic will be the focus of chapter 4, though a number of similarities will be addressed here. Secondly, including multiple forms of marginalization in the same study allows us to see how the different social boundaries compare in terms of their impact on the friendship. For example, how is race different from gender? And how is each of these different from sexual orientation? And so on. What's interesting is that there are notable differences between these social boundaries. In this chapter, we will examine how the socially constructed boundaries included in this study compare with regard to their overall impact on the friendship. There are, nonetheless, important similarities between different social boundaries. These similarities are the basis of a conceptual model for understanding these boundaries. Finally, the different types of social boundary I identify within the conceptual model have implications for the career of each friendship as it unfolds.

## Overall Impact of Social Boundaries on Friendships

The social boundaries of race, gender, sexual orientation, class, religion, age, and ability vary in terms of their impact on friendships. Each social boundary has unique qualities of its own that exert influence on the friendship dynamics. Not surprisingly, and as will be seen below, the research participants had much more varied and specific things to say about how the social boundaries played themselves out in the context of their friendships. Nevertheless, among the many varied responses, the assessment of the overall impact of the social boundaries fell into a spectrum of types of impact. Not everyone agreed that the differences between them and their friend had an overall positive impact on their friendship, meaning that their differences actually enhanced their relationship. In fact, less than half thought so. Others felt that the differences had no impact and still others admitted that the differences between them had a negative impact, meaning that their differences presented an obstacle that had to be overcome.

As one might expect, responses were highly varied and most of those interviewed had mixed responses, mentioning some positives, some negatives, and some areas in which the differences between them were rather neutral. Another interesting point to consider is that, within a single friendship, each friend could have a very different view of the impact of the social boundary on the friendship. One may feel that there was no impact while the other might think of the social boundary as being a source of bonding between them—something quite positive. While it is interesting to note the difference in perception, there was no consistent or recognizable pattern in these variations. For example, the higher-status friend and the lower-status friend were just as likely to say the social boundary had no impact or it was a source of bonding. Nonetheless, there were variations in the distribution of socially constructed boundaries within each type of overall impact (see Table 3.1) as well as corresponding variations in the distribution of types of overall impact within each social boundary (see Table 3.2).[1]

## Positive Impact—Enhancing the Relationship

As indicated in Table 3.1, 41 percent of the comments regarding the overall impact of the social boundary on the friendship were of a positive nature. In other words, the differences between the two friends were perceived by one or another (or both) friends as working to the advantage of the friendship itself. Some found the differences between them to actually be the source of bonding within their friendship. Others described their friendship with someone who is different as an eye-opening experience. Respect was another prominent theme: individuals described themselves as gaining much respect for their friend given the difference between them. (See Table 3.1 for the frequency distributions for each of these positive responses.)

When the individuals perceive the social boundary to be a source of bonding, there is an underlying belief that the differences between them are complementary: the two individuals match simply because they are different in this way. For example, Adam and Patricia—who are both straight—have been close friends for many years, though they started as colleagues. Adam feels that the gender difference between them has actually made their friendship more interesting.

> *I'm thinking if we were both men, we would both have the same strengths that we would bring into the friendship. Well, because she's a woman and I'm a man, we each bring a different set of strengths that make it more interesting and stronger. So, we bring a different mix to the relationship than you would have with two men, and maybe that's what makes it more interesting. It's too easy with a man to fall back on sports. You just simply say, "Oh, how about the Packers game?" You know, boom, you're off and running. With her you've got to be more thoughtful* [Interview 31B].

From Adam's perspective, his friendship with Patricia is more interesting because the gender difference between them actually makes them more compatible. As he says, they each "bring a different set of strengths" to their friendship, strengths that he attributes to their difference in gender.

Karen and Bill also have a long-standing, cross-gender friendship. Unlike Adam and Patricia, however, they are also different in sexual orientation. Karen feels that the difference in gender paired with the difference in sexual orientation makes them compatible.

> *Well, I think we're more like girlfriends. He's male, but I can talk to him about my sexual relationship with my husband, you know. I don't think that with a*

Table 3.1: Distribution of Social Boundaries Within Each Type of Overall Impact

| | Positive Impact: Enhancing the Relationship | | | | No Impact | Negative Impact: Obstacles to Overcome | | | | |
|---|---|---|---|---|---|---|---|---|---|---|
| | Source of Bonding | Eye Opening | Respect | Total | | Initial Hesitation | Be Mindful | Some Discomfort | Less Understanding | Total |
| **Race** | 18% | 17% | 40% | **21%** | **26%** | 13% | 14% | 0% | 0% | **9%** |
| **Gender** | 41% | 17% | 0% | **26%** | **19%** | 25% | 29% | 0% | 0% | **18%** |
| **Orientation** | 29% | 17% | 40% | **26%** | **33%** | 38% | 14% | 80% | 100% | **45%** |
| **Class** | 0% | 16% | 0% | **6%** | **7%** | 12% | 29% | 0% | 0% | **14%** |
| **Religion** | 12% | 16% | 20% | **15%** | **0%** | 0% | 0% | 20% | 0% | **5%** |
| **Age** | 0% | 16% | 0% | **6%** | **11%** | 12% | 14% | 0% | 0% | **9%** |
| **Ability** | 0% | 0% | 0% | **0%** | **4%** | 0% | 0% | 0% | 0% | **0%** |
| **Total** | 100% | 100% | 100% | **100%** | **100%** | 100% | 100% | 100% | 100% | **100%** |
| N=# of Friendships | 17 | 12 | 5 | 34 | 27 | 7 | 8 | 5 | 2 | 22 |
| Proportion of Comments on Impact (N=83) | 21% | 14% | 6% | **41%** | **32%** | 9% | 10% | 6% | 2% | **27%** |

*straight male it would have been quite that easy. It's nice to have a male friend that you don't have to worry about hitting on you . . . not that I think of myself as anything special, like that would ever happen, but it's nice to have a male friend who understands the testosterone and the male brain. But at the same time, I can vent about my husband and then he vents about his husband, you know. For me, if we've been this close and he was straight, I probably could have found myself more attracted to him and thought, "Oh, this is somebody I could dump my husband for." If he were straight, I could have walked down a pretty dangerous path, I think. So, in that respect, it's made a difference in our relationship because we probably wouldn't have evolved the way we did if he was straight* [Interview 12B].

The difference in gender makes them compatible in the sense that Karen gets the benefit of hearing about a male's perspective on, for example, relationships. At the same time, she recognizes that there may be some attraction issues in a cross-gender friendship when the two individuals become so close, so the difference in sexual orientation nullifies that possibility and makes them even more compatible. Both gender and sexual orientation work together as a source of bonding in Karen's friendship with Bill.

As seen in Table 3.1, the observation that the social boundary between friends was actually a source of bonding was more heavily weighted toward gender, followed by sexual orientation, with race and religion trailing behind. The fact that this type of impact is weighted toward gender takes on even more importance when considering that a number of the examples falling under sexual orientation were ones in which the individuals were *also* different genders.

A number of the comments made by friends indicated that the socially constructed boundary between them provided them with an eye-opening experience. In other words, they had much to learn and absorb from befriending someone who was different from them. These friends felt they benefited much from the friendship and that it was a growth experience for them.

Jessi and Tina are different in terms of their religious beliefs. Tina is Christian, though she is less interested in organized religious institutions than she is in her own spirituality. Jessi has a very non-traditional, new age belief system. Tina considers their conversations about their different spiritual beliefs to be an important marker that elevated their friendship dramatically. She explained that a genuine love and respect for the other person accounts for how they are able to deal with their different spiritual views. From her perspective, they are both very willing to find the similarities in the way that they think and listen with an open mind when discussing their differences. Jessi agrees that they have had much to learn from one another and that this has been an important part of their friendship:

*Our religious differences are like a source of conversation or debate where you are trying to get the person to see your point of view. To have someone to talk to and debate with you really strengthened both of us in our beliefs . . . to analytically talk to somebody and at the same time be able to analyze your beliefs*

*and to put them in order and to really try to figure out what you believe . . .*
*when you have to talk to somebody about it, it makes it more concrete. You can*
*hear your thoughts, so to speak. So, it was very important. It was very strength-*
*ening to our friendship because it was a give-give thing* [Interview 25B].

It is apparent that their conversations and debates on religion and spirituality
have been a source of much personal growth for both Jessi and Tina.

Bob and Jerry are almost thirty years apart in age and this difference has
been very eye-opening for Jerry who feels he has had much to learn from Bob's
life experiences.

*His life experience has been a part of our friendship. I mean, just his being sort*
*of like a teacher of life kind of thing almost. Learning from his experience and*
*stuff like that is probably the only way that age has really had an impact on our*
*friendship. I think it's great. He's a really good storyteller, I think, and he's in-*
*teresting to listen to. Hearing all about when he was growing up and all of*
*these Catholic experiences and all the stuff that he's done. I think that's really*
*interesting* [Interview 11B].

Jerry has learned a lot from Bob and has really enjoyed hearing Bob's stories.
What they have in common with Jessi and Tina is the fact that they have opened
themselves up to looking at the world through a different pair of eyes and they
have learned to appreciate the different perspective their friends have to offer.
Tim and Pam capture this same idea when discussing their friendship.

*TIM: I was thinking that our gender difference has helped us to see things from*
*a different perspective: you from the male perspective and me from the female*
*perspective.*
*PAM: I agree with that. It's helped our friendship develop and it seems like*
*something we were interested in, because it came up a lot.*
*TIM: I think a lot of times we just had discussions about, for example, the*
*stereotypical way that males act and the stereotypical way that females act in*
*society. I mean talking about society was like a pretty major thing for us. We*
*did it all the time* [Interview 26C].

Discussing and learning from their different perspectives helped Tim and Pam's
friendship to develop. The fact that the gender difference between them was an
eye-opening experience was an important benefit to them. Overall, the sense that
the difference between friends was an eye-opening experience was very evenly
distributed across the different social boundaries (see Table 3.1). No social
boundary was more or less likely to be an eye-opening experience, indicating
how valuable all differences are.

Some of those interviewed indicated that the difference between themselves
and their friend became a source of increased respect for one's friend. In other
words, when recognizing the struggle the lower-status individual goes through

or the open-minded character of the higher-status individual, the friend really comes to appreciate where she or he is coming from and this creates a high opinion on the part of the friend. Respect was most prominent with race and sexual orientation, followed by religion, and conspicuously absent for gender (see Table 3.1).

As seen in the opening paragraph of this chapter, Mike has developed a healthy respect for his friend Quinn given the challenges he has faced as a person from a working class background putting himself through college and struggling to get by. Christina too has a tremendous amount of respect for her friend and mentor Ellen. While Christina is Philippino-American and Ellen is white, she recognizes that her heritage doesn't automatically make her knowledgeable regarding issues of diversity. Ellen, on the other hand, does have that knowledge.

> *I find she's so savvy because she came of age in the sixties during the Civil Rights Movement. She's so savvy in talking about it: relations and ethnicity issues, just cultural diversity issues, in general, but mostly that it's so much a part of how she sees things. Cultural diversity is just how she sees things, that multicultural perspective, and that's something that I've been working on. And just because you're a person of color doesn't mean that you have that perspective. I've run into people who are fellow Philippino-Americans who just don't get it. So, Ellen . . . it's part of that kinship again. Like she got it* [Interview 34A].

Christina provides us with an example of a lower-status individual (racially speaking) who has come to respect the open-mindedness of her friend Ellen with regard to race and other issues of diversity. This sense of respect, together with the idea that social differences have become a source of bonding and represent an eye-opening experience, highlights the perceived positive impact that social differences can have on a friendship.

## No Impact

The perception that the socially constructed boundary made no difference on their friendship was also fairly common among those interviewed, though not as common as the positive impact already described. These friends felt as if the social boundary basically didn't even exist: there was no relevant difference between them and so the friendship couldn't have been affected in any meaningful way, for better or for worse. As can be seen in Table 3.1, this response was unevenly distributed among the different social boundaries, being weighted toward sexual orientation, followed by race. It was less prominent with gender, age, class, and ability. The perception that the difference had no impact was not at all evident with religion, indicating that religion was always seen as making a difference, for better or for worse (or even both), on a friendship.

Colin is an example of one who feels that the fact he is black has had no impact on his friendship with Kelly: *"I don't put a lot of emphasis on race with a friendship. I don't think it's a significant factor. I think if you have two black people or a black and a white person, they are going to be different regardless of race simply because they're two different individuals"* [Interview 1B]. In other words, from Colin's perspective, there's *always* going to be differences between friends, so why should race stand out?

Cynthia and Greg both agree that the difference in ability between them has had no impact on their friendship. Greg has had multiple sclerosis for about ten years and is confined to a wheelchair. Still, Cynthia does not think this has had an impact on their friendship. *"Well, I met him paralyzed. This is how I've always known him, so I've just rolled with it. You know, what are you going to do? It really hasn't affected our friendship. This is just how I know him"* [Interview 28A]. Greg agrees:

> *I don't know. It's a difficult question to answer, because she's never known me without being in a wheelchair. I was thinking . . . but yeah, I don't think that makes any difference at all beyond the fact that if she wants to hang out, she got to come here. And I don't think she ever felt awkward, either. I mean, I never got that vibe from her, you know. She's never been anything like that when hanging out. I'm pretty unobtrusive in my gimp and I'm pretty independent, so I don't ask my friends to do very much for me* [Interview 28B].

Both Cynthia and Greg attribute the lack of impact by the difference in ability to the fact that they met after he was confined to a wheelchair. Even so, Greg acknowledges that it means she has to go to his place to hang out, indicating that there is some impact even if they don't think it is a big deal.

Some of those who felt that the socially constructed boundary had no impact on the friendship seemed to recognize how unlikely that seemed, and so they explained their response by adding that they are simply used to having friends who are different in that particular way. Irene—who is black, but who was raised by white parents—provides one such example.

> *To me it's not a big deal having friends with a different race. To me, it would be a bigger deal to have friends of the same race. That could be a whole other interview, you know what I mean? That would be something to talk about. I really don't have any comments to make about the impact of race because all my friends are different from me. So, I don't really see any impact* [Interview 19B].

It is so normal for Irene to have friends who are not black like herself that she doesn't see race making any difference on her friendship with Bao.

While recognizing that many friends felt that the socially constructed boundary had no impact on their relationship, it is important to keep in mind that this is their perception in general terms only. There may have been a few examples where the social boundary did make a difference, but overall, they felt there was no impact. It is equally, if not more important to point out that this assessment is based on their *overall* perception: it does not mean that there was no impact at all. Indeed, chapter 4 will focus on the many ways in which social boundaries do have a very real impact on friendship dynamics regardless of whether it is actually noticed by the individuals involved. Sometimes the impact can be very subtle and easily taken for granted. In fact, while Colin said that race was not relevant for his friendship with Kelly, it became quite clear in their three interviews that race did, in truth, make a difference in their friendship, as will be seen later.

## Negative Impact—Obstacles to Overcome

Socially constructed boundaries are not always positive or even neutral in their impact even on successful friendships. As described by Korgen in her study of cross-racial friendships, "grappling with racial issues constantly early and often may severely harm an otherwise promising friendship" (Korgen 2002, 42). She then goes on to describe a case in which racial difference almost terminated the relationship. My findings indicate that the perception that the social boundary between friends had a negative impact on the friendship was less common than perceptions it had a positive or no impact. Given that the friendships studied represent the success stories—those friends that have continued to be friends despite or perhaps because of their differences—this finding is not surprising. Yet, as Korgen notes, "There is no way of telling how many [of these diverse] friendships once existed or started to develop only to be cut down by disagreements" over the social boundary in question (2002, 45). The fact that 27 percent of the responses to the question regarding the overall impact of the social boundary on the friendship indicated there was some kind of negative impact was nevertheless unexpected. Even in these success cases, the socially constructed boundaries did at times present the friends with obstacles to overcome or with which to cope. For some, the difference between themselves and their friend meant that there was some initial hesitation as the friendship began. Others expressed how they have to be mindful of the differences in order to not hurt or offend their friend. Still others expressed some discomfort with their friend given the difference between them. And a couple indicated that there was less understanding between the friends because of the social boundary, especially when compared to those friends who have no such differences.

In some friendships, the differences between the friends provoked some initial hesitation on the part of one or both parties. In other words, there were some doubts present as the friendship was first emerging, questions as to whether the friendship would actually work given the difference between them. Such initial hesitation was weighted more toward sexual orientation, followed by gender. This hesitation was relevant but less common for friendships crossing the boundaries of race, class, and age and was not mentioned at all when it came to friendships crossing religion and ability (see Table 3.1).

While out of the closet in his personal life, Dave is not out at work, where he met his friend Tom. Because he wasn't out with Tom initially, Dave observes that their friendship developed slowly at first while he assessed whether it would be okay to come out to Tom.

> *I think if anything our difference in sexual orientation slowed down the start of our friendship or it took longer to develop on the front end; but I don't think it's made any difference on the back end. I think what we've both discovered is we have changed the name* [Dave's label went from "straight" to "gay" when he came out] *but everything else is the same. There are many, many more simi-larities between us than there are differences* [Interview 6C].

While Dave feels that—overall—the sexual orientation difference between them has had little to no impact given all that they have in common, there was still that initial hesitation when they were establishing their friendship. The same dynamic was at work in the friendship between Lenora and Melissa. Lenora—who is black—had little experience in befriending white people like Melissa, so there was some initial hesitation on her part: *"I think it hampered our relation-ship in the beginning because I still wasn't used to talking to her because she was white; but now I treat her just like she's black or whatever she is. I don't even think she has a color. I don't even see her color anymore"* [Interview 5A]. The fact that there was some initial hesitation in these friendships but that, even-tually, the social boundary had no impact again highlights how these friendships go through different stages of development. Once more, this is a topic that will be elaborated below.

Some of those interviewed felt that they needed to be mindful of that differ-ence between themselves and their friend. In other words, they were conscious about making sure they didn't cause offense. Not that they were "walking on egg shells" when interacting with their friend. Instead, they simply were sensi-tive about how their friend might perceive their own actions in light of the so-cially constructed boundary between them.

Suzanne is very much aware of the fact that she has more financial re-sources at her disposal than her friend Jenny, so she is very mindful of that dif-ference between them.

> *I think financially some things play themselves out. There were some markers in Jenny's life—becoming Associate Dean—and my partner and I wanted to take her out for dinner and treat her as a congratulations. I knew we had to think about the type of restaurant we went to and we were aware that the res-taurant my partner and I would go to on our own would not be the same kind of place we'd go if Jenny were paying. It really highlighted how money is power.*
> *I remember when we first moved here, we got a Lexus SUV, and I was a little conscious of driving that to work at my campus. The college is so social*

*justice oriented and it was my first year, so I wasn't sure . . . I didn't know. I mean, I don't care what people think around here. I have the right to do the things I want to do. I give a lot of money. I care about social justice as well, but don't shoot me because I have money. Money can do things . . . a lot depends on what you do with it. So, I talked with Jenny about it, you know, "What do you think about that?" We'll be riding in a Lexus, talking about that and what that experience is like* [Interview 13A].

It is immediately apparent how Suzanne considers where her friend Jenny is coming from when choosing a location for dinner, even when it's her treat and a gift to Jenny. The second part of her story regarding the Lexus SUV indicates how she is conscious of her class standing among her colleagues in general. She wants to be mindful of the campus culture that is oriented to social justice. Interestingly, she doesn't keep her thought process on that to herself: she talks it out with her friend Jenny.

The previous example indicates how Suzanne—the friend who has more financial resources—is mindful of the class difference between herself and her friend. It is also true that the person with fewer financial resources is very much aware of the difference in class. Quinn, who we met at the beginning of the chapter, is a case in point.

*The class difference between me and Mike is apparent in the obvious ways, you know . . . they'll* [Mike and his wife] *pay for things when we go out. They see me as not being able to afford as much as they can. I think he was kind of raised with that mentality of achievement and that kind of thing more than I was, judging from the way he describes his background. I care about my values in terms of social justice and social service and things like that and I'm ambitious about those things, I'm not very concerned with achievement in terms of status. I'm just kind of more into community and of my relationships with other people and things like that. I would say I reflect a different value system than he may have been raised with, but it's like he seems to understand that and he doesn't really emphasize any kind of achievement things. And anytime I bring up my job search, he's like, "Oh, that's how it goes" and it just doesn't seem like it's a big deal. He doesn't seem to care about those kind of things, so oftentimes in our interaction, class doesn't play that big of a role. That's a curious thing because it's one of those things where I know it's there and I think he knows it's there, but it hasn't created any sort of barrier in the relationship* [Interview 15A].

It is evident that Quinn is highly conscious of the class difference between himself and his friend Mike and he thinks that Mike is conscious of it too, judging by the fact that Mike and his wife will pay for dinner and how Mike will try not to stress Quinn out about his job search. In this example, being mindful is all about the constant awareness of the difference between them. It is anything but an invisible boundary, despite the fact that Quinn feels it has never become an actual barrier to their friendship. As seen in Table 3.1, the feeling that one must be mindful with regard to the social boundary in the friendship was weighted

toward the combination of class and gender. When considering there were only
nine interviews focusing on class and thirty interviews on gender, the fact that
class stood out underscores the relevance of being mindful in friendships crossing class lines.

For a minority of those interviewed, the socially constructed boundary has
been a source of some discomfort in the friendship, although certainly not
enough to cause one or both friends to disengage from the other. Instead, there is
something about the difference between them that, while not perceived as a major concern, is kind of bothersome. The feeling of some discomfort was heavily
weighted toward sexual orientation, though one example was found in a friendship involving religious differences.

The friendship between Jordan—who is bisexual—and Shawn—who is
straight—is a telling example. Jordan didn't come out until well after becoming
friends with Shawn. In fact, he's never really told Shawn directly in conversation, although Shawn does know. They met through their common activities and
social network that involves a lot of sports and activities, such as triathlons, in-
line skating, skiing, and camping. For his part, Jordan perceives that Shawn feels
some discomfort, at least when his partner is along. He notes how they don't
double date like they used to.

> I guess we don't go on double dates really. We would do things like that when I
> was dating women, but since being back in Minneapolis and meeting my part-
> ner . . . So, out of respect there are things that aren't going to interest him now
> that I would go out and do. I'm more likely to go do things with him or his fam-
> ily or whatnot versus having him come into my world [Interview 38A].

Because of the sense of discomfort in getting together as two couples, Jordan is
much more likely to avoid asking Shawn to join him in his "gay world" and instead leaves his partner at home and joins Shawn in his "straight world."

In interviewing Shawn, on the other hand, I got a slightly different picture.
He noted that they do double date, although his perception is that it may actually
be Jordan who feels some discomfort in doing so. At the same time, though, he
does acknowledge that there may be some discomfort on his part as well.

> It probably becomes a little awkward if you brought a partner and we were all
> camping in the same tent. Then it might seem a little awkward for me. That
> hasn't happened, though that may be because it would be awkward for Jordan,
> too. My wife and I go out with him and his partner like any other couple, and
> we talk about the same stuff, challenging stuff, and the nitty gritty stuff openly.
> And that's fine; but you know, it could be awkward. Jordan's comfort level with
> it is . . . he doesn't try to put himself in too uncomfortable of a situation.
>
> I accept him and know who he is as a person, and I know his integrity. So,
> none of the other stuff scares me. That doesn't really bother me. And if it does,
> it would be such a small amount . . . it's not even that measurable. Whereas, for
> some people, it'd be very difficult, you know [Interview 38B]?

While Shawn seems comfortable having dinner with Jordan and his partner, he does distinguish this type of socializing from, for example, camping and sharing a tent. Then again, from his point of view, any awkwardness that exists is actually mutual. Moreover, the discomfort that is felt he perceives as minimal. At the same time, it is interesting that, however minimal it is, both of them mentioned it and they brought it up when it was comparatively rare for those interviewed to express any sense of discomfort.

Adam—who is Jewish—has also experienced some discomfort with his friend Jeremiah—who is Christian. Jeremiah is an immigrant from Africa and a colleague of Adam. When they first met, Jeremiah was absolutely thrilled to meet his first Jew ever, which initially took Adam aback, though he found the situation so novel—having someone immediately attracted to him as a friend because he was Jewish when he found most people to be somewhat disparaging of Jews—that he took a liking to Jeremiah as well. They quickly became friends. Jeremiah is ardent in his religious beliefs, which is fine for Adam until someone crosses the line into proselytizing.

> *Proselytizing doesn't happen often. It happened when I was younger, but I think it's pretty clear. Now with Jeremiah, I did get a little aggravated. I was very stung when that came up last week, 'cause he's never crossed that line really. He came to my office as he often does. Because he's grieving the death of his wife, I just stopped what I was doing for two hours. He and his wife were very close as you would guess in a community like this and there aren't a lot of outlets for him. But it's kind of the same for me being Jewish. So, I don't know . . . he turns every discussion to religion, which I find interesting. It's always fun to talk intellectually about things. The problem with him is he has such a passion and such a strong belief that no matter what you say . . . but I did get him off kilter a couple of times playing devil's advocate a little bit. But this was the first time I've heard this conversion business. He doesn't say that I need to change. He simply "knows that I will." Clever. I guess that expectation kind of annoys me a little bit, the idea that I'm not smart enough to be able to figure these things out for myself. But then again I look at him and he's such a be-liever; for him, it comes as naturally as brushing your teeth. But in all these years that's never happened before. I think it is the death of his wife that has him thinking about what happens when you die. I don't take it personally. Jeremiah is such a lovely guy, and he's such a rock and I know that he loves me* [Interview 32B].

The proselytizing happened only once in Adam's experience with Jeremiah, and it wasn't enough to harm their friendship. Still, it did stick in Adam's mind given the fact that he brought it up several times before, during, and after my interview with him.

Only a small portion of the observations made about the overall impact of the social boundary on the friendship indicated that there was less understanding between the friends because of the difference between them. In fact, examples of this were found in only two different friendships, which isn't really enough to indicate a trend. This form of overall impact was found exclusively with the boundary of sexual orientation. One or both friends indicated that, because of the difference in orientation, there were times when the straight friend just won't "get it:" they don't really understand what the experience of being a sexual minority is really like. In both of the friendships where the lack of understanding came up, it was the straight friend who was aware of it, though the gay friend also brought it up in one of those friendships.

Eric—who is straight—captures the sense of having less understanding of his friend Brad when he explains that, when he is with gay men he is "the other"—the one who does not fit in and who doesn't fully understand what it is like to be a part of the group. Notice that this passage also highlights the sense of discomfort he feels.

> *I'm socialized in this culture. I was raised Catholic and really had to overcome a whole heck of a lot to just make sense of that and always felt kind of guilty about things that you shouldn't be guilty about. I know that intellectually, but emotionally I can't do it. If I'm with a bunch of gay guys, those things would start to circulate in my mind, and I couldn't stop. It's like, if I go into a room with a bunch of women, I feel weird . . . out of place. I mean, I get along with women and I enjoy a lot of them, but I know I'm the other. So, there's always that sense of other. It's not an exclusionary sense in which you're not in the right caste or social class; but it's a sense of you don't share the same experiences* [Interview 7A].

Because he doesn't share the same experiences as gay men, Eric knows that he doesn't quite "get it" despite the fact that he is generally pretty open-minded. For his part, Brad also notes that there is less understanding between himself and straight friends like Eric, especially when compared with his gay friends.

> *I don't know that sexual orientation has necessarily affected our friendship in terms of the total thing. Even so, I don't think that Eric would have understood how I felt about Jim* [a man with whom Brad was deeply in love]. *He might have . . . I don't know that, you know. He would have never judged me about it and he would have been very caring, but I just don't think that most straight people understand how gay men think about one another or the context of what that means and some of the struggle of what that means. Part of this is generational; I mean, we're going back twenty-five years maybe, so the world's changed a bit. But I guess I don't think that I saw Eric as somebody that I would share those things with* [Interview 7B].

It is interesting that Brad has not given Eric the opportunity to try to understand his feelings for Jim in the first place. He does this because, from his experience, straight people don't really understand what being a gay man is like. Brad does admit that he might not be giving Eric enough credit, but his experience with the lack of understanding on the part of straight people won out.

It is also evident that Mark feels less understanding of his gay friend Dave. He notes that Dave has changed a bit since he left the military and doesn't have to be so closeted. Despite his claim that it doesn't bother him, Mark does seem a bit uncomfortable. Underlying this discomfort is the fact that he doesn't quite understand where Dave is coming from.

> *It can at times be a stressful issue, because I don't need to be constantly reminded of how good looking the UPS delivery man is or whatever. I'm just never going to see anything there, but I'll say, "Oh yeah, he looks buff" or "he's an in shape guy" or whatever. But that's where there's a disconnect. It doesn't bother me too much, you know. I just let it go and that's that. It's just, the longer he's out of the military, which has been a long time now, there has been a change in the . . . I don't know how to describe it . . . it's more free coming. Obviously, for all those years, he never could say anything like that ever. In the military, everything's hush, hush and under lock and key. And now when you hear it, it appears to be a bigger deal because you were used to hearing nothing like that. And that's just an example. Some things about the old way maybe wasn't all that bad* [Interview 10B].

For Mark, there is a bit of a disconnect between him and his friend Dave, a disconnect arising out of their difference in sexual orientation, particularly now that Dave is no longer constrained by the "don't ask, don't tell" policy of the military. At some level, Mark seems nostalgic for the friendship they had when Dave was closeted, indicating that he has less understanding for his gay friend compared to straight friends. This lack of understanding, together with the sense of discomfort, the need to be mindful of differences, and the initial hesitation some friends have felt indicate that, even among those friends able to overcome their differences, socially constructed boundaries can still have a perceived negative impact on the friendship itself. They present the friends with real obstacles to be overcome if their friendship is to succeed. Even so, such a negative impact was found in only a minority of cases, indicating that, for most of those studied, the social differences had no impact or even a perceived positive impact on the friendship.

## Comparing Social Boundaries

Thus far, I have identified the different types of overall impact of socially constructed boundaries on friendships as described by the friends themselves. In addition, we saw that there are variations in the distribution of social boundaries within each type of overall impact (see Table 3.1). At the same time, there are corresponding variations in the distribution of types of overall impact within each social boundary. These variations are presented in Table 3.2.

Table 3.2: Distribution of Types of Overall Impact Within Each Social Boundary

| | | Race | Gender | Sexual Orient. | Class | Religion | Age | Ability |
|---|---|---|---|---|---|---|---|---|
| Positive Impact: Enhancing the Relationship | Source of Bonding | 21% | 54% | 22% | 0% | 25% | 0% | 0% |
| | Eye Opening | 13% | 12% | 5% | 18% | 63% | 18% | 0% |
| | Respect | 8% | 0% | 7% | 9% | 0% | 0% | 0% |
| | **Total** | **42%** | **65%** | **33%** | **27%** | **88%** | **18%** | **0%** |
| **No Impact** | | **50%** | **19%** | **33%** | **45%** | **0%** | **64%** | **100%** |
| Negative Impact: Obstacles to Overcome | Initial Hesitation | 4% | 8% | 7% | 9% | 0% | 9% | 0% |
| | Be Mindful | 4% | 8% | 2% | 18% | 0% | 9% | 0% |
| | Some Discomfort | 0% | 0% | 14% | 0% | 13% | 0% | 0% |
| | Less Understanding | 0% | 0% | 10% | 0% | 0% | 0% | 0% |
| | **Total** | **8%** | **15%** | **33%** | **27%** | **12%** | **18%** | **0%** |
| **Grand Total** | | **100%** | **99%** | **99%** | **99%** | **100%** | **100%** | **100%** |
| N=# of Interviews | | 24 | 26 | 42 | 11 | 8 | 11 | 3 |

When looking at race as a socially constructed boundary, it is apparent that the responses describing the overall impact of race on the friendship were weighted toward no impact, meaning that fully one-half of those friends crossing this boundary perceived race as having no impact on their friendship, either positive or negative. Less than half, but a sizeable minority felt that the racial difference between them had an overall positive impact on their friendship. Most of those indicated that race became a source of bonding between them. Only a few friends indicated that having a friend of a different race was an eye-opening experience or a source of respect. Very few felt that race had a negative impact on the friendship, but when it was present it took the form of some initial hesitation or the desire to be mindful of the difference between them. And there was no evidence of discomfort or a lack of understanding between friends of different races. Such a distribution pattern may indicate that, at least among those with friendships crossing socially constructed boundaries, these individuals are more used to dealing with racial diversity or, and this is perhaps more cynical, they are more likely to downplay the impact in favor of being perceived as tolerant. Nonetheless, judging from the overall tone of the interviews and the sincerity among those interviewed, I favor the former assessment over the later.

By contrast, friendships crossing the gender line were perceived in a highly positive light in terms of their overall impact. This was especially true in the perception that gender became a source of bonding, an observation that emphasizes the view that men and women have complementary characteristics that match up in a friendship. Only a minority of the total comments indicated that gender had no impact. On the other hand, when compared to race, friendships crossing gender were a little more likely to provoke some initial hesitation or cause one or both friends to be mindful of the gender difference between them. Overall, and despite the fact that we are exposed to gender diversity much more than racial diversity in our day-to-day lives, it is apparent that gender is not something that can easily be taken for granted or overlooked, especially when compared to racial differences.

Friendships crossing the boundary of sexual orientation are especially interesting. The responses were evenly distributed between a positive impact, no impact, and a negative impact. Compared to the other socially constructed boundaries, sexual orientation elicited the greatest proportion of negative perceptions, presenting one or both friends with an obstacle to overcome. In terms of positive perceptions, areas in which the differences between the friends actually enhanced the relationship, it trailed behind race, gender, and religion. What separates sexual orientation from all the other socially constructed boundaries is that this is the only one where *all* identified types of overall impact are evident. Moreover, friends were much more likely to describe more than one type of impact operating simultaneously,[2] indicating that there were more mixed feelings about these friendships. As already noted, sexual orientation was the only social boundary to elicit the feeling that there was less understanding between the friends and, with the exception of a single comment made by an individual in a cross-religion friendship, to elicit feelings of discomfort. In fact, and this further separates sexual orientation from the other socially constructed boundaries, expressing a feeling of discomfort was the third most common response when asked to provide an overall assessment of the impact of the boundary on the friendship. Two thirds of these comments expressing discomfort came from friendships where both friends are male and in *all* of the friendships where some discomfort came up, the straight person (who was also always male) expressed such feelings while in one-third of them the gay or lesbian person also expressed some discomfort. By comparison, not one straight woman indicated that there was less understanding or a sense of discomfort in her friendship with a gay or lesbian individual. Again, this pattern seems to indicate that those in friendships crossing sexual orientation lines are more likely to feel conflicted than friends who cross other socially constructed boundaries, although this is much more likely to occur among straight men.

Religion was more polarized. It is the only social boundary for which no one indicated there was no impact; the overall impact was either positive or negative. Besides orientation, religion is the only other boundary that included an example of some discomfort. The overwhelming majority, however, indicated that it had an overall positive impact. This is especially true for those who perceive religious differences as an eye-opening experience. The responses among friends crossing lines of class, age, and ability were weighted toward no impact (although the fact that there was only one set of interviews focusing exclusively on ability makes that highly unrepresentative). Compared to race, gender, and sexual orientation, friendships crossing the boundaries of class, religion, and age were more likely to be an eye-opening experience, perhaps indicating that we have more to learn from these friendships.

Overall, while there were common types of overall impact of social boundaries on friendships, as assessed by the friends themselves, it is apparent that the distribution of the different types of impact varied for each social boundary. This makes it possible to compare the impact of race, gender, sexual orientation, class, religion, age, and—to a lesser extent—ability on the friendships. Such a comparison indicates that there are some areas of diversity—like race—that friends are more used to dealing with, while others—like sexual orientation—elicit a much more complicated pattern of responses.

While important and revealing, this focus on the overall impact implies that the relevance of the socially constructed boundary is consistent over time—a rather static understanding of the role played by differences within a friendship. Yet, this is not always the case. In fact, as alluded to in the previous section and as will be seen below, the impact of the social boundary often changes over the course of the friendship. Moreover, the social boundaries studied here have certain meaningful similarities and differences among them that play an important role in how friendships develop over time and what impact those socially constructed boundaries have at different times in the friendship.

# A Conceptual Model

Race, gender, sexual orientation, class, religion, age, and ability are all relevant for the dynamics within the friendship, but—as seen above—in very different ways. Still, there is a recognizable pattern among these socially constructed boundaries in terms of their impact on friendship dynamics—a pattern based on two dimensions: visibility and changeability. As one might expect, these dimensions are a matter of degree, so it is helpful to think of them as existing on a continuum from visible to invisible and from unchanging to changeable. These two dimensions form the basis of a typology that is helpful in understanding the relevance of socially constructed boundaries on a friendship.

The dimension of visibility varies from visible differences to invisible differences, each falling at opposite ends of the continuum. The question here is, "how immediately apparent (based on visual and/or auditory cues) are the differences between the two friends?" For example, if both friends dress and behave in gender-typical styles, then the gender difference between them would be instantly recognizable. Consequently, the social boundary between them begins to exert influence on the friendship even as the two individuals are first meeting each other and establishing a relationship. Recall the friendship between Adam and Patricia [friendship pair #31]: they instantly knew when meeting each other for the first time at work that there was a gender difference between them. There was no need for either one of them to subsequently reveal their gender identity. From the moment they met, gender played a role in their friendship.

This dynamic is true for all visible social boundaries, such as (in most instances) race, age, and those forms of difference in ability that have a visual (or audible) component. Class and religion can also be visible social boundaries depending on how one's class or religious affiliation is displayed. For example, a person can "wear" her money by driving a very expensive car or someone can display his religion by regularly quoting the Bible by chapter and verse. For Quinn [friendship pair #15], the class difference between himself and Mike is very visible given that Mike and his wife regularly pick up the tab for dinner. Their class difference was apparent from the day they met given that Quinn was still a student at the time and had to struggle to afford the trip on which they met whereas Mike and his wife could afford the trip quite comfortably. In the friendship between Cynthia and Greg [friendship pair #28], it was immediately apparent that they had a difference in ability given his confinement to a wheelchair. That difference exerted influence on their relationship from the beginning of their relationship, determining, for example, that they have to spend time at his home rather than her home.

Sexual orientation, on the other hand, could be completely invisible such that there are no outward signs to indicate that a person is gay, lesbian, or bisexual. Note that the assumption is made that—barring any outwardly stereotypical signs that a person is gay, lesbian, or bisexual—the person is straight. Accordingly, the presence of the social boundary is minimized or even non-existent *from the perspective of the straight person* as the two individuals meet and establish a relationship. When Dave and Mark met [friendship pair #10], Mark had no idea Dave was gay and Dave had no intention in revealing this aspect of his identity because of the fact they were roommates and both in the military at the time. It wasn't until years later, when Dave was no longer in the military that he revealed that aspect of his identity to Mark. At that point, this difference between them came out of the background and into the foreground (for Dave) and, from Mark's perspective, suddenly manifested itself and had to be dealt with. Again, this dynamic is true for all socially constructed boundaries lacking a visual (or audible) component. It is possible, for example, for a person's racial difference to go unnoticed depending on the individual's overall appearance and manner. The same is true for class, religion, and even age so long as visual (or audible) signifiers are missing. Recall the friendship between Jessi and Tina [friendship pair #25], who are different in terms of their religious beliefs. On the surface, there is nothing to indicate that they are different in this way. It was only through later conversation that they realized they had this difference between them.

The second relevant dimension for understanding the impact of socially constructed boundaries on a friendship is changeability, which varies from unchanging to changeable social boundaries. In other words, there are instances where a person can move from one social category into another and other instances where they cannot. For example, we don't generally think of a person changing race, which means that there is a consistent racial difference between the two friends.[3] This same dynamic is true for other socially constructed boundaries that are unchanging, such as gender (barring one of the friends being transgendered), sexual orientation (assuming the gay or lesbian individual is already out of the closet prior to meeting the straight friend), and ability (assuming it is a pre-existing condition that doesn't progress over time). On the other hand, it is important to notice the exceptions here. If a person changes genders, as was true in the friendship between Hugo and Debbie [pair #33], or comes out of the closet after the friendship is established, as in the friendship between Dave and Mark [pair #10], or has a deteriorating physical condition or a sudden change in physical ability (i.e., paralysis), then the friends are forced to handle the perceived change in status between them. The same is true for class and religion. If a person's class standing or religious affiliation changes (moving the two friends closer together or further apart in status), the friends must then manage that change in status. Recall the friendship between Suzanne and Jenny [friendship pair #13]. They come from different class backgrounds. However, as will be seen in the next chapter, Jenny's class status is changing and coming closer to that of Suzanne. As we'll see, Suzanne begins to mentor Jenny into the culture of her new, higher class standing. While the person who changed categories may still feel like the same person on the inside, who she or he is in the eyes of others does change and this forces the others, including the friend, to adjust.

This, in turn, forces a change in the relationship dynamics between the parties involved.

Given these two dimensions—visibility and changeability—it is possible to identify a conceptual model for understanding the impact of social boundaries on friendships. As seen in Table 3.3, there are four types of socially constructed boundaries: visible and unchanging, visible and changeable, invisible and unchanging, and invisible and changeable social boundaries. Those social boundaries that are visible and unchangeable, such as race (barring the above-noted exceptions), will have an impact when the two individuals first meet and begin to establish their friendship. In Lenora and Melissa's friendship [pair #5], the racial difference between them was immediately apparent and had the most impact when they first met and Melissa made friendly overtures: Lenora had to overcome her initial hesitation. After their friendship was well established, the racial difference moved into the background.

Table 3.3: A Conceptual Model for Understanding the Impact of Social Boundaries

| | | Changeability | |
| --- | --- | --- | --- |
| | | **Unchanging** | **Changeable** |
| **Visibility** | **Visible** | **Visible and Unchanging**<br><br>Impact early in friendship, not later. | **Visible and Changeable**<br><br>Impact early in friendship *and* later.... *If* there is no status difference when the friendship is established, the impact would be later in the friendship. |
| | **Invisible** | **Invisible and Unchanging**<br><br>Impact early in friendship, not later. However, this requires the lower-status person to announce the difference or the higher-status person to figure it out. | **Invisible and Changeable**<br><br>Impact is not early in the friendship, but later. |

Those socially constructed boundaries that are visible and changeable, such as age (barring the above-noted exceptions), will also have in impact when the individuals first meet and establish a friendship. Moreover, such social boundaries will have a continuing impact on the friendship dynamics in cases where these boundaries change gradually, such as age (such as in the friendship between Bob and Jerry, pair #11), or will have a sudden impact later in the relationship in cases where the social boundary can suddenly disappear (as in a religious conversion or a dramatic change in class status). For visible and change-able social boundaries, it is also possible for there to be no status difference be-tween the two friends when the friendship is first established and for a social boundary to gradually emerge (as in a degenerative physical condition) or to suddenly appear (as in having sex-reassignment surgery).

In the case of invisible and unchanging social boundaries, such as sexual orientation when the gay or lesbian individual is already out, the lower-status individual either has to announce the status difference between them (and this happens early in the relationship as the friendship is being established) or the higher-status individual gradually figures it out (which could potentially take some time). In the friendship between Karen and Bill [pair #12], Bill came out to Karen early in their friendship and they dealt with it immediately. Conversely, Shawn was put in a position of gradually figuring out that Jordan is bisexual [pair #14]. There never was a single "coming out" moment. In either case, while the actual status difference between them has not changed, the perception of one or both parties is adjusted in the early stages of the friendship.

Finally, when the social boundary is invisible and changeable, such as sex-ual orientation when the gay or lesbian individual is initially closeted, as Dave was when he met Mark [pair #10], the impact of the social boundary is not felt until after the relationship has already been established. Accordingly, the higher status individual (in this case, the straight person) is allowed to assume that there is no status difference between them as the friendship is established. As already noted, though, the gay or lesbian person's sexual orientation hasn't changed so much as the situation changes when he or she decides to come out and no longer pass for straight.

Overall, the visibility dimension is relevant for friendships when the two individuals are first meeting and establishing their friendship. It is at this stage in the friendship that the visibility of the socially constructed boundary has the greatest impact. The changeability dimension is most relevant for friendships after the friendship has already been established. After the relationship is under way, something happens to change the already established friendship dynamic, which then affects the future progression of the friendship. Consequently, the visibility and changeability dimensions have an impact on how a friendship de-velops over time, indicating that it is important to consider the stages through which a friendship will progress in light of the social boundaries that exist be-tween the two individuals.

## Stages of Friendship

It is not uncommon for those who study friendship to think of these relationships as emerging and developing through a number of stages: what might be called the "friendship career" (Spencer and Pahl 2006, 72). Friendships that cross socially constructed boundaries generally progress through stages in which the social boundary changes in significance. It is important to point out that the progression of a friendship crossing a socially constructed boundary is a matter of perception by the individuals involved. It is possible, for example, for the two friends to see it quite differently depending on their past experiences and whether or not they are passing as a higher-status person. Still, there is a general pattern evident in the friendships studied.

Initially, the social boundary is rather prominent in the eyes of one or both individuals, potentially making the initial steps toward friendship somewhat tentative. Over time, as they get to know one another, the comfort level of each friend increases and the social boundary recedes into the background. As they get to know one another, they are more likely to have discussions about the difference between them (see Rude 2009 and Korgen 2002), assuming they discuss it directly at all. On the other hand, this progression changes if the lower-status individual is passing for a higher status person when the friendship is initiated. In this case, the social boundary is invisible in the eyes of one friend and so from that perspective has no impact. For the friend who is passing, however, there may be some initial hesitation in forming the relationship. When she or he decides to "come out," the social boundary becomes much more prominent within their friendship. At this point, assuming the friendship continues, the friendship progresses much the same as for visible social boundaries such that the socially constructed boundary becomes less significant as the comfort level of both friends increases, an observation that confirms past research in this area (Rude 2009 and Korgen 2002).

For example, we've already met Kelly and Colin who are different in terms of race, so the social boundary between them is highly visible and will not be changing. Referring back to Table 3.3, the result is that race has an impact early in the friendship, but not later as the two friends acclimate to the difference between them. From Kelly's perspective, and unlike Colin, the racial difference between them was prominent in her eyes. Hence, in the early stages of the friendship, the race issue kept them from becoming closer than they might otherwise have become because Kelly was tiptoeing around the issue so as not to offend her newfound friend.

> *If I had met him on the street, I'd probably have been intimidated by him because he's a bigger guy, very broad shoulders, taller, big hands. . . So, I'd probably have that stereotype of, "Okay, keep your guard up, but just be friendly until you know what's going on." That kind of thing. I tend to judge the situation one on one. But I met him through my sister, so that wasn't a problem.*
>
> *Even so, it was my first friendship with somebody from a drastically different background, culture, and race than me. So, it was kind of like, "Okay, let's see how it goes and then, once we are comfortable around each other, we can start bringing up these issues because they may cause problems down the line or maybe it'll help us understand where the other is coming from. So, for a while, race went untalked about because I wasn't—and he wasn't—sure how the other would react when we started talking about it. And then once we*

*started talking about it, it helped the situation because it brought us closer to-*
*gether in a lot of ways* [Interview 1A].

From Kelly's account, it is clear that there was some initial hesitation on her part
due to the racial difference between them, although it helped that she met Colin
through her sister. Over time, though, as the level of familiarity and comfort
grew, the race issue actually began to bring them closer together than they might
have otherwise grown, becoming a source of bonding between them. Eventually,
they talked about it and in so doing they learned much more about each other
and one another's background.

> *Talking about our family and our cultural differences helps in bridging the*
> *gaps, I guess you could say. Like when we talk about stuff involving our differ-*
> *ences and race in general, sometimes we have different opinions about why*
> *things happen the way they do. But when we talk about it, I can understand bits*
> *of where he's coming from and he'll understand bits of where I'm coming from,*
> *so then we'll kind of meet in that gray area versus going, "Well, this is the way*
> *I see it and that's the way you see it and that's it!" We kind of gain an under-*
> *standing of where the other person is coming from and why we might think that*
> *way* [Interview 1A].

This stage represented a period of much growth in the relationship. Finally, as
the level of familiarity with one another increased to the point where it leveled
off, race receded into the background such that it no longer brought them closer
or kept them apart. In describing their friendship as it currently stands, Kelly
notes that *"race is not always the first topic of conversation or anything . . ."*
[Interview 1A]. Not that race disappears entirely; there are times when it comes
up, although this is generally a response to an outside situation such as a movie
with a lot of black humor or the reaction of a white person to Colin or a black
person to Kelly.

From Colin's perspective, the process did not work in the same way. For
him, the racial difference between them was not so prominent in the early stages
and so he did not find it inhibiting him in his interactions with Kelly. In their
paired interview, Kelly and Colin attribute this to the fact that he has had to interact with white people on a regular basis, so it is nothing new to him.

> *COLIN: I think race has been a bigger deal for her than for me. She knows that*
> *I am not going to be a white boy, so she's had to change a lot more than me.*
> *KELLY: Yeah. I think it goes back to as Colin was talking about before: he has*
> *to deal with white society all the time, but I don't have to deal with black soci-*
> *ety. It's not so prevalent in my everyday situation, and yes, I may have encoun-*
> *ters with people of different races, but it's not long-term or a more personal*
> *and in-depth kind of a thing. It's just kind of in passing. So, I wasn't ingrained*
> *with it every day and I didn't think about race the way I do now just because I*
> *didn't have to deal with it every day or as long. And so I think that's kind of*
> *helped me realize my stereotypes and what I needed to work on* [Interview 1C].

Colin has already developed a method for dealing with white people, a method that is so ingrained he takes it for granted, whereas Kelly—due to her comparative lack of experience in relating with members of other races on an intimate level, a consequence of white privilege—had to come up with a way to interact with Colin.

In this example, it was the member of the privileged group—Kelly—for whom the socially constructed boundary was most prominent. Nevertheless, this is not always the case. Sometimes the member of the marginalized group is self-conscious about their minority status even when their friend is not. Lenora is a young, black woman who was quite conscious of her marginalized status when trying to establish a friendship with her white friend Melissa.

> *In the beginning, race made a difference. I think it hampered our relationship because I still wasn't used to talking to her because she was white. The fact that I've only had a couple of white friends restricts my view on white people. Most white girls don't talk like me or dress like me or act like me. I'm more likely to talk to white girls who talk the way I talk and dress the way I dress and hang around and do the same things that I like to do. And Melissa has a lot of black friends, so she's been around black people all of her life [Interview 5A].*

For Lenora, her marginalized status vis-à-vis the privileged, white group has caused problems for her in the past. As a result, she easily makes the assumption that her marginalized status might be an issue when meeting people and establishing friendships.

In both of these cases (Kelly/Colin and Lenora/Melissa), it is the person who is sheltered within her own social category and who has little experience with members of the other category for whom the social boundary is prominent. And notice that this occurs regardless of whether she is marginalized or privileged: Kelly, as a white woman, is privileged but sheltered from much contact with those of other races and Lenora, as a black woman, is marginalized and also sheltered from much contact with whites. This shelter of similarity goes hand in hand with the discomfort of difference, so both Kelly and Lenora had to grow comfortable with the racial difference with their respective friends. By itself, this isn't surprising; but generally we think of this in terms of the privileged being sheltered. It is common among the marginalized to surround one's self with a supportive social network (or be forced into such a situation) of those who share the marginalized status or who are supportive despite any status differences. Such a supportive social enclave, while sheltering the marginalized, can also isolate them from the outside world, making it much less familiar.

For Lenora, given the visibility of her racial background, her marginalized status is immediately apparent; but this visible quality is not always true for the members of the subordinate group. It is possible to pass as a privileged individual, as in the case of sexual orientation (or race if the racial difference is not immediately apparent, or even gender in the case of those who identify as transgendered). Passing later necessitates "coming out" as a member of a marginalized group if one plans to create anything more than a superficial friendship. As seen in chapter 2, such was the situation with Dave who was quite worried about how his friend Tom might react, especially given that they were also colleagues in a profession Dave describes as being particularly homophobic. Passing as straight early in their friendship gave Dave the opportunity to size up his new-found friend to see if it would be okay to come out to a colleague. When his comfort level increased, he was able to do so. Thus, from his perspective, there was some initial hesitation on Dave's part and the social boundary between him and his friend was quite prominent as he considered coming out. From Tom's perspective, the difference in sexual orientation was not a big deal, though he recognizes that the point of coming out was significant for Dave.

In both of these examples—the case of Dave and Tom and the case of Lenora and Melissa, it was the member of the marginalized group for whom the socially constructed boundary was most apparent. What is interesting about this point is that it placed their respective friends—who are members of the privileged group—in the position where they had to "come out" as an individual who is okay with their marginalized status. They both made intentional moves to let their stigmatized friend know that they were sympathetic others or, in the language of Goffman (1963), "models of normalization" who do not consider them to have a stigmatized status in the first place. For example, Melissa made a conscious effort to indicate to Lenora that she was "black friendly," largely through subtle hints like references to black role models and specific aspects of black culture.

> I think either subconsciously or . . . I said something to let her know that we lis-ten to the same kind of music. Like, "Do you have that new CD?" Or some-thing where she can sort of realize that we're more alike. I'm sure I said some-thing like, "Did you see the new Denzel Washington movie?" and then she's like, "All right, she likes Denzel, too," you know. So, one thing after another led her to realize that we had a lot in common, which is important when you're trying to connect with someone. Sometimes I have to do that because otherwise I have . . . especially here, where I'm just one of so many white girls. And that's fine. If you don't, people don't understand that you have a lot of similarities if they just take you for what they see [Interview 5B].

Melissa recognizes that when people look at her they simply see a white woman, not a person who actually identifies more strongly with black culture than white culture. As a result, she actively drops hints to indicate her cultural affiliation.

Tom didn't drop hints *per se;* instead, he simply continued to treat Dave the same as he always did even as he began to figure out that Dave was gay. By maintaining the same behavior toward Dave, Tom was being very supportive.

> I think his being gay was a bigger deal for him because maybe he was more paranoid about losing our friendship than I was, because I knew and I was comfortable with it. For a while there, he thought maybe I didn't know and was

*wondering how I was going to react. He's been dealing with that for his whole life . . . worrying about people accepting him or not. So, I was getting more and more hints all along and finally it was so obvious that he figured I knew. He didn't see a change in my behavior, so it probably didn't bother him anymore. Then it finally got brought up and we talked about it; but by that time we did talk about it, I think he was already pretty certain that I was okay with it* [Interview 6B].

Unlike Melissa's experience, Tom had to "figure out" Dave's sexual orientation before he realized it was an issue for Dave. Only then did Tom take on that supportive role by not changing his behavior toward Dave.[4]

Overall, the prominence of the socially constructed boundary in the eyes of one or both individuals in the friendship makes a difference in the initial development of the friendship such that it may make the initial steps in forging a friendship more tentative. On the other hand, as the comfort level of these individuals increases, the relevance of the social boundary for the friendship begins to recede into the background. This change in the prominence of the social boundary is largely a matter of the individual's perception, as well as the visibility and changeability of the social boundary itself.

In this chapter, we have contextualized socially constructed boundaries within the friendships studied: What impact do the social boundaries of race, gender, sexual orientation, class, religion, age, and ability have on interpersonal relationships? There are important differences between the social boundaries studied here in terms of their impact on friendship dynamics. At the same time, by examining these boundaries at a more abstract level, it is possible to see a pattern in terms of their impact. Overall, it was apparent that the differences that exist between two friends are highly influential upon the friendship itself, even when they claim there was no impact. This topic will be taken up again in the next chapter, where we will focus on the interpersonal techniques used by these unlikely friends to negotiate the social boundary between them.

## Notes

1. While such distribution patterns cannot be generalized given the fact that this research is not based on a representative sample, the patterns are highly suggestive.

2. As indicated by the fact that N=42 (the number of different comments assessing the overall impact of sexual orientation) when the total number of interviews focusing on sexual orientation was 30.

3. Keeping in mind that race and all category systems are socially constructed, one recognizes that it is possible for a person's race to "change" in the sense that the classification system changes while the person does not. For example, my race "changed" between college and graduate school, not because I changed, but because the categories changed. When applying to college, the application form asked my race and included among its categories "White" and "Hispanic." I checked "white" because that's how I appear. When applying to graduate school, the categories for the same question included

"White, Non-Hispanic" and "Hispanic (regardless of race)." I then checked "Hispanic (regardless of race)" because I no longer fit into the "White" category when it was further qualified by the phrase "Non-Hispanic." In this sense, my race "changed." Still, from the perspective of everyone I knew personally, nothing changed. The relationships continued as they had previously. My race changed on paper more than anything else, and this affected the way in which I was "counted" by those collecting racial data.

4. As the cases of Melissa and Tom indicate, the conceptual model used to understand the impact of social boundaries on friendships might apply equally well to understanding the tolerance a person has for those who are different. For example, how visible or invisible is such tolerance? Both Melissa and Tom had to make their tolerance visible to their newfound friends, in effect "coming out" as tolerant people. Then there is the question of changeability: is such tolerance unchanging or is it changeable? Such questions raise interesting ideas that go beyond the data collected for this research project.

# Chapter 4

## Interpersonal Techniques
## for Managing Social Boundaries

Whether the individuals involved in diverse friendships realize it or not, they have to address and manage the socially constructed boundary in some way. Ironically, it is quite common for such friends to pretend the demographic difference between them does not exist (Rude 2009; Korgen 2002), but even this is a technique for addressing the difference. Whether the friends deal with it directly or try to ignore it entirely, "the friends actively [construct] a means to 'disarm' the topic, so that it would not come between them and harm their friendships" (Korgen 2002, 33). Disarming the topic fosters a sense of trust in one's friend—what Rude identifies as "racial trust" but could just as readily apply to gender, sexual orientation, and other social differences. In other words, the two friends "must work to demonstrate their . . . openness, but at the same time they must protect the relationship from . . . prejudice (their own and that of others)" (2009, 110). Such trust is a crucial element of a successful friendship (Rawlins 1992).

Throughout my interviews, it was evident that there is a great variety of interpersonal "techniques" for disarming socially constructed boundaries and establishing such trust, even when one or both friends felt that their differences had no impact or a positive impact on the friendship. At the same time, the term "technique" is somewhat misleading in that it suggests that the individuals are consciously pulling out some tool to help them in this situation, and this is not always the case. Sometimes it is merely circumstances, such as past experiences with members of the other group, the emergence of a shared history with their friend, or the fact that both individuals are marginalized although marginalized within different social boundaries (ex: one is a straight woman and the other is a gay man). Sometimes it is conscious, as in actively avoiding those individuals who are perceived to be unsympathetic to one's minority status, confronting those who have given offense, or agreeing to disagree. Among the strategies I found across my interviews, the most common include (1) a focus on the hidden commonalities between the two individuals, (2) "taking care" to be supportive and not cause offense, (3) meeting one's friend more than half way, (4) educating one's friend, and (5) the use of humor.

## Focusing on the Hidden Commonalities

The idea of focusing on what one has in common with another individual might be considered an elaboration of the idea that socially constructed boundaries are a matter of perception. Instead of dwelling on the differences between themselves and assuming that such differences represented barriers to friendship, many of those I interviewed enjoyed finding things in common and focused their attention on all they had in common with their friend and how those commonalities bring them together. Highlighting the commonalities allows the friends to sidestep the social boundary and focus on their common humanity. Erving Goffman (1963), in describing how individuals cope with stigmatization, notes that when a stigmatized individual surrounds him or herself with sympathetic others who do not share the stigma, these others tend to downplay the stigma, focusing instead on all the commonalities. This serves to "normalize" and humanize the stigmatized individual. In addition, identifying such commonalities "promotes treating each other as equals" (Rawlins 2009), equality being a key component of all friendships, but an especially relevant element of diverse friendships. Yet, this approach runs the risk of creating "color blindness" (see Korgen 2002), as if race—or any other social category—is inconsequential when, in fact, social scientists have clearly and repeatedly demonstrated that social differences such as race, gender, class, and sexual orientation do have very real and profound consequences at both the individual and societal level. There is therefore a subtle balance to be achieved between focusing on one's similarities with one's friend and recognizing the fact that the demographic difference between you is highly consequential, even if only outside the relationship.

Before getting to know one another, Irene and Bao initially made erroneous assumptions of differences between them based solely on appearances. In a moment of humor during their paired interview, Irene (who is black, but raised by white parents) mentioned that her first impression of Bao was that she was a "thug" and Bao (who is Hmong) thought Irene was a spoiled brat and therefore both assumed they would have nothing in common. Irene confessed,

> *To be honest, I was really intimidated by Bao at first. In my hometown, basically you're either white or you're Hispanic or you're me or my brother [black children raised by white parents]. And so I just thought that and it was really ridiculous. There was a lot of prejudice towards the community, and so I automatically kind of found myself thinking that she was a thug or whatever. And so*

*I was really intimidated by her at first and I was scared of her boyfriend too. But now I know he's just wonderful and I'm best friends with Bao* [Interview 19B].

For her part, Bao said, *"I think I told you [Irene] this before, but I didn't want to talk to you because I thought of you as this really bratty person, you know; but I got past that part"* [Interview 19C]. The irony here is that each one admitted to the other that there was a kernel of truth to their first impressions. Bao laughed at Irene's first impression of her as a thug and said, *"Honestly, at one point in my life, I was a bully—believe it or not . . . . Watch out!"* [Interview 19C]. For her part, Irene admits, *"I was bratty in high school. I was. I'm not proud of it at all, you know, but that was probably an accurate reflection of me at the time we first met"* [Interview 19C].

Eventually, there came a time when they had to share a car ride out of mutual necessity and this allowed them to get to know one another better and get beyond the initial stereotypes. Irene describes it this way:

*I was thinking, "what are we going to talk about," you know, because it was like two hours and I was just like, "should I try to sleep for two hours or something?" And yet I really got to know her on that car ride and how similar we were and how the differences that we had were so interesting; hearing how her culture is so different from mine and figuring out how we have a lot in common.*

*Her culture is so traditional and then the culture we're living in is so different from that. And it's kind of like you're torn between the two. Bao told me she's the only girl in her family who's in college and in her culture she should be married and have kids by now. She chose a different way, and so sometimes that's frowned upon. It's like "you're not Hmong enough," you know. And I feel the exact same way. I've had that struggle my whole life: not being black enough or not being either one or the other. You can't just be yourself—who you are. Often I was just kind of in between. So, I found that really big similarity with her, which makes me really intrigued by her* [Interview 19B].

Bao confirms the relevance of this similarity between them by saying,

*Irene went through a lot of discrimination here as an African American person trying to fit in with the African-American group. She feels she fits more with the Caucasian group and it's the same with me. So, I think we're in the same kind of situation where we feel like we don't really belong one way or the other; where we're kind of in the middle of both cultures and both worlds* [Interview 19A].

This much more personal connection arising out of the car ride allowed them to see what they had in common: both feel like "minorities within a minority." Irene, while African American, was adopted and raised by white parents and as a result is not considered "black enough" by many other African Americans. Similarly, Bao has been told by members of her own immigrant community that she is not "Hmong enough" because she is going to college and then graduate school rather than getting married at a young age and starting a family. At the same time, neither one of them feels like a full-fledged member of mainstream society. So, they are both minorities within their respective marginalized groups and this has become a primary source of the social bond between them. They are able to identify with one another's situations in a way that most others can't.

This example highlights the importance of common experiences in bringing those from diverse backgrounds together, a key aspect of intergroup contact theory (Allport 1954). Similar interests and values also figure prominently in this focus on commonalities and I could give many examples of these. Another interesting case has to do with finding commonalities within apparent differences. Deborah (who was raised Christian but who converted to Judaism) and her friend Fatima (who is Muslim) have many interests in common: books, movies, philosophy, learning new things, travel, unique shops, and teaching. Given all these similarities, religion certainly is not the focus of their friendship; still, they are not afraid to "go there" with regard to discussing their religious traditions as they come up in their everyday lives. In the process, they discovered that even in the context of religion—the social boundary that separates them— they have commonalities that intrigue them both. Deborah explains that

> *I think we still would have been friends even without the religious difference between us; but, if anything, I think the difference has had a positive impact on our friendship in that it has brought an awareness of rituals and lifestyles different than my own. It's just added another layer that's enriched our conversations. And I think what amazed us most is the similarities that we saw between our respective religious traditions, whereas one would think there would be more differences.*
>
> *For example, I remember Fatima showed me her wedding album, and that was probably the first time that I realized she was Muslim. We talked about that just a little bit, because one of my interests is rituals and traditions. That's something that really intrigues me: why people do what they do. The one thing that Fatima and I realized fairly early is that there are a lot of similarities between Judaism and Islam, such as in the rituals surrounding babies and the naming ceremony. In Orthodox Judaism, in the marriage ceremony, you walk around the huppa, but they also have some sort of a canopy and they walk around and say prayers. Again, you'd think they'd be very dissimilar, but there were things that we noticed that are similar.*
>
> *Of course, there are many, many differences. They are different religions; but, when you're in their home and having a meal with them, there's no difference. I think the hate and distrust are more politically based than religiously based. To me, personally, it's not a religious war. It's political and it's land and it's all those other things, but it's being disguised in the name of religion* [Interview 17A].

Fatima echoes these same sentiments, although she frames it in terms of spirituality and philosophy.

*Our friendship wasn't really based on religion. It was just based on the per-*
*sonality, you know, and how we kind of clicked and have fun together. I'm in-*
*trigued by religion and I like to know more about it, but our friendship is not*
*based on that. When she invited me for her son's bar mitzvah, however, I think*
*that was the most fun experience I had, you know, because I'd never been in a*
*synagogue before. I found it to be fascinating. I didn't know a whole lot about*
*Judaism before I met her, but I think I've learned a lot about it, you know, like*
*in the sense that I find it to be very similar to Islam. And thinking about what*
*they value and especially . . . even the rituals are quite similar. We compare*
*notes, you know: "Oh okay, so you believe in this and I believe in that." So, we*
*have open discussions and kind of share our beliefs. We don't talk about spe-*
*cific religions so much as about more spiritual things. She's very spiritual. I*
*like to talk about philosophy and about the spiritual and the life after and those*
*kinds of things, and she does, too. So I think it's very interesting and it's fun to*
*talk about it. We can talk about religion and the spiritual part of the religion*
*very comfortably* [Interview 17B].

When the differences come up, they enjoy talking about them. These are comparative discussions that oftentimes unveil the surprising similarities between
the two religious traditions, such as similarities in ritual. I found it interesting
how often Deborah brought up these similarities. When we focus on such areas
of commonality, differences become less relevant and meaningful. As observed
by Korgen, the friends are then "surprised to find how much they had in common with each other" (2002, 17). The similarities are endowed with meaning,
not the differences. I did ask Deborah if they avoided the differences and she
said no. She's never felt the need to edit what she says with Fatima. Naturally,
she knows there are differences in the two religions; but what have become
prominent for her are the similarities. For her part, Fatima also mentioned how
they focus on the similarities in their religious practices, noting how both traditions separate men from women, place importance on windows facing East, and
the value of helping one's neighbor.

What was most striking to me was that they seemed to bond more closely
with one another because they are both religious minorities living within a predominantly Christian culture. This again underscores how, like Bao and Irene,
the common experience of being a minority can create a strong bond between
friends even if they are different from one another along the same lines. While
my sample is not statistically representative, it is suggestive that in 28 percent of
the friendship pairs,[1] *both* individuals are minorities within at least one of the
dimensions included in this project. Even within those friendships where only
one member is a minority, there is a general focus of attention on what the two
have in common rather than on the differences between them. Such a focus on
the commonalities is a way of holding the door open between them and allowing
the friendship to develop and strengthen. At the same time, it is important to
point out that the individuals I've interviewed are not afraid to see and even
celebrate the differences. Relating this back to the previous section, the differ-

ences are not perceived as threatening; instead, they are considered an asset of the friendship.

## Taking Care

Over the course of the interview process, I noticed how many of the research participants took care to be supportive of their friends with regard to the differences between them and not cause offense. In other words, they develop a sense of "protocol" (Rude 2009). In several cases, this meant actively not talking about the differences. Most other cases, however, did not involve such active avoidance. Instead, one or both individuals may avoid emphasizing the difference between them. In the case of friendships across genders or sexual orientations where the issue of attraction might be of concern, actually establishing *relational* boundaries in order to bridge the *social* boundary is an effective technique in taking care of the friendship and not allowing the difference to become a problem.

Taking care was first evident to me when I conducted the paired interviews in which the two friends were brought together to openly discuss their friendship in light of the differences between them. In a few interviews, I noticed that one or both friends might be much more subdued in their expression when talking about what might be perceived as a "sensitive issue," kind of like walking on tip-toe. I would not go so far as to say they were uncomfortable; they were simply being more sensitive. For example, in his one-on-one interview, Dave was quite animated and passionate when describing his views on the kind of woman who carries a "chip on her shoulder." He did this in order to contrast it with what his friend Miriam is like.

> *Miriam knows how men think. I mean, she's not a bitch. There's so many women I work with in my business who are just bitches, and that's the easiest way to describe it. They've got a chip on their shoulder and, you know, "Daddy wanted a son and I came with indoor plumbing versus outdoor plumbing and I'm just as good as any man, and I'm going to prove it to you." It's like, "Honey, get over it. You know what, I don't fucking care." But Miriam is better at her job than most of the guys, and she knows it and the guys know it, so she's never had to prove anything to anybody, and she doesn't have this chip on her shoulder where she's trying to prove how good she is. She doesn't need to because she knows she is. She walks the walk so she doesn't have to talk the talk. And so many of the other women that I know and work with are running their mouths so much, but then they can't back it up, you know. So, they want what you've got, but they want what they want, too: "I've got mine and I want yours as well." And I deal with this all the time. I'm just like, "You know what? You want this equality bullshit, but yet you're not willing to share. You want mine as well." That just irritates the living hell out of me; but Miriam doesn't push*

*any of those buttons. If more women were like her, I think the world would be a much better place* [Interview 8B].

While his animated tone of voice does not carry over into the printed word, his colorful language and passion certainly do. Later, Dave made virtually the same point that "women want it both ways" in his paired interview with Miriam except that he was much less animated about it, instead emphasizing the equality that has been achieved and that he has accepted.

> *I think that women are getting more and more equal, which I think is fine. I think men have mostly gotten over it; but I think women want it both ways. It's the Hillary Clintons of the world who absolutely just drive me into the stratosphere because they want it both ways. They want Smith College* [for women] *because women have special learning needs, but they want women to get to go to the Citadel* [historically for men] *because they want to be part of the little boys' network. In my opinion, you can't have it both ways. They want mine and they want theirs, and that's okay; but I can't have mine because I'm excluding them. It's kind of like in professional sports. If I was a TV reporter as a man and I want to go into the women's basketball locker room, I'd be a pervert. I'd be a bigot. I'd be in jail. But yet you have female sports reporters who want to take a TV camera and go down into the football locker room, and they're trying to sue to get to do it because it's their God-given equality right, and "I'm being discriminated against cause I'm a woman and I don't have equal access." Well, wait a minute. It cuts both ways. You can't have it both ways, and that's the part of this that drives me up a tree* [Interview 8C].

In the paired interview, Dave presents a more level-headed argument when making his case and his tone is much less accusatory as reflected in the toned-down language. In Miriam's presence, Dave is taking care to not be too inflammatory and insensitive.

Taking care not to cause offense is much more obvious when the two friends actually avoid discussing some aspect of the difference between them. This approach is actually quite common in the literature on diverse friendships (see Rude 2009 and Korgen 2002). In discussing their religious differences, for example, Deborah and Fatima never really got around to speaking about Palestine. Fatima describes it like this.

> *It gets harder for Muslim people to know Jewish people because of the Palestine-Israel conflict . . . so, we really don't talk Israel and Palestine. I don't like to bring the topic up. I think we don't want to create a friction because we might have different viewpoints. I doubt it, knowing her; but I just don't want to talk about it. We do talk about the children who are suffering, but we don't talk about the policies of the government and who is right and who is wrong. It's just something that I really don't want to talk about* [Interview 17B].

Fatima goes on to say that she really believes that Deborah has liberal views and therefore might be much more sympathetic to the Palestinian side of the issue, but she doesn't care to test the water. Their friendship matters much more to her than a debate on the Palestinian-Israeli issue.

Cynthia and Greg also chose not to talk about the difference between them, which in this case is one of ability. Greg has had multiple sclerosis for ten years and is confined to a wheelchair. While this difference between them is not a taboo subject and Cynthia has certainly thought about Greg's condition a lot, they have talked about it only rarely, focusing on the disease itself. Cynthia knows that Greg is a bit touchy about his disease and is easily offended. She respects that feeling and doesn't push it with him.

As an example of Greg's sensitivity about MS and his confinement to a wheelchair, Cynthia tells a story.

> *This little kid came up to him a few months ago—a kid like five or something. And his mom was around, standing there. The kid came right up to him and asked, "Why are you in that chair?" And Greg took offense to it, and he told him he should really mind his own business. I couldn't believe it. I would think that most people in that situation would just say what happened; but he was kind of pissed off, you know.*
>
> *I said, "He's just a little kid," and he's like, "So? It's none of his business." I was like, "okay," you know. It's like, "all right." I think he was more mad that the mom let the kid ask or something, I don't know. But yeah, I couldn't believe it; and I said, "Come on." And he's like, "Fuck him! It's none of his business." I mean I think Greg definitely has issues being in a wheelchair, but he's also accepted it. He's just pissed, of course. I would be pissed* [Interview 28A].

Cynthia's desire to take care with regard to the ability issue in her friendship with Greg actually started before this event took place, even before she met him. When she first learned she would be meeting him and that he was in a wheelchair, she thought to herself, *"Oh, I hope I don't say something stupid"* [Interview 28A]. So, Cynthia was already sensitive to the issue. However, Greg's touchy nature has made her that much more careful. She has also been in situations where she has felt the sting of Greg's reactions.

> *When I was in a car accident last winter and I couldn't walk for like six weeks. I was bitching about it and he'd say stuff like, "Yeah, doesn't that suck," you know. He'll say little shit like that once in a while. Another time I was going off about having to walk all that way or something, I don't even remember what I was talking about. But he said something like, "Well, at least you can walk." I was just like "Sorry, sorry," you know, and he's like, "I'm just fucking with you." But I think he is serious on a certain level, like, "Shut the fuck up. Quit bitching that you have to walk," you know. And I just don't think about it. So, I feel like sometimes I should just really watch what I say as far as bitching about walking or something like that, you know* [Interview 28A].

So, Cynthia is highly conscious of Greg's feelings and seeks to avoid saying anything that might offend him. As one final example, she tells of a time when a group of her friends invited Cynthia (and through her, Greg) to go camping: *"But everybody knows he can't go. I mentioned it one time, but he didn't say anything about it either way. But sometimes I feel like we don't talk about that because he can't participate anyway, so why bring it up in front of him"* [Interview 28A]. Cynthia's sensitivity toward Greg's feelings is obvious. Nevertheless, this is one of very few cases in the research where there was an active avoidance of directly focusing on the social boundary between them in order to not cause offense.

In more typical cases, one of the friends may avoid drawing what she or he considers to be too much attention to the difference. For example, Suzanne, who is a part of the upper-middle class, is sensitive about overt class displays when she's conscious of the fact that she's from a different class background than her friend Jenny, who comes from a working class background and is now entering the professional middle class. Suzanne tries not to "wear" her money. For example, while she wanted to show Jenny pictures of the place she was staying on vacation, Suzanne didn't want her to see the website and thus be able to figure out how much the place cost.

> *We went to Mexico for a week and part of the time we were at this hotel where we had a private pool in our suite. It wasn't a big pool, but—no, it was a big pool in my view: it was like eight by twelve feet. It was incredible—right out on the bay. And I was like, "I'll show this to you on the website because I don't want you to know how much money it's going to cost." And she's like, "Why?" I'm like, "Because it's wrong to spend that kind of money, but we're going to, and I'll just show it to you on the web"* [Interview 13A].

In the end, she didn't show Jenny the pictures at all because the class difference between them would have been too conspicuous. *"I chickened out and I didn't want to show it to her on the web, because I didn't want her to memorize the website and then look up and see how much we spent. So that was an uncomfortable thing"* [Interview 13A]. In one sense, I got the impression Suzanne was trying to shelter Jenny so that she didn't feel bad when Jenny saw what opportunities were available to her. In another sense, I got the impression that Suzanne was trying to spare *herself* from becoming too self-conscious or even embarrassed, at least at some level. Hence, this technique raises the question of how much of it is "for their own good" and how much of it is for "her own good?"

The most interesting technique for "taking care" to not cause offense has to do with creating relational boundaries in order to overcome the social boundary between the two parties. As also observed by Rawlins (2009), this was a technique often employed in those friendships where there might be a question of one or both parties being attracted to the other, as in friendships across the socially constructed boundaries of gender and sexual orientation. While Affifi and

Guerrero (1998) note that many cross-sex friends avoid talking about "loaded" topics such as dating or sex, Rawlins argues that it is of crucial importance "to communicate clear definitions and boundaries within the relationship" (2009, 115). They need to have a mutual definition for their friendship and this agreed upon definition establishes appropriate boundaries for how to interact. In friendships where attraction is a possibility, it is important to de-emphasize sexuality (Samter and Cupach 1998). At the same time, though, the topic avoidance observed by Affifi and Guerrero may be counterproductive in that it simply increases the (potentially sexual) tension between the two friends. Establishing appropriate boundaries within the friendship is therefore quite different from avoiding the topic altogether. Instead, it is important to maintain "open communication about the boundaries and definitions of their relationships, noting there's always a point where persons have to state where they're at, to keep roles clearly defined" (Rawlins 2009).

For example, Katie tells the story of the emergence of her friendship with Ed. Very early on, they had a sexual encounter. Later, they came to a mutual agreement that neither one of them wanted to be in a relationship and instead decided to be friends.

> *I just found myself wanting to like be Ed's friend, you know. I guess he just seemed like a nice guy and that kind of drew me to him. At one point, we went to Florida over Christmas break and stayed through the New Year. On New Year's Eve, we both got really drunk and we had kind of a little sexual experience. It became a joke on the team, because some people came into the room with a video camera, so we had to deal with that together and it was kind of embarrassing, but also really funny. So, we had that common experience and we could laugh about it, you know, like defend ourselves and joke around and stuff. It brought us closer and we started hanging out more and more. When we got back from Florida, we decided we had to have a talk, to get it out in the open and decide what we were going to do about that. And we both agreed that we didn't want to be involved in a relationship at all. That's not what either of us wanted, but we still want to be friends. We liked each other and stuff like that, so we decided that we were going to still hang out every once in a while just like friends do* [Interview 4A].

By simply having "the talk," Katie and Ed began to create relational boundaries between them in order to establish what kind of relationship they were going to pursue: a friendship as opposed to a romantic relationship.

Barbara and Janice provide more specific examples. Barbara (who is straight) and Janice (who is lesbian) both described actions they take in order to avoid "sending the wrong signal." They are both aware of the social boundary represented by the difference in sexual orientation combined with their similarity in gender. Barbara described how she doesn't take her joking around so far that it might be misconstrued as flirting while Janice also avoids doing anything that might be interpreted as sexual interest on her part.

*JANICE: I would stay 100 miles away from any sexual dynamics between the two of us.*
*BARBARA: Right.*
*JANICE: . . . Out of fear of giving the wrong impression, fear of, you know, whatever.*
*BARBARA: You know, I do love Janice. I mean I do. She's a wonderful person and given how I feel about the whole thing, it does enter into a situation where, now don't get nervous, but you know what I mean . . .*
*JANICE: You just don't want to flirt. You don't want to flirt, you know.*
*BARBARA: At risk of being misunderstood or leading someone on.*
*JANICE: Yeah.*
*BARBARA: Right, whereas I don't worry about that with a gay man. I can flirt with a gay man, but he's not going to think I'm coming on to him. But if I flirt with her, it could be interpreted differently and you don't want to go there. You don't want to mess up the friendship. So it's more similar to being friends with a guy than it is being friends with a girl. It's not a hurdle, but it does probably set some boundaries. It's like, it's implicit. It's implicit sort in the relationship.*
*JANICE: Yeah, it's not a hurdle. The only hurdle for me was [inaudible], that's the only thing.*
*BARBARA: There's that boundary that's there, that we both know is there, but doesn't affect anything, yet we know we don't go near it maybe [Interview 22C].*

Establishing and not crossing this relational boundary is done not so much out of avoidance or fear as it is a matter of "respecting boundaries" and respecting the other person. They have a common understanding of how to manage this boundary. Interestingly, this common understanding was not generated through active or direct negotiation. Instead, it is a mutual understanding generated by a simple recognition of the status/identity of the other person and an understanding of the possible negative repercussions for crossing that relational boundary.

## Meeting One's Friend "More Than Half Way"

In our culture, we have a generalized belief that "meeting them half way" is an effective technique for addressing differences and (potential) conflict. In the case of friendships that bridge socially constructed boundaries, however, it was apparent that in many instances the individuals involved go more than half way in an effort to reach out to others in order to establish and strengthen their friendships. Sometimes this means taking the time to understand where another person is coming from rather than simply dismissing him or her. At other times, going "more than half way" actually means identification with or even assimilation to the privileged group.

Making an effort to understand where another person is coming from can take patience and persistence. In the cross-gender friendship between Pam and

Tim, Pam finds it easier to become emotionally close to other women because—
stereotypically—she finds them generally more open to expressing their feelings
and covering intimate topics.

> *My girlfriends that I can talk to, we just really feel understood and you really
> learn from them. Janet, a really good friend of mine, is just so completely
> aware of her own thoughts and feelings. It's just so educational talking to
> someone like that because they're a complete person. They're giving more of
> themselves.*
>
> > *I don't think men feel less. I just think they're less aware of it, and that's a
> stereotype, and I could be wrong. But it's a barrier, I think. You shouldn't be
> ashamed of your feelings, but don't be a victim of them either. There should be
> an awareness of your feelings and how they influence you* [Interview 26A].

Despite her feelings, she does not give up on men. Given enough time with a
man—and this is the case with Tim—she can see the emotions that lie unex-
pressed beneath the surface.

> *People have said he's kind of odd at first. He's sort of robotic almost in the
> way that he'll interact: more of a monotone voice and he has a very hard time
> expressing emotion. Over the years, he's kind of loosened up a little bit with
> me. And he's actually this incredibly affectionate person and very loving, but
> sort of restrained—noticeably so. But he's really great, you know. And if you
> are at all sentimental, or give him a hug or something, he totally responds to
> that. It's just not something he initiates. It's almost like he's forgotten how* [In-
> terview 26A].

Over time, Tim also became more comfortable talking with her at an intimate
level. The key here is Pam giving men like Tim enough opportunity to show
who they are below the surface, which implies patience and persistence on her
part. Without these characteristics, by inference, many women would give up on
men because what women define as intimacy within a close friendship is a long
time in coming.

Fatima has also had to exercise much effort at understanding her friend
Deborah. While the focus of their interviews was on their religious differences,
there was also a significant cultural difference given that Fatima immigrated to
the United States from Pakistan while Deborah was born and raised in this country. From Fatima's perspective, Deborah is typically American in that it is culturally acceptable to cancel or back out of a commitment if it is no longer convenient for her. This is something that Fatima had to become accustomed to
because for her, once she's committed, she's committed no matter how inconvenient it may later become.

> *In my culture, when we commit to do something, we do it anyways even if it's
> really, really inconvenient, you know. But I think in American culture, if it's not*

*convenient, you won't do it. That's sometimes hard even though it's only hap-
pened once or twice; but that's how it is. If it wasn't convenient, she would
cancel. But when I looked at the whole picture, there were things happening
with her life that were hard for her to handle. But that was the most difficult
part of our relationship.*

*I think I'm becoming like that, too. Now, if things are not convenient for
me, I say no; but when I was younger, it was hard for me to do that, even
though it might have been 100 percent inconvenient—but that's how I grew up.
But now I say no if it's not convenient for me and my family* [Interview 17B].

Fatima realizes that Deborah's behavior is not personal, but rather cultural. And
so this difference has not endangered their friendship. In other words, she made
the effort to try and understand where Deborah was coming from. That understanding helped resolve any conflict she might have experienced over the difference. Not that she likes it, but she does understand it and doesn't take it personally.

Some individuals go "more than half way" in meeting the member of the
other group simply because they do not particularly identify with other members
of their own group. This is the case for one or both friends in 38 percent of the
friendship pairs,[2] indicating that such a lack of identification is a notable trend
among those whose friendships extend across socially constructed boundaries,
though this lack of identification with one's own group is a matter of degree.

In some cases, this lack of identification can go both ways, as we already
saw in the case of Irene—who wasn't "black enough"—and Bao—who wasn't
"Hmong enough"—where neither one of them identified with their own group.
Christina, in discussing her friendship with Ellen, also describes how other
Philippinos jokingly refer to her as not "Philippino enough." She made a point to
mention that she does not particularly identify with many other Philippino individuals. She has a strong attachment to her Philippino identity at an intellectual
level as evidenced by the fact she is seeking a graduate degree in literature, spe-
cializing in contemporary Philippino-American literature; but she highlighted
the aggravation she has with other Philippinos due to their lack of awareness of
the politics of race and assimilation.

*Growing up, I've always had mostly Caucasian friends and not much knowl-
edge of the Philippines. But then my own awareness of race and ethnicity was
bolstered in college, and then I became very much Philippino-American, you
know, helping form a group there. But I still feel like it was so segregated, you
know. I mean we were in the Asian Student Union, but we were independent of
them. Then I realized I wasn't always comfortable with the Philippino-
Americans because they weren't interested in the political things that I am. I
became frustrated with them, you know* [Interview 34A].

Now, just as when she grew up, she says, *"Here [in the Midwest] my friends are mostly white."* Again, going "more than half way" in meeting a friend who is different may simply be the result of not identifying with one's own group.

For some, meeting one's friend "more than half way" goes beyond not identifying with other members of one's own group and reaches the point of actual adaptation or even assimilation. This possibility is much more typical of the marginalized individual, but it does not exclude members of the privileged group. Adaptation implies that the individual molds him or herself to be more like those from across a particular socially constructed boundary whose company she or he is keeping. Outside of such company, they go back to acting like other members of their own group. Such adaptation is epitomized in the friendship of Jordan (who is bisexual in terms of sexual behavior, but prefers not to be identified with any such label) and Shawn (who is straight). Of the two, Jordan seems to be the "chameleon," as they put it, meaning that he is the one who adapts himself to his social context. If he's going out with gay people, the way he dresses is tailored to that audience. Same thing if he goes out with straight people.

> *JORDAN: When I go out to the bar with [gay] friends, I dress differently than when I go out to the bars with you [straight] guys. I think that you portray yourself a different way depending on the environment you're going to be around. There's a bit of chameleon going on.*
> *SHAWN: I think you got to flex with the environment a little bit.*
> *JORDAN: You know? It keeps chameleons alive and half the other stuff that runs around the woods, right?*
> *SHAWN: They fit with their seasonal environment.*
> *JORDAN: And that's how they survive* [Interview 38C].

While Jordan acts as a chameleon, Shawn doesn't change to fit the situation. When they used the "survival of the fittest" analogy to explain how such adaptation enabled Jordan to blend in and survive, they inferred an image of straight people as "predators." Such an image has many interesting connotations: Jordan, the sexual minority, is the one who assumes responsibility for adapting to his surroundings and going "more than half way" in their friendship.

Assimilation goes a step further in that the individual is not just adapting behavior to the other group while in their company and then switching back; instead, the individual actually *becomes* a member of the other group and never switches back. This is often because the individual has little or no exposure to other members of his or her own social category. For example, in the friendship between Wilson (who is biracial—black and white) and Frank (who is white), Wilson has grown up in largely white neighborhoods and gone to schools that were mostly white. As a result, he has not had the opportunity to identify with blacks at all and, by default, has basically shouldered all the responsibility for crossing the racial boundary by making himself fit in perfectly with white culture.

> *I've actually been around white people for my whole life. I've never really been outside of that. I mean a lot of my friends say—and we have a joke between Frank and me—that Frank's blacker than me . . . I mean it's just weird. God, I don't really have a lot of friends of color. I mean Oscar, he's probably the only one. I even date white women because I'm more comfortable with it given that I haven't been around other races. My dad, who is black, could sit down on a bench with some black guy and have a conversation, but not me* [Interview 21B].

By his own admission, Wilson "acts white" and thus does not challenge his (white) friends by making them adapt to a different way of thinking, behaving, or talking. As a result, Frank has not had to change any of his expectations in order to accommodate Wilson's difference in race. Wilson has done all the work for him. Such assimilation, though, is due to the fact that there is a complete absence of other close black friends in Wilson's life.

In 73 percent of the cases[3] where one or both individuals do not identify with her or his group, it was the member of the marginalized group who did not identify and who adapted or assimilated to the privileged group. In only four cases was it the friend in the privileged category who could not identify with her or his own group. So, as a contrasting example, it was already pointed out how Melissa made a conscious effort to indicate to Lenora that she was "black friendly." As seen in chapter 2, Melissa finds it easier to identify with blacks and Latinos because, growing up and going to school where she did, they represented a disproportionate number of her peers and an integral part of her social circle.

> *I think it started out with my best guy friend Allen, like the boy that I've been friends with since second grade. He's mixed and so in junior high he sort of had to define himself as black or white and he identified himself with blacks. My white friends were like, "I don't know why you hang with him all the time and why you hang out with the black kids all the time." So I just opted to leave. I would say hi to them, we were still friendly; but looking at it, they were like tennis players and soccer players and that's not me. I don't care about those things. I wanted to go watch my friend Allen. He plays basketball at UNC now in North Carolina. I'd much rather watch basketball than watch tennis. It's like just little interests* [Interview 5B].

As a result of her experiences and her closeness to her biracial friend Allen, who identifies as black, Melissa began to hang out with other blacks and is now less comfortable among whites like herself.

More often than not, in the pairs I studied the member of the marginalized group reached out and met their friend "more than half way." Meeting one's friend "more than half way" by taking the time to understand where a person is coming from seems the most equitable approach. Even then, such potential balance was absent. In the examples I found, one person is making more of an effort at this than the other; and again, it was typically the person in the marginalized group—Pam, Fatima, Jordan, and Wilson—who had to have patience and be persistent with the member of the privileged group—Tim, Deborah, Shawn, and Frank. The power of privilege is evident even within those friendships that are successful in bridging social boundaries.


## Educating One's Friend

Given how many people point to ignorance as a major reason for everything from stereotypes to bigotry, educating one's friend about one's own culture was quite common—43 percent of the cases[4]—and represents an "active learning process" that is an integral part of many of these diverse friendships (McCullough 1998). Such education is often, though not always, one-sided (Rude 2009; Korgen 2002). It is the members of the marginalized group who typically take it upon themselves to educate their friend. This is largely the result of the fact that the marginalized have a "double consciousness" (DuBois 1961) in that they have learned the culture of their own (marginalized) social category, but at the same time have learned to get by in the culture of those in a position of privilege. Such double consciousness is required in order to succeed in a world dominated by the privileged.

For example, Colin has explained much to Kelly about his experiences as a black man and Kelly, for her part, has expressed much interest in learning about his experiences. Kelly describes an experience they had that left her a bit baffled.

> *Sometimes I have a hard time understanding why he doesn't react the way I would in a racial situation. Last summer, we were driving downtown, the windows were down, and a Caucasian guy rolled down his window and did the white power signal out his window. And that was my first REAL experience with racism. And Colin was like, "Yeah! Whatever!" and kept driving like it was no big deal. And I'm like . . . I would be writing down his license plate number. So I wondered, "why aren't you upset by this?" and he's like, "but it happens all the time." And so sometimes it takes me a while to process that. He's kind of habituated to being discriminated against this way so it's not that big of a deal for him to see something like that* [Interview 1A].

Experiences like this one have created greater understanding between them and, as Kelly reveals, *"I would say it has definitely brought us closer together because we talk about stuff a lot more"* [Interview 1A].

While dramatic events like the one described by Kelly can be powerful experiences, it is everyday life that seems to bring out the most learning on her part because this is where she is immersed in a culture that is new to her.

*Most of our differences, in terms of cultural differences, weren't apparent until a little bit later and we started to talk about things more. . . the differences and the similarities too; but mostly we talk about the differences because, instead of having a gap, it'll bring us closer. I've become involved in African-American culture—stuff like watching the TV shows, hanging out, going to fraternity events, that kind of stuff* [Interview 1A].

Kelly then goes on to provide some examples of what she has learned with regard to cultural differences that she sees as tied to race.

*Sometimes we were like, "Let's go see a movie. What do you want to see?" and he might pick a movie that I wouldn't necessarily have picked—even though I enjoyed the movie. It opened my door to African-American movies I might not have watched, like "The Original Kings of Comedy." Not that he forced me to go to the movies, but it gave me a different perspective. A lot of the culture you pick up through TV shows. Like I'd pick up little words here and there when I'm watching "A Different World" in the morning when I'm getting ready. I'm like, "Oh, my God! Colin does that!" [laughs] and so that's kind of my slow process of getting into his culture more. At first, I was like, "I don't even know what they're talking about" and Colin would have to explain it all the time. Now I know what they're saying when they say, "Oh, that's tight!" or "this is my dog!" You know what I mean? Not in the pet sense but as in "we're good friends." Colin just thinks it's hysterical to see a Caucasian person using those same words and phrases. As I pick out more slang, I understand everything better. And it, you know, brings us closer together too. It helps to talk about it and get another person's perspective. I know he can't speak for every African-American or every male; but it opens up my mind more and doesn't limit my thinking.*

*A significant part of this process is getting involved with his family a bit. I think his mom is pretty hesitant with him being in an interracial couple with my sister, but I've helped out his mom a few times and I've watched his nephew a lot. From watching his nephew, I've seen some of the differences regarding how he was raised and why she might do this versus my parents who might have done that. So, his sister is now like, "Oh! She's cool!" so I think I've even broken down some of her stereotypes of how a white person is too—that we're not ALL self centered [laughs] and focused on ourselves all the time* [Interview 1A].

It is clear that Kelly has learned much about African American culture over the course of her friendship with Colin, most of it simply by being a part of his everyday life.

Again, this kind of educational role is often one-sided. Because Colin and other marginalized individuals like him live in a world dominated by the privileged—in this case, whites—they have no choice but to learn about the culture of the privileged group. Colin, and all those in his position, are exposed to the culture of the privileged group on a daily basis and cannot afford to take that culture for granted since it is the privileged who have the power. By contrast, those in a position of privilege don't *have* to learn what it is like to be a member of the marginalized group. When asked whether he or Kelly focused more attention on the racial difference between them, Colin, without hesitation said, *"Me!"* and followed that up by saying, *"She doesn't have to"* [Interview 1B]. By saying this, he is alluding to the fact that those in a position of privilege are able to take their status for granted and do not have to bother understanding the cultures of marginalized groups if they don't want to. The result is that the friend who is in the marginalized group is much more likely to be called upon to play the role of educator.

Continually playing this educational role can wear on the marginalized individual if he or she is called upon to perform it too often, though for Colin this really depends on the other person's approach.

> *If you keep on doing it and say, "I don't like the fact that black people can call each other niggers and when I do it, I get in trouble. That's not fair," I don't really like that approach. But, if you're like, "Colin, I'm just curious why they do it," that's okay. To me, presentation is important and shapes how I will deal with them. If you come to me and you think you already know the answer, and you're just trying to get me to agree, I'll be like, "Go read a book." First of all, you're not going to find a book but I mean it'll take a book to respond. I just don't want to deal with it. But if you genuinely want to be educated, I'll tell you. Then I don't mind doing it* [Interview 1B].

Kelly is one of those individuals who have been able to approach Colin in a genuine and respectful manner. This has made all the difference for them and the development of their friendship.

While it is oftentimes the marginalized individual who educates the privileged person, there was one case of a member of the privileged group doing the "educating." We've already met Suzanne (who is upper middle class) and Jenny (who is only just entering the professional middle class). Jenny noted how Suzanne has introduced her to Suzanne's higher-class culture. This is particularly true in the context of social functions since Jenny feels a bit uncomfortable in these situations. This is how Suzanne describes it:

> *One time, my partner and I were going to a fundraising dinner. Actually, she was on the corporate committee for the dinner. She was like, "let's buy a table and invite people to come. We'll have fun . . . Do you want to invite Jenny?" And at first I was like, "Hmm, nah, I don't think so." She's like, "Why?" I'm like, "It's $100 a plate and that's a lot of money for newcomers. I don't think Jenny would want to pay that money. I don't want to make her feel uncomfortable. Do you want to ask her?" It turns out the president actually had two tick-*

*ets and his wife could not go, so he asked Jenny if she wanted to go. So, she ended up going.*

*I was thinking about it all week. So, when talking about it, I prepared her. I went over specifically what it's going to be like. The way people dress and the whole thing. I'm like, "Yeah, it's going to be interesting," and I just laid it out. I'm like, "Jenny, these people have money and it's not unusual for the MC to ask, 'Who has more money to give tonight? $2,500? Who will stand for $2,500?' And people do. 'Who will stand for $1,000?' and people do. They make a lot of money that way." And so I wanted her to know, so that it wasn't a horrible experience.*

*She was glad I told her because it gave her a little forewarning. Afterwards she said, "I'm really glad you told me. I'm just glad I knew what it was before I went"* [Interview 13A].

It is clear from this example that Suzanne is making an effort to prepare Jenny for a level of fundraising and personal philanthropy with which she is not yet familiar: everything from the style of dress to the size of the donations beyond the $100 a plate. Jenny also has a story to tell in which she learns from Suzanne how to interact with those from the higher class that she is entering.

*I remember Suzanne and I were having this conversation when I was deciding to apply for this current position [as Dean]. We knew it meant I would have more interaction with our Board of Trustees and things like that. For the most part, the Trustees are all white men who have a lot of money. So, I ask Suzanne, and I always kind of call her my coach, "Coach me about your people. I mean, what is it that I need to be thinking about?" And so we'd talk about different things. Suzanne knows that, where I'm from, when you're talking to people who're older, you address them as "sir" or "ma'am." It's just such a part of who I am and that cracks Suzanne up. But when it comes to the Board of Trustees, she's like, "You can't be saying sir to them." And I was like, "But they're old enough to be my grandfather!" And she was like, "But you can't." And I'm like "Well, why can't I?" And she was like, "It's a class and race thing. You want them to know that you are their equal." And so this was really interesting, and that's where it gets complicated for me, because that goes against my way of being and how I look at elders. And she was like, "I get that, but this is how it's going to be interpreted . . . it subordinates you and puts you in a different role. You want them to see you on their level"* [Interview 13B].

Jenny is learning a lot from Suzanne about moving into a new world that is characterized as "higher class." On the other hand, one could argue that such education is more than simply instructing one's friend. Instead, one could think of it as "assimilation in process," linking the management techniques of education and meeting more than halfway together.

It is apparent from these examples that, while education is a common and effective technique used to bridge the gap between members of different groups, it is still the position of privilege that is being supported in this process, just as it was in meeting one's friend more than half way. Again, it is typically the marginalized individual who is expected to educate her or his privileged counterpart. They are the ones "shouldering the burden" and making the effort to educate their privileged counterparts, assuming they don't outright assimilate to the dominant culture. Even in the case of Suzanne and Jenny, it is the culture of the group with higher status that is reinforced and even strengthened. This once again emphasizes that the power of privilege plays a significant role even within these friendships that bridge the gap between different social boundaries.

At the same time, though, such education plays an important part in creating bridging ties between diverse groups of people. Going back to intergroup contact theory, Allport (1954) recognizes that education fosters roletaking and empathy between members of the in-group and the out-group. Rude (2009), whose research focused exclusively on race, identifies this as "racial empathy." For the purposes of this study that includes multiple social boundaries, we might better label this phenomenon "empathy with diverse others." While such empathy is not the only form of learning that takes place within these friendships and is the most difficult to achieve (Rude 2009), it is arguably the most important. The roletaking and empathy described by Allport and Rude are crucial for the emergence of social affinity (Vela-McConnell 1999) and fostering both social bonds and social cohesion, a topic that I will take up again in chapter 5. Because of the socially transformative potential that friendships—and especially diverse friendships—have, Rawlins (2009) considers ongoing learning in the context of these relationships to be an "ethical requirement" of friendship.

## The Use of Humor

> Maybe a laugh is like a sigh. A form of release that connotes pleasure. We can for a moment give up the facade of polite speech and the pretense of liberal rational society. There is joy in this. Yet perhaps—as with sighing—we are also informed by the knowledge that the break is temporary. We laugh loudly for a moment, we sigh deeply for a moment. And then the world keeps on turning. Yet, while our laughter is temporary, its persistence may be promising. Maybe it signals that despite our best efforts we are not so sure about ourselves and the serious world in which we live (Atluri 2009, 213).

Humor is a common theme running through past qualitative analyses of diverse friendships, representing a form of "indirect engagement" with the socially constructed boundary (Rude 2009). It indicates that many people feel comfortable enough to use it despite the sense by many social scientists and critics alike that humor about race, gender, sexual orientation, and so on is inherently problematic. It was brought up (oftentimes without even being asked) as a technique for managing differences in a surprising 33 percent of the friendships I studied.[5] What is unanticipated about this is that using humor based on social inequality goes directly against what is considered acceptable among those who consider themselves to be culturally sensitive and progressive individuals—that is, it certainly isn't "politically correct." From this perspective, race-based humor, for example, is an expression of racism (Atluri 2009; Barnes, Palmari, and Durrheim 2001; and Coleman 2000). And much the same could be said about humor that is based on gender, sexual orientation, or any other socially constructed category. C. G. Prado, a columnist writing for *Personal Ethics*, explains the rationale behind political correctness.

> What underlies the sometimes sound, sometimes silly reworking of |politically correct| language is the Sapirs-Whorf hypothesis that thinking is shaped by language; that linguistic categories define conceptual ones. The idea is that discourse doesn't just convey thought but partly determines it. So the theory is that if you get people to talk in nonracist and nonsexist ways, they'll soon think like and be nonsexists and nonracists (Prado, August 2, 2006).

This point is in keeping with the phenomenological perspective in sociology (Berger and Luckmann 1967): what we say—language—has the power to shape reality. From this point of view, the use of humor that targets members of certain social categories both helps to create and perpetuate a social environment in which racism, sexism, heterosexism, and so on are acceptable. This understanding leads many to condemn such humor. For example, Kai Thaler wrote an op ed piece in the *Yale Daily News* in response to a campus outcry regarding a parody targeting certain groups. He explains,

> Humor about social issues is always likely to offend someone. This is a simple fact. Generalizations will be made, stereotypes will be used, and even if the attempt of the joke is to satirize that stereotype, its very presence . . . seems to draw an immediate defensive response (Thaler, September 27, 2006).

Despite warnings like this one, such humor continues. In fact, one will often witness individuals targeting their own social category with their humor. Many find this form of self-deprecating humor to be acceptable because it represents the member of the targeted group reclaiming his or her power from the members of the privileged group. In his book *Stigma* (1963), Erving Goffman notes how behavior like making a joke about one's self diffuses the tension others may have surrounding one's personal qualities, in this case one's status as a member of a marginalized group. It allows the individual to take a negative symbol—a word like "queer," for example—and change it into something positive. The result is that the members of the privileged group—straight people—are no longer able to effectively use the term to deride gays and lesbians. Some critics, nevertheless, find that even this form of humor is problematic.

I know [racist and sexist jokes targeting one's own group] are supposed to pass as self-deprecating humor, and audiences are supposed to be aware of that. It's also supposed to be a kind of power-play, an adoption or usurpation of the inherent prejudice, much the same as gays adopted the previously offensive word, "queer," and feminists have done the same with other terms. But it doesn't work with humor. The reason is that . . . the jokes still get told and so the put-downs are achieved. The fact that the jokes are told by members of the targeted groups, in the spirit of poking fun at themselves, may work with some members of an audience, but there'll be a lot of others who ignore or forget who told the joke and just savor the dirty dig. In this way, stereotypes are continued and supported and eventually work against the targeted group and the joke-tellers themselves. . . . Racist and sexist jokes are put-downs, period, and they're ethically wrong regardless of who tells them (Prado, Personal Ethics: Suite 101, comment posted December 20, 2006).

Even for Goffman, self-directed humor that is used to manage and cope with stigma demonstrates the user's acceptance of her or his inferior status—that she or he will not make any claims for a non-stigmatized status—thus maintaining the social order of society (Lemert and Branaman 1997).

Not all would agree, however. Some consider such humor to be a form of folklore in which the person using this form of humor is actually outmaneuvering the oppressors (Atluri 2009; Rude 2009; and Ryan 1999; for examples, see Jones 1991 and Mo 1991) and critiquing the system of oppression itself by revealing its inner hypocrisy (Rogin 1996). This form of humor parodies the stereotypes that comprise it and makes fun of those who use them (Barnes, Palmari, and Durrheim 2001). Some choose to distinguish between humor about social categories and humor that actually reflects bigotry. For example, in the same article in which Kai Thaler critiques such humor, he also says that "racist humor is not funny. Humor about race can be. The line between the two is a thin one and its position is dependent upon one's own perceptions" (2006; see also Goldstein 1995 and Gould 2007). Two issues are key here—the nature or style of the humor and the perceptions of the audience—although everything seems to hinge on perceptions.

It is important to note that much of what I found written on the topic of humor targeting race, gender, sexual orientation, and so on, assumed that there was a wide audience for the humor. It assumed the humor was used in public where the user has little influence over who hears it and therefore has much less control over the perceptions of the members of the audience—perceptions that are likely to vary widely. On the other hand, in the context of private relationships like friendships the speaker knows exactly who is in the audience. Rude notes the importance of this "contextual dimension," explaining that, "critical to the negotiation over what is funny and potentially transformative and what is offensive and potentially oppressive is the position of the speaker relative to the listener" (2009, 129). The friends, over the course of their relationship and past interaction, have developed a common understanding or definition of the situation that provides a context in which to interpret the use of humor. In other words, there is far more control over perceptions of such humor in a relationship between two people, particularly if the use of humor is kept between themselves. Indiscriminately labeling humor based on social categories as "politically incorrect" is a blanket statement that removes the humor from its context. As all sociologists recognize, understanding the social context is very important. A racist joke told by a stand-up comic during a show is very different from such a joke spoken in private between two friends, one of whom is a member of that race.

Given this point, perhaps it is not so surprising that, in one-third of those friendships studied, the friends discussed how they effectively used humor as a means for bridging the difference between them. In fact, the use of such humor serves multiple functions: (1) it provides a non-threatening way to introduce the social boundary into conversation, (2) it establishes and affirms the non-prejudiced attitudes of the speaker, and (3) it can ease the tension that might arise because of the sensitive nature of the social boundary (Barnes, Palmary, and Durrheim 2001). All of these functions were apparent in my interviews and their personal experiences defy many of the social critics. Given some of the subtleties mentioned by the critics, though, what might not be surprising is that in two of these friendships, there were times when the use of humor went "too far." For this reason, it is evident that many friends who use humor place unspoken limits on it. Of the twenty-seven friendships where the use of this form of humor did not come up as a technique, one or another member of the friendship was directly opposed to the use of humor in only two of them. Such data indicates that there is a significant gap between what is deemed acceptable in the academic literature and the lived experiences of those who were interviewed.

Returning to the case of Kelly and Colin, both parties brought up their use of humor, but Colin better explained its importance. He emphasized how both parties need to keep a sense of humor in dealing with their differences. Otherwise, when those differences are highlighted, one or the other party might take offence. At the end of his interview, Colin summed up his perspective and provided an example:

> *I think the biggest factor [allowing us to break down race and bridge the racial gap] is that we can joke about each other's races. Like Kelly could say, "Where's your home brothers? They're never on time." Such a question indicates there's a cultural barrier there; but if I can just laugh it off, then the barrier comes down. So, I can throw it back at her. I think white people are the most time-conscious people I've ever met in my life. I think the clock in their world is fascinating. And so, I joke with her. I'm like, "Man, whoever invented the watch made the best invention of all time, 'cause white people just loves watches. You can't go into a room without a clock on the wall." Meanwhile, my people don't give a damn about time. They don't care. But white people . . . oh boy; and I joke with her* [Interview 1B].

So, Colin feels that members of both races just need to lighten up about race. Kelly echoes his perspective by explaining that *"being able to joke about our differences as far as race is like an icebreaker. It helps to not only be closer to them, but just to understand another culture better"* [Interview 1A].

Amanda takes this point a step further when talking about the use of humor with her friend Doug (the focus here was on gender, but they are also different in terms of sexual orientation, Amanda being lesbian and Doug being straight). She notes that Doug is willing to use humor to confront others who might disparage her for her gender (especially given the fact that she works in a field dominated by men) or her sexual orientation: *"When we were working together, there were moments when he took somebody to task for saying something about me, either my gender or my sexuality. I know he's done that"* [Interview 14A]. They also use humor with one another and, in so doing, they have "named the difference."

> *Um, I think to a certain extent we've named* it *[and that has allowed us to break down the gender barrier]. We've named it and I think we've usually named it through humor. We've either done that 'cause that was very safe or because it was no big deal, making it easy to kind of dismiss it and just be like, "This isn't an issue." So, I think we've broken down the barrier to a certain extent just kind of by naming it. I think we both know it's there and I don't think it was a big deal to either of us. We didn't have to work through it together* [Interview 14A].

For Amanda and Doug, naming it takes the power of the social boundary away so that it doesn't keep them apart. This point is so important that, for Amanda, it was one of the summative reasons for the success of their friendship.

Ted and Jeremy use a lot of racial humor in their relationship, particularly Ted. In fact, Ted (who is black) will often use racial humor to test a person whom he's just meeting. As Jeremy (who is white) describes it,

> *What a flirt . . . the sparkle, flashing eyes, and then testing the comfort limits with humor, seeing how far you'll let his joking go. His sense of humor can be a little naughty and challenging. Then he'll pull back if he sees he's crossing a line and making you a little uncomfortable; but he likes making you a little uncomfortable, too. Just a little . . . And then you realize that behind the humor there's this great person who really has a lot of experience in life* [Interview 40B].

Left to his own devices, Jeremy would not use racial humor. Nonetheless, through his interaction with Ted, a culture of such humor has developed within their friendship.

> *I would never deliberately joke around about race with most of my friends; but with Ted and I, I can't believe some of the things we joke about. I remember*

*surprising myself when something slipped out of my mouth that was just . . . it would have been something out of Ted's mouth. I can't even think what it was, but it was something like a joke about* Driving Miss Daisy *humor or something. I'm like, "I don't believe I just said that." But when we do it, we don't even think about it. It depends on whether there's malice intended, I believe. Intent can make or break it [the use of racial humor].*

*And it's one thing if it's just the two of us talking and we've discussed race or what he's experienced and explained to me, but then he's comfortable joking around with some racial humor in front of his parents or other friends. My immediate instinct is don't joke about it even if it's just joking because I don't know where this other person's humor level is. We can get away with stuff like that with each other, but we talk about it, too. So, I think we know that aside from the joking, we know how the other one really, really feels about it, you know . . . about whatever it is we're joking about* [Interview 40B].

It is clear that Jeremy has some unofficial "rules" about racial humor in mind, including not engaging in such humor in the presence of others who are not a part of the culture that he and Ted have created within their friendship. When we started talking about this rule directly, Jeremy realized that such a rule isn't just about protecting outsiders from what they might consider offensive (a good thing) but it is just as much a way of denying the validity of the friendship culture they had created. At that point, he began to question this unspoken rule by relating it to his experience as a gay man.

*How many things that you're comfortable with in life are you not going to do because they're not [comfortable with it]. Oh, God, welcome to the life of a gay man . . . On many levels, you know. Try being a gay man. God knows many aspects of being gay—which aren't even big deals—make other people uncomfortable. And so we change pronouns. We don't talk about whatever because it might make somebody else uncomfortable; but it's just real life for us at home. And now all of a sudden we got the friendships that have racial differences, and we're comfortable joking around and friendly banter or whatever. But we're doing the same thing: we protect others from discomfort* [Interview 40B].

At this point, Jeremy began to worry that he was engaging in self-censorship when he avoided using racial humor with Ted in the presence of others. He worries that such self-censorship inhibits his and Ted's freedom of self-expression.

The role of humor is much more nuanced in the case of Dave and Mark. Their friendship started in the military and they ended up as roommates for a couple years. Now, they live in different parts of the country, but still speak regularly. In their joint interview, they both identify their "sick sense of humor" as a major reason why they have stayed friends for years beyond the time when they would see each other on a daily basis. Later in the same interview, they identify humor as the key to the success of their friendship. What makes this interesting is that, at least early in their friendship, their humor—particularly Mark's—was quite sexist, racist, homophobic, and so on. In fact, Dave (who is

gay) has a fondness for identifying Mark as an "equal opportunity bigot" while
Mark (who is straight) explains, *"Some of our prejudices are very similar, which
leads to a similar sense of humor"* [Interview 10B]. Here's how Dave describes
Mark and his sense of humor—and keep in mind that Dave says this with affection in his voice:

> *Mark tended to be a little irreverent. When I first met Mark, he hated everybody
> including himself. He was the world's number one bigot. I mean, it didn't mat-
> ter what it was; nothing was off limits. He hated everybody, you know. I don't
> care if you're gay, black, Jewish, Catholic, white, Hispanic, Irish or whatever
> . . . and he's Irish. He was an equal opportunity bigot. And, you know, I'd be
> the first to admit, ninety-nine percent of his jokes were funny and, like I say, he
> was not discriminating against any particular group of people. He was dis-
> criminating against everybody and would even make jokes about himself. So, I
> mean, he was an equal opportunity bigot* [Interview 10A].

Perhaps not surprisingly, I was a bit taken aback by this impression I received of
Mark and so felt compelled to ask whether Dave thought his jokes were more
about words than actions.

> *No, they were mostly words. He just had a big mouth, still does. But at the same
> time, I don't think anybody had ever confronted him. Nobody ever said, "If
> you're going to talk the talk, you got to walk the walk." I think he realized on
> his own that he was talking the talk and he wasn't walking the walk and that
> "I've got to make a decision here. Maybe I need to rethink this a little bit and
> change"* [Interview 10A].

Adding to the complexity in the use of humor in their friendship is the fact that,
for the first few years of their friendship, even as they were roommates in the
military, Mark had no idea that Dave was gay. So, of course, I had to know how
the off-color jokes about gays went over with Dave.

> *He was never ugly to me personally and that's why it never bothered me. He
> wasn't ugly to me as an individual. Had it been directed specifically to me, that
> would have been unacceptable, but it wasn't directed specifically to me. It was
> just in general.*
>     *When you think about what a bigot he was and how he was so angry at the
> whole world and everybody, it's amazing to me that our friendship has en-
> dured. I fully expected that, when he realized I was gay, he just would not be
> able to handle it. Instead, he realized, "Oh my God! Here's one of my closest
> friends and I've been just a horse's ass for the last two years. Is this guy going
> to want to be friends with me? Have I offended this person?" And what has
> been amazing is to see the transformation in him to being well read, well spo-
> ken, quite articulate, knowing about gay issues, because he actually knew
> somebody like that. Mark is a very, very straight, very locked and cocked, up-*

*tight, conservative, military officer, and so for him to make that transformation*
*is I think nothing less than remarkable* [Interview 10A].

What I find to be particularly significant in this example is how Dave was able to separate the off-color jokes that Mark told from the intentions of the person saying them. This could only happen in a relationship where there was genuine trust and familiarity with the character of the other person. Without knowing exactly where the other person is coming from and what motivates him or her, it would be difficult—if not impossible—for a person with a more open-minded value system with regard to diversity to hear such jokes without taking offense. In other words, the friendship itself provides a crucial piece of the context from which the individuals derive meaning from the jokes and interpret them in such a way that they are deemed acceptable. Outside of this kind of intimate context such jokes are potentially very damaging, given—as described at the beginning of this section on humor—the lack of control the (public) speaker has over the audience and how the members of the audience perceive the use of humor.

Despite the fact that the friendship provided a context in which such humor was perceived as acceptable by Dave, he was still worried about how Mark would react when he eventually found out that Dave is gay. Instead, Mark experienced this transformation in his attitudes toward gays and lesbians as a group: *"Before, I didn't know anybody who was gay. Now it became a personal issue. It's easier if you don't know anybody. Once you have a buddy or some other people who you actually respect and then you find out, you go, 'Oh man, I better revisit that issue'"* [Interview 10B]. Moreover, Mark did not limit his change in attitude to Dave alone. Instead, he generalized it to gays and lesbians as a group.

*I guess because I figured if they could . . . you know, you start with one and then you build from there and you get a group that I believe represents probably ninety percent of the rest of them in the service; if that's the case, it doesn't matter . . . it's just not a problem* [Interview 10B].

In fact, this transformation did change the style of humor Mark uses, at least with regard to gay jokes in the context of his friendship with Dave. I asked Dave whether Mark still tells gay jokes in his presence.

*He hasn't for a number of years, not that he's not welcome to 'cause generally he's got some pretty funny ones. But no, I've noticed he hasn't made any; but he doesn't make any of those kind of off-color jokes. I think he's kind of grown up, and I think he's realized that he's a big boy and big boys don't do that* [Interview 10A].

This change in Mark's views and behavior indicates that, at some level, he knew that the jokes he told in the past went too far even if he didn't intend to hurt anybody and even though Dave himself never felt targeted or hurt. As a result, the normative standards for jokes—at least the gay jokes—changed in the context of their friendship. It was apparent Mark desired to show his respect toward Dave by changing his behavior in light of Dave's coming out to him as gay. He valued their friendship too much to risk allowing off-color gay jokes to come between them. On the other hand, this does not mean that sexual orientation is no longer a source of great humor between them. The humor has simply moved away from random jokes to laughing about specific situations in which they find themselves where sexual orientation plays a significant role. In their paired interview, they told a story that got both of them laughing.

> *DAVE: In Provincetown, we're sitting at this bar and he has several drinks. We met a very nice F-18 pilot—Peter. He was buff, he lifted weights, he was cool, and he was great to talk to.*
> *MARK: Yeah, and he was decent and didn't have the attitude; just a general regular good guy.*
> *DAVE: Well he just thought, he absolutely . . . he was like, "Hmm, who's your friend?" I'm like, "Leave him alone, he's straight." "Oh yeah, okay, uh huh. He's your friend." "Look, he's straight." "Uh huh." So, Peter's like licking his chops looking at Mark, and Mark's sitting there just oblivious to what's going on around him as far as . . .*
> *MARK: The dynamics . . .*
> *DAVE: . . . the dynamics of what's going on. So somehow or another oral sex came up and Mark's saying, "Well, you know, after six gin and tonics I wouldn't care who was giving me a blow job." Peter stands up and says, "Bartender! Six gin and tonics here." And Mark's like, "Huh?" And I said, "Bartender, stay there. Peter, sit down and shut up. And Mark, keep your mouth shut." And Mark's saying, "Huh?" And Peter's looking at me like, "Dude, you're shooting me down here, you know. You're causing me major problems." I knew Mark was going to get even more toasted than he was already, and the next morning he was going to wake up with a hangover and go, "Oh my God! What the fuck did I do?" What kind of a friend would I have been to throw him to the wolves, have him wake up in some friend of mine's hotel room going, "Oh shit! What have I done?"*
> *MARK: Too much to lose, not enough to gain.*
> *DAVE: And he, it would have fucked him up. I mean it would have fucked him, and because he is a close friend, I was like, I was not about to let that happen. If it was somebody . . .*
> *MARK: It had been Roger on the other hand. And it was the big brother, little brother thing.*
> *DAVE: Yeah, but he was, I'm going to say he was so naïve, because that wasn't his thing. He was in over his head and didn't know it. He'd never been in that situation before. I mean literally they were looking at him like a piece of chopped meat, and there was a line. Literally, they would have formed a line and said, "Oh I'll buy a ticket for that!" And he's like, "Huh?" I was just like "No, we are not going there for all those reasons." And we've laughed about that.*
> *MARK: Numerous times* [Interview 10C].

This detailed example from the interviews of Dave and Mark highlights much of the nuanced complexity in the use of humor that focuses on a particular socially constructed boundary as a means for building connections between two individuals living on opposite sides of that boundary. The success of this technique depends largely on the friendship culture and the definition of the situation created by the two friends in the course of their interaction. At the same time, the case of Mark and Dave also highlights how the use of humor walks a very fine line between what is deemed acceptable and what is considered offensive.

In most friendships where humor is used to bridge the gap, they were successful and the "contextual dimension" of the relationship allowed them to take what might otherwise be considered offensive and redefine it as comical. Still, it is important to take account of the "relative power" between the two friends when considering this contextual dimension. Such a "power-blind" approach to using humor can jeopardize the relationship (Rude 2009). In two of the cases studied, there was a point where the use of humor went too far. We've already seen how, in the case of Wilson and Frank, Wilson has actually assimilated to white culture. In their friendship, they rarely talk about race in a serious manner. Instead, they have dealt with race almost exclusively through a teasing form of humor. For example, given Wilson's biracial identity, Frank will taunt him saying that "he only gets half the jokes" in a black comedy movie. Wilson considers Frank to be very outgoing and funny and sees this shared humor as a reason why they are such good friends.

> When I first heard Frank's comments, I'm like "What did he say?" For example, he'd leave a message on my machine, saying something about the "N word"—nigger—or something and I was just like, "Whoa," you know. But after a while, once I got to know him, I knew he was joking around. And I never really heard it directed towards me in the least. When we first started hanging, I think he said something about, "I'll joke or be dumb and say some things, but I want you to know that I'm just goofing around with my friends." He made a point in telling me that, so I felt more comfortable around him then [Interview 21B].

When asked why what Frank says doesn't offend him, Wilson explains, "*Because we're good friends and I've known him so long. From his body language and how he says it, I know he's just joking. He's a humorous guy. I don't know . . . it just doesn't bug me*" [Interview 21B]. For his part, Frank describes race as a "tool" he and Wilson have used to fuel their humor.

> It's definitely been a tool that we've used to joke about. Like he would call me a racist and I would make some black joke or whatnot. It's actually . . . we'd joke about it more than care about it. It works because both of us are pretty trusting in the fact that him being black and me being white didn't really matter that much so we could joke about it [Interview 21A].

Even so, there are times when Wilson gets uncomfortable with Frank's joking around.

> *At times I wish he wouldn't goof off like that, especially when other people are around. Generally, I don't care. I can tolerate it, but other people might not. Or if it was totally inappropriate, I'll get angry. But he knows me well. He knows I'll be vocal if it bugs me and he'll stop then. You just got to be firm with Frank and he'll stop. I don't get angry a lot around this, so he knows that if I'm angry, he should just calm down. Sometimes he might feel uncomfortable when he feels it's just a joke and I'll just come back and say, "Why'd you say that? What do you mean?" And he'll feel uncomfortable sometimes with me bringing it up and say, "Why's it important," you know, "We're friends. Who cares"* [Interview 21B]?

The problem for Wilson was that Frank didn't seem to think that Wilson had any problems with the jokes he made. Korgen points out that the use of humor within diverse friendships gives the "surface impression that the two friends are on an equal playing field. The only indication that the field is still slanted is the fact that . . . insults are more likely to injure" the marginalized friend than the privileged one (2002, 39-40). Wilson noted that there were a couple of comments that had "hurt a little" or at least given him pause. It's apparent here that, while this doesn't always happen, there are times when Frank's joking does create tension within the friendship. Wilson has been angry with him before and has learned to confront him. This will often work, but there are times when Frank resists. Nevertheless, Wilson does feel that Frank is making an effort to be respectful: *"Because sometimes I've called him on it, I think Frank is more cautious now; so I think he's making more of an effort. But I've also made an effort to speak my mind when he's out of line"* [Interview 21B].

Wilson also said that there were comments that Frank made that would have bothered him if someone else had made them. When asked why, he said he trusted that Frank didn't actually have any prejudices and said that Frank had actually taken him aside on more than one occasion and let him know that it was all just joking and he really didn't mean any of it. On the one hand, this use of humor seems to indicate a high level of comfort with one another regarding the issue of race. In their paired interview, they indicated that it actually allows them to address the issue of race in a way that is not threatening.

> *FRANK: It's like South Park. I don't know. Personally, I think the reason why I joke about it is it's just a way of defusing an issue. Maybe it's our way of confronting race and letting each other know that it's not a really big deal.*
> *WILSON: Yeah, I can see that definitely* [Interview 21C].

On the other hand, the almost exclusive use of humor in dealing with race in their friendship allows them to virtually ignore the issue at a more serious level (see Rude 2009 and Korgen 2002). Consequently, while humor has been a means by which Frank and Wilson have bridged the racial difference between them, given the fact that there are times when tension arises, it is clear that Wilson and Frank have not been entirely successful in creating agreed upon limits to the use of humor.

Pam and Tim also use good-natured banter and ribbing in their cross-gender friendship. In their paired interview, they agreed that what makes this friendly banter between them possible is the amount of trust they have in each other's intent. They both know that neither one of them would ever say anything intentionally malicious. For example, Pam has strong feminist views and is not shy about voicing them and challenging people around her. While Tim agrees with her fundamental desire for gender equality, he'll tease her about being a "man hater." It is said lightly, with humor, and you can almost hear the quotation marks around the word or phrase. Even so, there was a point when Tim made a more general, gender-focused joke that, as she described it, made Pam's blood run cold.

> *I think the most thoughtless thing he ever said to me—and I can't believe he'd even say it to anyone—was a story from when he lived in Colorado or maybe it was just some story he'd heard about. It was a total college town. Anyway, there was a girl walking alone at night and a bunch of these college guys saw her and one of them yelled, "Let's rape her!" He thought that was funny, and I didn't at all. I remember very distinctly him telling me this, and I was just like, "Are you kidding me?" He's like, "Well, you know, I just think it's funny when people screw with people's heads. She should know better than to walk alone at night." And I was just like, "Oh really. So you're teaching her a lesson." I just got . . . it really bothered me. I don't think that's typical of him and I think I remember him getting very serious, 'cause he realized I took it really seriously. And I remember . . . and I don't really think that that's how he thinks; but that came out in such a casual way that it was like it's not something he was thinking about and still, you know. And that's actually very atypical of the way he treats women and thinks of them, and he's probably the most open-minded person as far as women goes that I've ever met in practice* |Interview 26A|.

After I completed this set of three interviews, I was reflecting on what Pam had said about this situation and decided to ask her a follow-up question about it in order to unpack the subtleties where being called a "man hater" is funny and acceptable but the practical joke was not at all funny. Here's her response:

> *I've thought about it and I think the major difference is that I know that Tim is kidding when he calls me a man-hater. At the same time I realize I invite being called that because sometimes I make provocative comments like, "Men are the reason we have war and violence, etc." I realize that these are irresponsible statements and therefore I am able to accept what is an equally irresponsible comeback.*
>
> *The rape comment was something that, at the risk of being dramatic or overreacting to the situation, I consider a form of violence against that girl and*

*women in general. The thoughts and feelings that Tim and his friends must have had in order to make such a comment and find it amusing go to the heart of a problem that I think is very serious and important. I find nothing even remotely amusing about threatening a woman who is walking alone with rape. I find it highly offensive and see the situation as part of the far greater problem of violence against women and sexism in general.*

*When Tim makes fun of me as a man-hater, it's a playful exchange of two people who are comfortable making fun of each other. When Tim told the story about the woman, it betrayed his fundamental feelings about who men and women are and what their roles are—even though I've since concluded that Tim really hadn't thought through what he was saying and doesn't honestly think something like that is funny. In fact, he may have initially thought the story WAS similar to him ribbing me about being a feminist. After my reaction, I think he reconsidered* [Interview 26A].

Pam described how, after Tim first told the story, she distanced herself from him for a brief period because she needed to reassess where he was coming from. Since then, however, they were able to talk through it and Pam explained how, for her, the joke wasn't funny at all because it touched on a very real and very serious problem that women face—violence: a problem she believes can never be taken lightly.

These two instances in which humor has been taken too far—the case of Wilson and Frank and the case of Pam and Tim—support the point made by critics that such humor is, for example, "always going to offend someone" (Thaler 2006). Ultimately, the person in a position of privilege is demonstrating his or her power relative to the other. This seems to be done unintentionally, but it becomes problematic for the friend who is marginalized nevertheless. On the other hand, these two cases were in the minority. In 83 percent of the friendships[6] where humor was used, it was used in a way that was mutually acceptable and there were no reports of any resulting friction within the friendship.

Friends who use humor do so as a means of bridging the socially constructed boundary between them. Throughout this discussion, I have suggested that these friends will often establish rules to bind humor within limits of acceptability. The use of such rules reflects Goffman's metaphor of "life as ritual" (Lemert and Branaman 1997 and Goffman 1967). Such rituals serve a cohesive function, bringing people together and creating social order, much like Durkheim's work on religious rituals (Durkheim 2008). For Goffman, though, the social order unfolds at the micro level of social interaction and thus represents the "ground rules" of social life. Individuals engage in performance as they interact and the social function of such performance is to maintain this ritual order. For this reason, friends who use this form of bonding humor develop rules that guide their interactions, placing conditions and constraints on the manner in which the interaction unfolds. Without such rules, the ritual social order can easily be broken, undermining the social cohesion established within the friendship.

Humor can easily be taken too far and create tension or even jeopardize the friendship, as was seen in the last two examples above. These rules tend to be based on common understanding and are therefore left unspoken, although they are no less compelling as a result. Instead, they arise out of the friendship culture established in the course of interaction over the history of the friendship and their tacitly agreed upon definition of the situation in which humor is used. As the Thomas Theorem tells us, if you define a situation as real, it will be real in its consequences (Thomas 1928). If humor based on social categories of race, gender, sexual orientation, and so on is defined by the friends as acceptable within the context of their friendship, then it is perceived in a positive light so long as both parties follow the rules of humor they have established.

What are the humor rules that friends use to successfully guide their interaction and banter? Some are unique to each friendship. Still, after a careful analysis of the data in this study presented above, it is clear that there are a number of unspoken rules that most if not all friends follow in their use of humor:[7]

1. *Trust and familiarity must be established first.* Friends rarely, if ever, use humor based on social categories immediately upon meeting someone for the first time. Instead, they build the friendship—the intimacy, the trust—and then, as their comfort level with one another rises, they feel free to introduce humor. With familiarity it is easier to interpret the intentions of another person. The use of humor must be motivated by benign intentions and must not be malicious; perceiving intentions accurately takes familiarity and trust.

2. *Outsiders are not welcome.* The use of humor is acceptable only between friends where such trust and familiarity are present. Outsiders are not allowed to use such humor because knowledge of the others' intentions is unknown. In this way, humor is used as a form of "in" joke that helps to solidify the bond between the friends (Korgen 2002). Also, the use of humor based on social categories is largely kept away from outsiders who might overhear the exchange and is relegated to the context of the friendship pair alone. Otherwise, the friends have less control over how the humor and they themselves are perceived.[8]

3. *The use of humor must be mutually acceptable.* If only one friend defines such humor as acceptable, there will be problems if the other decides to use it. Moreover, not only must the *use* of humor be mutually acceptable, but also the *kind* of humor allowed. This point will be discussed further below.

4. *The use of humor must be tempered with mutual respect and affection.* It is very important that this style of humor not be taken personally; therefore, humor targeting specific individuals is much less acceptable than humor that is much more general and does not target an individual, particularly one's friend. In other words, the use of humor based on social categories must be done for no other motive than pure fun.

Beyond these four fundamental rules, there are additional rules that vary from one friendship to another. In keeping with the third rule, these variations have to do with the subject matter, or the *kind* of humor used. Some friends agree that they may joke only about each other's social category. Other social categories are off limits. This is the case with Irene and Bao, who direct their humor toward themselves, especially focusing on their common experiences of being minorities within minorities because they are not black or Hmong "enough." For example, upon noting the demographics of the people around her, Bao might say, *"There sure are a lot of Asians around here"* [Interview 19A]! In saying this, she is separating herself from the Asians around them, which simultaneously highlights what she and Irene have in common. Irene has done the same thing. What helps is that in this case they are both minorities, even if different ones, and it is more acceptable to make jokes with one another than for a majority member to do such a thing, even if only in fun. In contrast, Sam and Rodney (among others) only make jokes about other races, not about each other's race. That way, they ensure that they don't break rule four identified above. Finally, some friends restrict their use of humor to actual situations in which they find themselves and where their social categories are relevant. This was most evident in the case of Dave and Mark, described above, where they tell a story about a gay man's trying to get Mark drunk and Mark's not realizing what was going on. In sum, the function of these rules—the four fundamental rules seen in all friendships where humor is used and the additional rules that may vary from one friendship to another—is to protect the friendship from damage through unintentional offense and to maintain the ritual order of social interaction (Goffman 1967).

Again, humor was used in one-third of the friendship pairs included in this research, mostly with success (problems arising in only two of those cases, both of which were described above). In only two of the remaining friendships did one or another friend outwardly oppose the use of humor, indicating that they were clearly in the minority. Barbara (who is straight) is generally opposed to the use of such humor with her friend Janice (who is lesbian). While she has laughed when a minority friend made such a joke and on a rare occasion might even bring one up herself, she considers this rather exceptional for her and her comfort zone.

> *You know, I struggle with that one because, you know, a black will call another black person a "nigger." And well that's okay, they're both black. But I don't know how I feel about that, because I'm like, "Oh, gosh." That seems like it's such a bad word, and it has such negative connotations. Why would you ever want to use that, you know? But at the same time I guess if the people within that relationship feel comfortable with that, then I guess it's their choice. I would not feel comfortable with it.*
>
> *I mean, I don't even think I joke around with my brother [who is gay] about it. My husband will joke around with my brother about it; they kind of*

*have a little ribbing sort of relationship there, and that's fine. But I think that even though it's a joke, there's a grain of truth |as in intent| underneath it. And so sometimes I think there are issues that are too sensitive to joke about. People who do may not really be prejudiced, but I think it just reflects a willingness to say that we can make fun of this, and I just don't think that's okay.*

*I just think there's some things you shouldn't ever make fun of, and there's certain words you shouldn't use. You know, like I would never call someone a "fag." I wouldn't call my brother a "fag." I would just never do that, even if the person was okay with it. I just wouldn't do it. Certain words, like "nigger," I could never use . . . I mean I would kill myself if that word ever literally came out of my mouth. So, there's certain things I just don't feel comfortable with; but I know a lot of people feel like a joke is a joke and you can make fun of anything, and it's not a big deal, but I'm just kind of weird about that, I guess.*

*I would be very cautious about joking around 'cause I would be afraid no matter how close a friend you are, it's a sensitive issue for them. And you never know what mood . . . you may be hitting them on a day when they just had someone say something nasty to them. So, I would be very cautious about that* |Interview 22B|.

Barbara knows that such humor is present in other friendships, but she feels that, even if there is a mutual understanding, there might actually be a kernel of agreement with whatever stereotypical attribution is made in the joke. For her, this is true even if it is the minority individual who initiates such a joke. So, her choice is to avoid initiating such humor altogether. She'll go along with it if the friend initiates, but she won't initiate it herself. The stakes are too high and she values her friendships too highly.

Overall, it is evident from the data that the experiences and views of the individuals in these friendships that bridge socially constructed boundaries of race, gender, sexual orientation, and so on indicate that the downside of using humor that focuses on these social categories is threefold. First, it sidesteps the issues of race, gender, sexual orientation, and so on so that serious dialogue is minimized or avoided entirely. Of course, dialogue is not always necessary or even required to understand one's friend and where he or she is coming from. Still, such dialogue has the potential to add more depth to the relationship and each individual's understanding of the other. In addition, using humor of this nature becomes tricky when there's the possibility that outsiders may overhear. If outsiders do not understand the established friendship culture and common definition of the situation, they could take it personally—if they are a member of the social category targeted by the humor—take offense, or even come to believe such values are more widely acceptable, even among those who do not share the same definition of the situation. Finally, as Barbara notes above, the social category one belongs to may be a sensitive issue for an individual and the use of such humor may become problematic. It might not always be a sensitive issue; but there may be extenuating circumstances that cause the individual to become more sensitive than she or he usually is, opening the door for hurt feelings. Beyond these identified problems with the use of such humor, there are also the downsides addressed by social critics: the lack of control over how this form of humor (at least in public situations) is perceived and the fact that any put-down within the humor is achieved regardless of how it is perceived.

While acknowledging the problems in using humor to bridge diverse social categories, it is even more apparent from the experiences and views of those interviewed that humor serves a positive function in most friendships where it is present. As already discussed, using this form of humor requires trust and familiarity between the individuals involved. At the same time, such humor—when it follows the rules that emerge in the friendship—actually enhances both trust and familiarity, resulting in a strengthening of the social bond between the two friends. While it is arguably a downside of this style of humor that it allows the individuals to sidestep the issues of race, gender, sexual orientation and so on, it is equally clear that humor allows the friends to "defuse" any issues related to these socially constructed categories that might be viewed as problematic by outsiders with different values. By using this form of humor, the individuals ensure that race, gender, sexual orientation and so on do not become problematic in the context of their friendship. Finally, as Amanda noted in her interview and as was explained above, humor focusing on social categories allows the friends to "name the difference," taking the power of social differences away so that they are not and do not become a barrier between the two individuals, even if it is a barrier for others in our larger society.

An important goal in my research on diverse friendships has been to understand how people bridge the social distance between them. My findings suggest that, regardless of the socially constructed boundary in question (race, gender, sexual orientation, class, religion, age, and ability), there are a wide variety of interpersonal techniques available—some used intentionally and others merely arising out of the specific circumstances—that the two friends may use to successfully bridge any differences between them based on socially constructed categories. These techniques are used to disarm the differences (Korgen 2002) and establish trust between the two friends (Rude 2009; Rawlins 1992). Rude observes that "the key . . . to a successful [diverse] friendship would seem to reside in managing a delicate balancing act between engaging with issues of [diversity] and deemphasizing or downplaying [these] differences" (2009, 133). Central among those strategies I found among those I interviewed is an intentional focus on the commonalities between the two individuals, "taking care" to be supportive and not cause offense, meeting one's friend more than half way, educating one's friend with regard to the social category to which one belongs, and—surprisingly—the use of humor. Not all of these strategies, however, are used with equal success within the different friendship pairs and most friends use multiple strategies simultaneously.

# Notes

1. Eleven of the 40 friendship pairs.
2. Fifteen out of the 40 friendship pairs.
3. Eleven of the 15 cases.
4. This technique was found in 17 of the 40 cases—43 percent.
5. Thirteen of the 40 cases.
6. Eleven of the 13 cases.
7. These rules for the use of humor represent a composite view incorporating the experiences of all those friends who utilized humor in the context of their friendship.
8. In only one case (Interviews 40A, B, & C) did the two friends involved seem to have differing rules regarding the use of humor; even so, it has not caused a problem because both parties understand the character of the other. Ted (who is black) likes to use humor to test other people's boundaries and limits, especially when he is getting to know them. He enjoys the mischievous approach and uses it all the time. On the other hand, Jeremy (who is white) seems to prefer to limit the use of such humor to those times when it is just the two of them. Not that the humor itself bothers him; it's just that he is uncomfortable including other people in it when he does not know how they will react or what their comfort level is. In other words, Jeremy seems much more conscious of how such humor will create an impression among those who are not "in the know." Still, the difference in their views on the use of such humor doesn't cause any problems between them beyond some discomfort on Jeremy's part. In fact, Ted knows well the reaction Jeremy will have and so teases him intentionally. It seems to be a part of their playing around with one another.

# *Chapter 5*

# "Bridging the Gap" Through Friendship

This book has focused on two very important sociological topics: diverse friendships and social cohesion. More importantly, it has focused on the intersection between these two topics: the unlikely friendships between those who, outside of the context of the friendship, live on different sides of a socially constructed boundary and who are nevertheless able to establish bridging ties between them, nurturing the social cohesion between diverse peoples that is so crucial in an increasingly multicultural global village. Accordingly, the friendships studied represent two successes: (1) at the interpersonal level, the success of the friendship itself and (2), from the societal perspective, success at bridging the socially constructed differences between them, and in so doing challenging the system of stratification as it currently exists. Let's look at each of these in turn, starting with the friendships themselves.

## The Personal Significance of Friendship

Not surprisingly, there were many reflective moments in the interviews conducted for this research project, especially when the individuals thought back on the significance of the friendship and then described what it had meant to them. At times, these were very sentimental statements where the individual might even choke up when speaking of his or her friend. Now and then, in the paired interview, the friends took it upon themselves to bring up how important each is to the other. These were quite personal, intimate moments that I was honored and privileged to witness. The vast majority of what was said about the meaning of these friendships had very little to do with the social boundary that the friends have crossed, highlighting how there is much, much more to these friendships than the fact that the two individuals come from different backgrounds. They have full, multi-dimensional relationships and are everything that a truly close friendship should be.

Eva has nothing to say with regard to her straight friend's support of her as a lesbian when asked what their friendship has meant to her. Instead, her focus is on the amazing support that Nicole has provided her over the years, even though they live in different parts of the country and only get to see one another about once a year.

> *Our friendship has meant a whole lot, you know. She's the one I just know that I can turn to, whatever's going on. And she's someone who I know that, if we don't talk for several months, it doesn't mean that we're not thinking about one another. I think about Nicole often. I just don't pick up the phone every time. And unfortunately life, work life in particular, has both of us extremely busy. You know, Nicole called me a few weeks ago and left a message, saying, "Hey, I've been thinking about you. Just wanted to say hey." She pointed out just what I said that "even though we haven't talked in months, I've been thinking about you. Just wanted to let you know." And it's so good to know that I have that in my life. She's very important to me. I would do anything for her, and I feel like she would do anything for me. I guess just knowing that gives me great peace of mind and helps me make my way through the world* [Interview 36A].

For her part, Nicole has nothing but a deep-felt appreciation for Eva.

> *Our friendship is definitely something that I treasure. I share a long history with Eva and throughout the entire time I have been her friend, not one single time has she disappointed me or made me feel uncomfortable or feel bad about who I am or what I'm doing in my life at the time. She's always been incredibly supportive of every step of my life and has been, you know, very happy for me when good things happen and celebrates the choices that I make in my life with me. And that's really a gift that, you know, doesn't always happen. She's incredibly generous in that: never jealous, never petty, just always very real and truly open and caring about everything* [Interview 36B].

Eva and Nicole, both in their forties, have been friends since they met as first-year students in college. Their friendship has stood the tests of time and separation in large part based on how mutually supportive they are and the effort they put into maintaining the friendship.

The majority of the responses[1] having to do with what the friendship meant to each individual were in the same vein as what Eva and Nicole had to say about each other. People regularly cited the support they received from their friend and, in more general terms, simply explained that their friend meant a lot to them. Others discussed how the friendship affected their own personal development or described how their friendship was fun, interesting, and enjoyable. Lenora is one of those who describe how her friendship with Melissa has led to her own personal development. Almost as an afterthought, she also mentions how she and Melissa have fun together, another dimension of her friendship that she values very much.

> *This friendship has taught me a lot of things about myself that I never thought of before. My friendship with her has made me grow as a person and made me value my family more because I see how she is with her family. I want that kind of a close relationship with my family. She's helped me and my friendship with her has hopefully made her grow as a person, too. I think that we look at things more openly. I know I do. I try to look at all sides now. It's also been a fun relationship. We always have fun with each other* [Interview 5A].

A few people mentioned how they learned about friendship itself or even described how the friendship confirmed their sense of self. Melody has much to say regarding what she has learned about friendship.

> *It has been challenging, and it has broadened my horizons, been eye opening. I guess being a friend is easy, but having a friendship isn't as easy because a friendship is . . . You've got to maintain, you've got to commit, you've got to be in it for the long run, you've got to stick with each other if you move away, you know. Under any circumstances, you've got to stick by each other. A friend is sort of in the now, like when your friend is right there; so that's the easy part of being a friend. The hard part is maintaining the friendship, and I think that's where those two are quite different. One is joyful and spontaneous and the other is sort of long term and more work* [Interview 29A].

Responses having to do with the fact that the friendship itself bridges a socially constructed boundary were in the minority,[2] an observation that stands in contrast with past research (Korgen 2002). I expect that the difference results from the fact that I did not ask the friends directly and instead wanted to see if they brought it up themselves, an indication of how truly important this outcome would be for the individual who spontaneously brings it up. More often than not, only one of the two friends provided a response with such a reference and then it was usually the person in a position of privilege who mentioned how the friendship has allowed him or her to become more open-minded with regard to issues of diversity. This finding is entirely consistent with past research (Jackman and Crane 1986; Korgen 2002). Recall, for example, the friendship between Mark and Dave. This is the pair who met in the military while Dave was closeted, even when they were roommates. Only after leaving the military did Dave come out to Mark who then had to confront his own homophobia. Mark describes how this experience has changed him.

> *It's been a very eye-opening experience. It's probably been good for personal growth in different ways for each of us, but I think it's been good for me. It's been a unique experience, and like I said before, I never saw it coming. I never would have fathomed in a million years that would be in my life and I'd be forced to deal with an issue like that because the place and the time in which*

*we met was very homophobic, although I don't even necessarily agree with that*
*word. It forced a lot of personal growth in a very short period of time and that*
*wasn't easy. It's been good. It's actually meant a lot to me and will continue to*
*as well* [Interview 10B].

Mark feels that this was a growth experience for both of them and Dave also
describes it as such throughout his interview. When asked what the friendship
has meant to him, though, Dave spoke in much more general terms without a
single reference to the difference between them.

*Well, it's very important. It's one of my richest, deepest, most important friend-*
*ships. It's an important chapter in my life. It's an important part of my life, you*
*know. It's one of my very closest friendships. They say in a lifetime if you have*
*five good friendships, you've done very, very well. Well, he's one of those very,*
*very close five friendships. I look forward to maintaining this friendship for a*
*while* [Interview 10A].

Again, more often than not, it is the privileged who make a point to note how
having a friend who is different from them has been a growth experience. Perhaps the reason for this imbalance lies in the fact that the marginalized have had
to live in a world dominated by the privileged for much if not all of their lives.
The opportunity to learn and grow from such an experience is not restricted to a
single relationship but represents the totality of all interactions with those in a
position of privilege (Dubois 1961).

One apparent exception is the case of Quinn and Mike, both of whom express how their friendship has led them to be more open-minded. Recall that the
difference between them is one of class, Quinn being from a working-class
background though he has just completed a college degree in his late twenties
and Mike being a part of the professional middle class. The irony here is that
when Quinn refers to himself becoming more open-minded as a result of their
friendship, it has nothing to do with the class difference between them. Instead,
it has everything to do with their religious difference: Quinn is Christian and
Mike is Jewish. So, what their friendship has meant to each of them is not an
exception to the overall pattern after all. Quinn, the person in a position of religious privilege, has become more open-minded from having befriended a person
of a different religious faith tradition, while Mike, from his comparative position
of class privilege, has become more open-minded as a result of that particular
dimension of his overall status. Here is what each of them had to say, starting
with Quinn:

*You know, despite the fact that we're talking about the class difference, I think*
*it's been important for me to be a friend and learn about somebody from a dif-*
*ferent religion. So, I think that our friendship has been a great deal about kind*
*of overcoming differences and succeeding at being friends in spite of our dif-*

*ferences. So it's, you know, it's enjoyable, interesting and just kind of reward-*
*ing to overcome those differences* [Interview 15A].

Simply overcoming the differences, religious and class-based, has been an interesting and rewarding experience for Quinn. Mike too describes it as interesting.

*Our friendship has allowed me to be more open to the possibility of rich friend-*
*ships with people with whom I have superficial differences. It was one of those*
*rearview mirror kinds of things that I never thought about the differences until*
*we had really kind of established a friendship. [Only then did I ask myself],*
*"Oh, but you know, why is this thing working, 'cause I am this and you're*
*that?" Well, that's kind of interesting* [Interview 15B].

Still, Mike doesn't leave it at that. In describing what his friendship with Quinn
has meant to him, he goes on to describe how he has learned about friendship
itself and to describe their friendship as enjoyable simply because "I like this
guy."

*What it has meant to me is it has made me a better friend. It's taught me how to*
*be a friend. It's taught me how to give, and it's taught me how to take, which is*
*sometimes a challenge for me, which has not only been good in the context of*
*my relationship with Quinn, but is transferable. It has made me a better person.*
*And, aside from the friendship, I just like this guy. He has such heart and soul.*
*He has such integrity. He is so bright. He is so articulate. He is so kind. He is*
*so gracious. He's got a tremendous range of skills. I am fascinated to see how*
*his life is going to play out. Even if we weren't friends for whatever reason,*
*he's someone I will always be curious about* [Interview 15B].

Irene and Bao also present us with a case in which a marginalized individual describes how the friendship has made her more open-minded. In this situation, however, they are *both* members of racial minority groups, Bao being
Hmong and Irene, who feels she has learned from the racial difference between
them, being black. The reader may recall how Irene's first impression of Bao
was that she was some kind of thug, a very misleading impression.

*I think she has really shown me the value of being accepting of people, I guess,*
*and the importance of not judging them by your first look and your first thought*
*because there could be an awesome relationship behind this that you could*
*miss out on. I would have if I had kept going with my little insecurities, scared*
*of little thug Bao, you know. I've just learned that it is important to get to know*
*people* [Interview 19B].

Bao also speaks of how she has developed as a person as a result of her friendship with Irene. Yet, for her it has nothing to do with the fact that they are different races.

*I think it's definitely one of those relationships where—I think especially now at this point in my life, it's such a crucial point of where I'm trying to find myself and I'm changing and transforming and all that stuff—I think that she's one of those friends I know that I'll probably remember even if I don't keep in touch with her throughout my life. I'll always remember her as one of those people that I shared all that experience of becoming who I'm going to become, changing myself as a person. I think that I'm always going to remember her as that person who has been there and gone through that process and has seen me change and all that stuff. Not too many friends actually see that, you know. It's also been one of those friendships that you're going to remember, always remember, even if you don't keep in touch with them in the future. You'll always look back and be like, "Yeah, I remember I had this friend once that . . . ," you know* [Interview 19A].*

There were only a few examples[3] of a marginalized individual making a point to highlight the social boundary being crossed in his friendship when asked what the friendship has meant to him. As one might expect, this was done as a sort of appreciation for how his friend simply accepted him as he was, allowing him the freedom to simply be himself. Such was the case for Bill, who is gay, when speaking of his straight friend Karen. Karen allowed him to be gay in a town where that has been a particular challenge. Moreover, Karen made it possible for Bill and his partner to become gay fathers by volunteering to be the surrogate mother for their child.

*Well, when you put it in context to what she's given us, given me, you want to just . . . her love for me has allowed me to become a father. But, you know, if you take my son out of the picture, which is hard to do, she's allowed me to be me, you know, more so than I would without her being part of my life. She's just reinforced the fact that I'm a human being and I have value in this world. A lot of people have done that for me, but she's certainly played her role in her acceptance of me as a person. That's fortified me* [Interview 12A].

Karen also expresses how important Bill has been in her life, although she does it without reference to the difference in orientation between them, simply focusing on all the support Bill has given her over the years.

*[This friendship has provided me with] emotional stability. Just knowing that no matter what else is going on in my life, there's always Bill. Unfortunately, I can't even say that about my husband. And don't get me wrong, I love my husband. He's a great guy, heart of gold; but you know, I just can't always count on him because he's my forty-year-old child. He just doesn't get me sometimes and Bill does. So, no matter what chaos is going on in my life, he's always there. I would hope that I'd be able to be as strong for him as he has been for me in my times of crisis, but then I don't know. You never know what you're going to do until you get into that instance, and somehow you always forge ahead* [Interview 12B].

More often than not, it is the privileged friends who describe how their friendship has changed them for the better. The marginalized, in contrast, have had much more experience in dealing with those who are different. In those few instances where the marginalized refer back to the fact that their friendship is bridging a social boundary, they are either in a friendship where both parties are marginalized or, as in the case of Bill, are expressing appreciation for the privileged simply allowing them to be themselves.

## The Experience of "Breaking Down Boundaries"

The friendships studied here represent the success stories: those who were able to move beyond any differences in terms of social boundaries and maintain a close friendship. So, what has made these friendships successful in terms of breaking down those boundaries and bridging the socially constructed differences between them? As we learned in chapter 4, there are a number of interpersonal techniques that the friends use to navigate the difference between them, such as the use of humor or focusing on the commonalities they share. Naturally, these techniques can be seen as centrally important in actually breaking down the boundaries represented by the demographic differences between the two friends and bridging the presumed gap between them. But what is the secret to their success in accomplishing what others might see as a rather daunting task?

Before answering this question, I should point out that the question, while it is important sociologically, makes the assumption that there are "boundaries to break" and "gaps to bridge." Certainly, this is true in terms of the structure of society, as highlighted in much of this book and in countless other works of sociology. Yet, many of the individuals interviewed for this project would beg to differ. Fully one third of the responses either directly challenged this assumption about boundaries and gap or alluded to the fact that they didn't exist for the friends. Hugo is one of those who directly challenged the assumption, saying, *"You know, I'm going to pick on you, James. That construct that you gave—that it's a boundary and that it has been broken down—is a white image. For us, there never was a boundary"* [Interview 35C]. Hugo argues that the talk of socially constructed boundaries and breaking them down is a white image. In one sense, he has a point. However, not all sociologists who developed our understanding of stratification are white. Instead of a "white image," I would say it is a sociological image. The concept of the socially constructed boundary is a fundamental analytical tool within sociology, as is social stratification. Nevertheless, this conception is much more meaningful to sociologists than it is to everyday people living their normal lives. Now, both Hugo and his friend Lisa are a racial minority, which makes it easier for them to say there never was a boundary between them because they share their minority status, even if they are different in terms of race; but Hugo was far from alone in making this point. Brian is one of many others who made a similar point, saying, *"I never perceived the boundary in the first place. So, I guess I can't answer that because I just don't feel like any boundary was broken down. Even though it might have been, I never pursued the boundary to begin with in terms of Caroline and our friendship"* [Interview 39B]. Notice that Brian acknowledges the point of my question, indicating that there might be a social boundary present even though he never perceived it as such, highlighting the difference between a sociological understanding of the situation and his strictly interpersonal experience of it.

One person who did acknowledge boundaries did so in a way that had more to do with "mental barriers" rather than socially constructed boundaries in the sociological sense. Eva, who is lesbian, speaks of the mental barrier within herself as she struggled to accept her sexual orientation and then be comfortable enough to tell her friends.

> *I don't feel like we really had a barrier or anything to break down. I feel like I just needed to be okay with myself and then be able to express to Nicole a little bit more of who I am by coming out to her. I feel like the barrier was more in me, in getting to that place. I guess it could have been a potential barrier, but Nicole's immediate response of acceptance made the potential barrier just disappear. Actually, when I think about that with another friend of mine—Beth—I think in that case there is a barrier [given her right-wing religious values and prejudices about homosexuality]; but I think Nicole's willingness to accept me, accept this about me, even if it's only to a degree, has helped kind of break apart the barrier, although I think there still may be a little bit of rubble from that barrier* [Interview 36A].

For Eva too, there were no experienced social boundaries. Instead, she faced "mental barriers," both her own—as reflected in her need to come to terms with being lesbian and then working up the courage to tell her friends—and those of her friend Beth (who was not the friend interviewed for this study).

Understanding differences in terms of socially constructed boundaries or social stratification so that groups of people are separated from one another and awarded differing levels of social and economic status as well as levels of power is a useful analytical tool for understanding the macro dimensions of society: the overall social and hierarchical pattern which characterizes any given society. Nonetheless, at the level of interpersonal interaction, such analytical tools have little if any meaning to individuals, except perhaps for sociologists who can't get the big picture out of their own minds. What does matter are the lenses we use when looking at the people around us: our values, attitudes, beliefs, stereotypes, prejudices, and so on—the "mental barriers" cited by Eva above, or the lack thereof—all of which, as discussed in chapter 2, are shaped by our past encounters, group memberships, institutional contexts, and society in general. This again connects us to the bigger picture, but most of us do not think in those terms. Instead, we see ourselves as acting independently from those around us.

None of this is to say that macro sociology is irrelevant to understanding these friendships. As we've seen throughout this book, that is far from the case. Instead, such an analytical framework is used for precisely that: analysis by sociological researchers. Beyond that, it has little meaning or direct influence on individuals in the context of their everyday interactions. Hence, when the contextual factors fall into place—our cultural, institutional, group, and individual contexts—and provide us with the opportunity to meet and befriend those who are different from ourselves in whatever way(s), the rest is up to us irrespective of the existing system of social stratification. Recall that a fundamental characteristic of friendship is equality between the two individuals (Rawlins 2009; Rude 2009; Korgen 2002; Pahl 2000; and Bell 1981). Such equality does not refer to identical positions within the stratification system. Instead, it refers to the perceptions and approach of the individuals befriending one another. Their approach is first and foremost one of dealing with each other as one would deal with any other person irrespective of any differences between them. So when, in interview after interview, the research respondents claimed that there were no boundaries between them, that there was no gap, they were not simply glossing over their friendship to give me an image of a smooth and unblemished relationship. Nor were they ignoring the harsh reality of a world in which there are vast inequalities with tremendous consequences for all groups; they were highly cognizant of the racism, sexism, homophobia, and so on that still exists in our society. Instead, they were revealing their view of the world and the people inhabiting it: a world in which, regardless of the cold facts of stratification, the person standing before them as their friend, while different, was an equal in their eyes. Dennis makes this point flat out when speaking of his friend Ann Marie: *"I mean, I always saw her as an equal"* [Interview 14C].

Acknowledging the point that social boundaries and bridging the gap are fundamentally sociological and not necessarily reflective of the daily, lived experiences of those interviewed, it is still important to understand how these friends have succeeded in a world where such friendships are still relatively rare. The vast majority of the responses[4] had to do with (1) dealing with each other as people rather than as members or representatives of a social category and (2) simply talking about the differences between them, which subsequently allows each friend to see the world from another perspective and learn from the experience. Basically, the friends would confront the difference and then move on with their friendship, although sometimes this required one or both individuals to enter "the comfort zone," which takes time and the development of trust.[5]

Dealing with one another as people is predicated on the friends not even perceiving a socially constructed boundary as a boundary in the first place. Instead of a member of a racial group, or a gender, or a sexual minority, or what have you, they see each other first and foremost as people, which is not the same as the "color blindness" critiqued by other scholars of diverse friendships

(Rawlins 2009; Korgen 2002). This is Matt's conclusion when asked the question about breaking down boundaries and bridging the gap.

> *I guess basically we just deal with each other as people. And when you do that, you can bridge any differences. You're just people regardless of your background or your orientation or your race. Just dealing with someone as another person on that level is probably the best way to bridge a gap together* [Interview 2B].

This point of view—dealing with one another as people—was expressed by both those in a position of privilege, like Matt who is straight referring to his friendship with Sarah who is bisexual, and those who are marginalized, like Lenora who is black when referring to her friendship with Melissa who is white.

> *I think we brought down the racial differences because we were intelligent enough to see past the racial difference and look at the person, the personality and the drive of the person, and you realize that race really doesn't mean anything. What matters is how the person thinks, the way the person is. She's cool and I like her for who she is. I don't care what color she is. So, we maintain our friendship. I think we broke that down and bridged it by just basically maintaining our friendship by making it grow and by just staying in contact with each other. I think I see her race less and less every day* [Interview 5A].

Dealing with one another as people rather than as members of a social category is key to breaking down social boundaries at the interpersonal level.

Talking about the differences between one another was also cited as a reason for the success of these friendships. Almost one-third of the responses[6] focused on talking about the differences and learning to see from the friend's perspective, resulting in the roletaking and "empathy with diverse others" we learned about in the last chapter. In fact, Hugo argues that ignoring the differences or pretending they do not exist or are not relevant is actually more problematic than helpful. *"I think that Debbie and I have never been afraid to talk about it. And I think when you act like the gender difference doesn't exist, it creates more problems. And we know it exists, so we talk about it when we think it's going to create a problem"* [Interview 33C].

In many cases, the friends talk about it when one or another friend is confronted with a challenging situation having to do with the difference between them or by their own ignorance of the other's experience. Consider the friendship between Miriam and Dave. They both bring up talking about their gender difference when it is relevant and, in so doing, they hear from a different perspective and learn from the experience. Miriam poses this in terms of disagreements.

> *First of all, I think our gender difference is not that big of an issue and if there was anything that came up where it would be, like where we had a difference of*

*opinion about something or you know, one of us did something that the other one didn't like, we talk about it. We don't just let something go. If there was something that came up that we didn't like, we would say something about it. He might disagree. He'll definitely give me the male point of view on it, and then I can either take it and agree with it or agree to disagree. So we just talk about it. But to start off with, it's not that much of an issue* [Interview 8A].

Dave focuses less on the disagreements themselves than on the conversations that allow them to see and learn from each other's perspective.

*I think we talk about it and then I get her perspective. Like in the military, we talk about the guys from a woman's perspective and we talk about the guys from the guy's perspective. We talked about the women from the guy's perspective and we talk about the women from the women's perspective. Women tend to pick up on things that men miss and vice versa* [Interview 8B].

While Dave alludes to the learning he gains from listening to Miriam and getting her perspective as a woman, Quinn is much more direct in detailing what he has learned about his own biases from his ongoing conversations with his friend Mike about class and the class difference between them.

*People don't typically make friends outside of their class, but I guess in some ways it's helped me realize that you shouldn't be judgmental about it. If I find out somebody lives in the suburbs, like in an upper middle-class outer suburb and has a decent amount of money, that doesn't necessarily make them a bad person, you know. I realize that the thing is more complicated than that. And in that way, I guess for me anyway, it makes me realize that this struggle doesn't always necessarily have to be about conflict, you know: us against them. There can be cooperation, and a lot can be accomplished with a diplomatic approach. And that's just kind of like a personal insight. I don't know that that's necessarily something that's helped bridged classes in general* [Interview 15A].

Overall, simply talking about the differences is widely used as a strategy by those in these diverse friendships. While it seems obvious, keep in mind that just under a third of the participants mentioned this approach as compared to dealing with each other as people, which represented almost 40 percent of the responses.[7] We live in a society in which it is often considered discourteous to ask questions about what makes us different from one another. Instead, while we are hyperaware of those differences, we pretend they do not exist, which, as Hugo noted above, is more problematic than anything else. Attempting to sweep the differences under the rug within polite society does not allow us the opportunity to learn and grow from these experiences, much less see the world from a perspective that is different from our own.

Because of these norms of polite society which prevent many of us from talking to one another and especially asking questions, it takes a while for us to relax and enter the "comfort zone" in which it is acceptable to talk about the differences. Naturally, this takes time and the development of trust within the friendship. This is true for Bill and Karen with regard to their difference in sexual orientation. In their paired interview, Bill brought up talking about their differences and Karen went on to describe the relevance of their being comfortable with their own sexuality and, presumably, with each other's sexuality—comfortable enough that they can talk about it.

> *BILL: We break down the boundary by talking about it for one thing. That's definitely . . . anything you're unknowing about or uncomfortable with, you talk about it and you learn. That's probably the most important.*
> *KAREN: Yeah, being open and honest about it and just being comfortable enough with who I am and Bill being comfortable enough with who he is that allows us to sit down and be able to talk about it. It's a combination of all those things. We're both comfortable enough in our own sexuality it allows us to be able to sit down and talk openly and honestly* [Interview 12C].

The idea of entering the "comfort zone" is also well described by Eva above when she recounts having to overcome her mental barriers to accepting the fact that she is lesbian. Only then was she able to tell her friend Nicole about her lesbian identity. Overcoming her mental barriers allowed her to enter the "comfort zone" described by Karen. Reaching that zone allowed Eva to simply confront the difference between her and her friend Nicole and then move on.

> *EVA: I think we broke down the boundary just by meeting it head on, just by saying, "Hey, you know what, Nicole, this is who I am," and by Nicole's reaction to that: complete acceptance. I mean, it's amazing. From my perspective, there was no question that I was going to tell Nicole, but there was certainly some anxiety over doing so, and the desire to have everything be okay. But the thing is, you know, it's just not an issue. It's not an issue for us. It's something that we had to bring to the surface and . . .*
> *NICOLE: Yeah, I don't know that there's a whole lot that I could add to that.*
> *EVA: And I'm very grateful and thankful for that.*
> *NICOLE: As am I* [Interview 36C].

Once Eva was comfortable enough to come out and address the difference between her and Nicole, it was like they were "over the hump" and could move on with their friendship. In fact, having this conversation enhanced their relationship, bringing them closer together. Accordingly, talking about the differences, even in a society in which it is not generally considered polite to do so, is of considerable importance. Talking about the differences and dealing with one another as people rather than as members or representatives of a social category, coupled with the interpersonal techniques described in chapter 4, cover the ways in which individuals see their own actions making a difference in breaking down socially constructed boundaries and "bridging the gap." This is where the individuals exercise their own agency, deciding for themselves how they are going to relate to people who are different. In so doing, they raise their social consciousness about issues of race, gender, sexual orientation, class, religion, age, and ability. Moreover, they are better able to roletake with diverse others and develop that "empathy with diverse others" that is crucial to mutual understanding. As we've seen, this becomes a transformative experience for the friends who then can become rolemodels for others. Such consciousness and empathy—as well as the transformative action and rolemodeling—are key components of the social affinity that lies at the heart of social cohesion (Vela-McConnell 1999). We'll explore more of these connections below.

From a sociologist's perspective, though, the individuals are only part of the story. One must also consider the social context in which these friendships occur, as discussed in chapter 2. Such contextual factors are often beyond the awareness of the individuals who actually act through that context, much as a fish is not likely to notice the water in which it swims. There were very few exceptions to this point. Only four people[8] made any reference to the social context in which these friendships occur. It is the sociological perspective that reminds us that our social context first provides us with the opportunity to meet and befriend those who are different from ourselves. These opportunities are a necessary step in breaking down the social boundaries and bridging our differences.

## Friendship and Bridging Ties

We have seen how demographic differences represent socially constructed boundaries that divide people based upon them. Our cultural values and belief systems, such as the idea that men and women cannot really just be friends, serve to create these invisible, but no less profound boundaries. These boundaries are then made more concrete in our institutional arrangements, such as our work environments where those with different levels of education are separated one from another through status and even the spatial arrangement of the office. Our neighborhoods are highly segregated by class and, despite all efforts to the contrary, largely segregated by race, and sometimes even by religion, age, and sexual orientation. Such divisions cannot help but carry over into our own social circles and groups, as evidenced by the data presented at the beginning of this book indicating how homogenous our social circles, particularly friendship circles, tend to be.

As argued in chapter 1, these micro and macro level divisions weaken the social affinity that is required for a cohesive society in which diverse groups of people are brought together through a sense of mutual obligation and reciprocity. Using the terminology of Robert Putnam (2000), we have historically pursued the bonding social capital that strengthens the solidarity within homogenous in-groups of people at the expense of out-groups and neglected the bridging social capital that creates broader connections among many diverse peoples. However, studying diverse friendships allows us to learn how such bridging ties can be established at the micro level of interpersonal interaction, effectively tearing down the socially constructed boundaries that segregate one group from another one relationship at a time. Friendship ties are only one of many possible mechanisms promoting bridging social capital and social cohesion and these interpersonal bonds are insufficient in and of themselves in contrast to the claim made by Spencer and Pahl (2006) and noted in chapter 1. Nevertheless, as dyadic relationships, friendships represent the fundamental building blocks of larger groups and ultimately social structure itself (Simmel 1950) by providing connections to larger, interlocking social networks that are fundamental to society (Putnam 2000), making the study of friendships sociologically significant. Thus, with an eye toward the more general issue of social cohesion, the guiding question in this book has been to explore how those who have close friendships with diverse others establish and maintain those social bonds.

In chapter 1, I argued that, in order to reach the potential of diverse friendships to strengthen social affinity and forge the micro-level social bonds required for macro-level social cohesion, two conditions must be met: at the structural level, there must be opportunities to meet diverse others and, at the interpersonal level, the individuals involved must be able to bridge or tear down the socially constructed boundaries that exist in society such that feelings of anxiety, fear, or prejudice do not interfere in their relationship. Accordingly, breaking down these social boundaries created by demographic differences requires an approach that extends from the structural level all the way down to the interpersonal level and back again, recognizing the fact that these are mutually reinforcing (Binder 2009; Hewstone 2005). It will require "a concerted effort on the structural and the individual level to greatly increase opportunities" for diverse friendships (Korgen 2002, 103), and ultimately to foster and strengthen social cohesion.

Starting with the structural level of analysis, recall that 82.5 percent of the friends studied met within diverse institutional settings (see chapter 2). Given this pattern, it is clear that structural changes that promote diversity and intergroup contact must continue. Only then can the positive role of intergroup contact exert its influence, reducing levels of prejudice and opening the door for individual-level openness to increasingly integrated social settings. Recognizing the "friendship potential" identified by Pettigrew (1997) and prefigured by Allport (1954) as a condition for favorable intergroup contact, we also need to acknowledge the specific "potential of friends" to reinforce—and perhaps even function as a catalyst for—social change. These relationships foster a common in-group identity between the two friends that replaces the dichotomy between "us" and "them" with a unified "us" (Gaertner and Dovidio 2005; Rude 2009).

There has been much empirical support for the positive impact of intergroup contact, but the results are not definitive. The benefits of intergroup contact are often circumvented by the "spontaneous self-segregation" of people in social settings that are otherwise "optimal for intergroup contact" (Tredoux and Finchilescu 2007). Such self-segregation typically occurs as a result of intergroup anxiety and what are called meta-stereotypes (Finchilescu 2005; Goff, Steele, Davies 2008): the fear on the part of in-group members that those in the out-group believe that they themselves are prejudiced in some way and this fear prevents the members of the in-group from connecting with members of the out-group. Consequently, bringing together diverse groups of people is not always effective in bridging socially constructed boundaries. And the fact that social distance is often entrenched within systems of power (Rawlins 2009) is admittedly daunting. Nevertheless, there are sufficient and increasing numbers of success stories to engender a sense of hope and optimism and the friendships studied here clearly demonstrate that socially constructed boundaries are not insurmountable.

Those who want to create a world in which social boundaries no longer exist despite our differences need to be cognizant of both the structural and interpersonal dimensions of division within society. They need to confront the value and belief systems we have so well internalized that focus on the differences between various groups of people to the exclusion of all we have in common. They need to continue to chip away at the segregation that has hold of our institutional settings, re-conceptualizing how we can organize social life in such a way that does not require the separation of groups based on status. They also need to promote a group culture that is accepting of diversity within their social circles.

Yes, the larger social context is of crucial importance (Allan and Adams 1998; Adams and Allan 1998) in bringing people from diverse backgrounds together; but this point is not intended to minimize the relevance of the interpersonal efforts to break down socially constructed boundaries and bridge the gap. In fact, these efforts represent a critical step, although they can occur only after structural conditions have been met. As seen in chapter 2, there must first be opportunities to meet and interact at a personal level in order to befriend those who are demographically different from ourselves. Once the opportunity presents itself, individuals are then able to act through their situational context, guided by their own personal experiences, values, attitudes, beliefs, and so on and then by the interpersonal techniques employed by *both* parties within the friendship. Hence, there is an interplay between the structural context on the one hand and individual agency and interpersonal dynamics on the other which either promote or prohibit the emergence of friendships that cross the lines of social stratification within our society. The pieces at all levels of social context— from the structural to the interpersonal—have to fall into place in some very specific ways in order to promote the emergence of these relationships, which may explain why there are comparatively few such friendships. As our society changes in favor of greater equality and integration, however, the number of such friendships has begun to increase (Korgen 2002). This trend is reinforced by individual willingness to participate in these friendships. As will be discussed at the end of this chapter, this emerging trend in turn may actually promote further social change in our system of stratification, setting up a self-reinforcing cycle that will ultimately challenge the current stratification system.

Sociologists recognize that social stratification is a fundamental aspect of every known society. In other words, despite all the utopian visions written about in the past, such as St. Thomas More's *Utopia* (1516/1964), we cannot imagine a realistic social system that is not stratified in some kind of way. Perhaps this view is what gave rise to the dystopic visions of subsequent writers, such as Aldous Huxley who wrote *Brave New World* (1932). The fact that social stratification will be present, though, does not require that this system be static. In fact, stratification does change over time: it changes form and it ebbs and flows so that it is sometimes much more vertical and at other times more horizontal. Alan Wolfe highlights the benefits we receive from a certain amount of social stratification and the accompanying presence of social boundaries:

> In the absence of social boundaries, . . . we could never belong to anything with texture and character. Yet if the boundaries between particular groups are too rigid, we would have no general obligations. . . . We would live together with people exactly like ourselves, unexposed to the challenges of strangers, the lure of cosmopolitanism, and the expansion of moral possibility that comes with responsiveness to the generalized other (1992, 311-312).

Nevertheless, the fact that social boundaries and social stratification exist and are an integral part of all social systems does not mean that we are expected to stand by and accept their negative consequences. Even Wolfe notes that "boundaries are both here to stay but also here to be crossed" (1992, 323). The friendships included in this book represent a highly effective means of crossing these socially constructed boundaries and challenging the stratification system as it currently exists.

## Do Our Friendships Make a Difference?

Earlier in the chapter, I highlighted how the individuals within these friendships consider one another to be equals irrespective of the social stratification system existing within our society—a system of inequality. In other words, the reality of stratification and inequality that exists within society as a whole has little to no bearing on the way in which these individuals perceive and treat one another because, while understanding that social stratification is highly useful analytically speaking, it has little direct bearing or meaning for these individuals as they interact with one another in their daily lives. It is this same casual approach that allows these individuals to interact as equals regardless of the reality of social stratification. Recall from chapter 2 how Jerry described Bob and him as being "thoughtlessly friends" [Interview 11B]. This is precisely the approach taken by all the people studied: they are in effect saying, "Despite the fact that, in the larger scheme of things, there are very real inequalities between us, we are going to completely disregard that reality and create one of our own, one in which we are *in fact* equals." It is this blatant disregard for the larger reality of social stratification that poses a direct threat to such a system. In classic sociological understanding, definitions have very real consequences. And in this case, individuals are defining each other as equals. In so doing, they are creating a reality that is in direct opposition to the existing system of social stratification. They are posing a direct challenge to the reality of social inequality by refusing to accept that reality and instead pursuing an alternate reality in which equality does exist.

Remember the point made by sociologist Ray Pahl that there is pressure within stratified societies to "avoid the formation of friendships between social unequals" (2000, 162). The reason is that such friendships undermine the legitimacy of such inequality. Rawlins argues that "pursuing equality" characterizes friendships and represents an ethical practice of friendship. At the same time, the pursuit of such equality within friendships represents a political practice and outcome. As such, the equality that characterizes friendships is an important tool for effecting social change: "Standing as equals embodies a challenge to hierarchical social structures. The tendency of friendships toward equal treatment is therefore a fundamental political potential. . . . It flies in the face of the status quo" (2009, 194). This is why those who benefit from the stratification system often discourage friendships between those of differing social status (Hutter 1978; Rawlins 2009). This sense of equality and the challenge it poses to the status quo is not simply an ideal. Allport first documented the positive effects of equality in reducing prejudice as well as the reverse: "differential status . . . is an active factor in creating and maintaining prejudice" (1954, 274). Given its obvious importance, Allport identified status equality as one of his four conditions allowing for the reduction of prejudice in his nascent intergroup contact theory.

While any single friendship is basically a private relationship between two people, it is still witnessed by the people around those individuals. Moreover, as these friendships crossing the lines of stratification and based on equality increase in numbers, a *pattern* of interpersonal relations emerges that is also witnessed by the people around them. Such a pattern becomes a tacit public statement calling the system of stratification into question at its most fundamental level. While still relatively rare, these friendships represent a counter culture (Pahl 2000)—a culture of equality that exists in direct opposition to the larger society characterized by inequality. As noted in chapter 1, such a counter culture poses a threat to the established and taken-for-granted order of our larger society and has the potential to move our society in the direction of increased egalitarianism.

The threat posed by friendships that successfully bridge the socially constructed differences of race, gender, sexual orientation, and so on is a grassroots form of opposition to the prevailing status quo. In other words, it starts with the friends themselves. Beyond that, the friends represent potential role models for those in their social circle and for those strangers who simply witness their friendship. Their larger social circles are generally supportive of the friendship, which might make one question the effectiveness of such friendships as role models paving the way for a more equitable society. Still, just because these social circles are more tolerant does not mean that such boundary-crossing friendships are common within them. In fact, it varies. While some social circles are tolerant, they often have no other examples of such friendships. The potential for role modeling is much higher in these social circles. In other group contexts, such diverse friendships abound and are mutually reinforcing, providing higher levels of support for diverse friendship networks.

Given the potential of these friendships to create social change from the bottom up, I asked the interviewees whether they thought that friendships like theirs make a difference in this world of inequality. Their perceptions, even if inaccurate, are informative regarding how people feel about their ability to create change in society. Moreover, I also asked if they had any specific examples of how their friendship may have had an impact on those around them. Some, like Adam, expressed initial surprise that this could even be a possibility: *"Wow, could we be that important? I can't imagine. I suppose it's possible. I just never thought of us as being poster children"* [Interview 31B]. Nonetheless, such surprise quickly gave way to sometimes tentative and at other times quite confident responses. As one might expect, there was a full spectrum of responses.[9]

Those who felt that their friendships made no difference provided very practical explanations for why they thought so, starting with simple visibility, as when Janine said, *"Well, most people think I'm straight"* [Interview 20B]. The issue of visibility was first brought up in chapter 3 in the context of the conceptual model for understanding social boundaries. Visibility was one of two dimensions for distinguishing socially constructed boundaries in terms of their impact on the friendship itself. Some social boundaries, like race and gender in most cases, are instantly recognized by visible cues while others, like sexual orientation and religion, are not so readily apparent. In the context of the friendship itself, invisible differences required self-disclosure in order to be made visible. This is also relevant here. If the difference between the friends is not visible to outsiders, how are outsiders to know of it and perhaps benefit from the presence of a friendship crossing that particular social boundary? Janice is also quite aware of the relevance of invisibility with regard to sexual orientation, as is her friend Barbara.

> *I think the problem is that it's not an obvious thing where they can look at us and say, "Oh, gay-straight," you know. If you're black-white, it's obvious. There is nothing that necessarily distinguishes a person who's homosexual and*

*so people may not ever realize that here's two people who have a friendship across that boundary. It may never occur to them. That's why I think it is important for people to be out, and I know that's hard for people, but I think it's important, although that's easy for me to say* [Interview 22C].

Deborah felt the same way with regard to the religious difference between herself and Fatima.

*I don't think our personal relationship has made an impact, because we're not that visible to that many people. There are probably lots of closet Jewish-Muslim relationships out there. I don't know. I hope that at some point those kinds of relationships do change perspectives of people, but I don't think our relationship has. I mean, I don't think so* [Interview 17A].

Before their friendships can make a difference, those who are crossing invisible boundaries like sexual orientation and religion have to make their differences known to others.

Even if the differences between friends are obvious, as in most cases of cross-racial and cross-gender friendships, outside witnesses have to actually be thinking about those differences at the level of the interpersonal relationship *and* in light of the macro dimensions of the social boundaries in society. Some of those who felt that their friendships made no difference had little confidence in the ability of those around them to be thinking out the issue so closely. Kris and Kim both feel this way.

*KRIS: I don't know. I mean I guess I would be inclined to say no in that most people aren't that analytical about it and say, "Oh, look at their friendship and . . ."*
*KIM: I'm just saying that I've never really thought about it, and if I had to say that people think about it, I'd be like, "Wow, do people really think about this"* [Interview 37C]?

Kris and Kim don't believe that people really pay all that much attention. Neither does Barbara: *"I would hope our friendship would [make a difference], but I just don't know if it does. I would like to think that people would look and say, 'Oh, look how this works. They're great friends and it doesn't matter.' But I just don't think people pay enough attention or think deeply enough about that type of stuff"* [Interview 22B].

Others, like Colin, look at the evidence in the world around them. He doesn't see race relations improving all that much, so logically speaking, how can friendships like his with Kelly be making a difference?

*Our friendship is nothing new. I mean, there are hundreds of millions of people who have had friendships based on differences of race, gender, or whatever; but we still have some of the same problems from the same wounds thirty, forty*

*years ago. So I guess, being white you can afford to be more optimistic and say,*
*"Hey it's going to work out and it's going to get better." And it's like, no, it's*
*not getting better. No, we're not getting beat up, but now we can't get a job. So,*
*the problem is still here* [Interview 1C].

While Colin is overestimating the number of friendships that cross socially constructed boundaries like race, he does have a point with regard to the state of
race relations. While the overt racism of the Jim Crow Era is largely a thing of
the past, that does not mean that racism and other forms of prejudice are not
present in much more subtle but no less pernicious forms.

Colin doesn't believe that their one friendship, out of the many that are out
there, could possibly make a difference in and of itself. The same could be said
of many of those who don't believe their friendship can make a difference in
society. Irene is of the same opinion except that she pictures her friendship with
Bao as adding to the larger phenomenon of friendships crossing the racial
boundary.

*I don't think we're changing the world by being friends and I don't think peo-*
*ple are going to be like, "Oh, I just saw a black woman and an Asian woman*
*together. That was beautiful." You know? I just don't think like anything that*
*significant is going to happen, but I think that the more you see it, the more*
*normal it becomes and the fewer head turns you'll get. I think it just kind of*
*adds to the hundreds of other relationships that are interracial that people see*
*and are starting to become more accepting of* [Interviews 19B and 19C].

This is where a glimmer of optimism enters the picture. While acknowledging
that, in the big picture, their one friendship does not make that big a difference,
Irene recognizes that it does contribute to the visibility of interracial friendships
taken *as a whole*. Taken together, these friendships exemplify a cultural shift
toward increased tolerance. Bao agrees with her friend Irene in terms of the big
picture, but she also acknowledges the relevance of the small picture.

*Yeah, I agree in terms of society itself: I don't think our friendship makes a dif-*
*ference. But I think in terms of our personal lives maybe it does, including our*
*families or whoever and we're role modeling for our nieces and nephews or*
*brothers and sisters or whatever. I think it does have an impact on them, you*
*know. But in terms of society, like Irene said, I don't think they're looking at us*
*and thinking, "Wow, they can be friends"* [Interview 19C]!

This is the crux of the issue and it is the same for most social problems. When
we as individuals think of the big picture of racism, sexism, homophobia, and so
on, we feel daunted and overwhelmed by the sheer size and complexity of the
problem, not to mention a very long history. We wonder what a single individual or pair of friends could possibly do in the face of such a vast problem as racism, for example. We think that, unless we're a Rev. Martin Luther King, Jr. or

a Rosa Parks, we can't possibly make a difference. We feel ineffectual and powerless; what social psychologists have termed "learned helplessness."

We see ourselves as having power or relevance only within the limited circle of our own lives and those with whom we come into contact, and sometimes not even then. Sam's view of the relevance of his friendship represents this perspective. *"On a micro level, sure [we can make a difference]; but to overturn racism in this vast country, no. But for every other person who sees our friendship, they might wonder and might ask. With any person that I might engage in a conversation about race, I hope to have some kind of impact there"* [Interview 30C]. Suzanne also has little faith in her and her friend Jenny's ability to change society through their example.

> *I think our friendship has an impact on the people who are close, but when you say the word society . . . I have such a disdain for society, because how do you change it? You don't. It changes so slowly. How do you make changes? It's just hard. So, that's too global* [Interview 13A].

Lenora is yet another person who fits this pattern.

> *I really don't think it's making a difference. Maybe it's helping some of the people around us, maybe making them think, "If she has a relationship with her, why can't I?" So, maybe it's helping people around us, but I don't think it's helping the world or the culture in the United States. We don't have access to go other places with our friendship and tell people about it or show people how we attract each other. We don't even think, "Maybe we should show people how we act." We don't think about that on a conscious level. We just interact with each other here* [Interview 5A].

Lenora is alluding to how she does not believe that she and Melissa have any power to systematically influence other people and change their perceptions. She just sees Melissa and her living their lives and pursuing their friendship without conscious intention to set an example for others. She feels that without such intent and the ability to reach a wide audience, she and Melissa could not possibly hope to make a difference in the larger scheme of things.

This is where there is an error in our thinking. We assume that, in order to address a macro problem like racism, sexism, or homophobia, we have to address it at the macro level and only at that level, a sort of top down approach. This is where placing our heroes on well-deserved pedestals does us a disservice. Figures like Rev. Martin Luther King, Jr. appear to us as demi-gods who were at the very top of their respective movements and, with almost supernatural ability, were able to make changes at the highest levels while everyone else simply followed along. This, however, could not be further from the reality of the situation. As Howard Zinn describes in his book *You Can't Be Neutral on a Moving Train* (1994), such movements have their roots in average, everyday people like you and me. Such movements were *grassroots* movements, coming from the bottom up, not from the top down. Heroes like Rev. Martin Luther King, Jr. and Rosa Parks were carried up in a much, much larger wave comprised of thousands of people. They did not act alone and they did not even start out as leaders. Instead, they *emerged* from the masses of other people and became symbols of a much larger movement. These masses of other people were already struggling in their everyday lives before there ever was a "movement," simply trying to live their lives as they saw fit. That is no different from those I interviewed who were "thoughtlessly" pursuing their friendships despite the fact that those friendships cross various social boundaries. Simply because they are living out their everyday lives does not mean that their actions, their friendships, are not radical when compared to overall friendship trends. Recall Adam's initial surprise by my question: *"Wow, could we be that important"* [Interview 31B]? The answer is yes, and that would surprise many of those who were interviewed who, through no fault of their own beyond that "learned helplessness," simply take the larger implications of their friendships for granted.

The optimistic 43 percent of those interviewed did appreciate that their friendships can be influential, recognizing that even influencing the people around them makes a difference. While it might not change the whole world overnight, they, like Frank, see their friendships as mattering: *"While our one friendship isn't going to change the world, I think other friends of ours would say, 'You know, it's awesome that you're good friends' and that they would open their mind more to being friends with somebody of another race"* [Interview 21A]. When those interviewed spoke of "opening people's minds," they weren't just referring to people in a position of privilege. These friendships opened the minds of *both* the privileged and the marginalized who thought that such friendships were not possible. Dave, referring back to a party attended by many gay men, but at which he had a straight male friend as well, tells how his gay friends could not believe the straight one was really straight.

> *I think that you change perceptions on both sides of the fence, and I think that we changed the perceptions of about fifteen different people on my side of the fence, which I think was important for them. I think there was some role modeling and they realized, "Oh, yes. You can have [straight] friends and you can have . . . da da da da* [Interview 6C].

Melissa says much the same thing about her friend Lenora's other friends.

> *[A lot of Lenora's black friends] haven't gotten that close to white people before. Even though Lenora was the initial one to be like, "Okay, I accept Melissa," her friends were given a more intimate opportunity to see what kind of person I am, and they don't have to make the big choice of whether or not they can hang out with me. In their head, they're thinking, "Okay, Melissa's different than most white girls." But, in the end it's just the same revelation that Lenora had: who's to say this [white] girl's not different and everyone can hang out together? It's like they see it. I think sometimes the more you see it,*

*the more comfortable you get and then the more comfortable you are with do-*
*ing it yourself* [Interview 5B].

The benefit of these friendships is not just for one group or the other. It benefits those on both sides of the socially constructed boundary.

In expressing their optimism about their friendships making a difference, the vast majority spoke about it at a theoretical level without concrete examples. Brad is typical in that way.

*If friendships like ours didn't exist, change wouldn't happen. I firmly believe I*
*can be a catalyst. I can create awareness. I can paint a picture or whatever. I*
*think we see a very human thing. If you have somebody that you really love*
*dearly and you see something that's hurting them, you're going to be much*
*more willing to say, "Well, let's do something about it," you know. I think that*
*when you have that experience of somebody you know and they're hurting, then*
*you're going to get your ass in gear* [Interview 7C].

The abstract quality of Brad's response is immediately apparent: he believes, *in theory,* that his friendship with Eric has an impact on those around them. While very confident in their responses, most of those interviewed who said that their friendships made a difference actually had a difficult time when asked if they could provide an example where this has happened, an observation that is consistent with past research on diverse friendships (Rude 2009). Perhaps because the impact, in most cases, would be invisible, as in a change in attitudes and perceptions, it easily slips by undetected.

On the other hand, a few were able to provide such examples. Immediately following Brad's statement above, Eric gave a more concrete example focusing on his sons and what they learn from their father who has a very close friend who is gay.

*I think of my sons in particular, the generation coming up. They know that I*
*have a friend who's gay, okay. They hear a different kind of conversation. With*
*other friends of mine, they may be closed to sexual orientation, but because*
*they're open to me, that gives a wedge where it throws some doubt into their*
*minds with what they do* [Interview 7C].

Mark provided a much more in-depth example of his friendship with Dave making a difference for others in his social circle.

*Oh, yeah, absolutely. Our friendship breaks down barriers, which is a cliché of*
*sorts, but it really does, especially given the military culture where we met. I*
*mean, it's obviously made a difference in my life as far as the way I look at*
*things. I think when he and his partner came to my wedding, those guys who*
*were there in their dress uniforms, all the other military guys, I think maybe*
*they changed a little bit. That was a pretty manly, testosterone-ridden crowd*
*there—classically masculine. The first thing these guys would have expected*

*me to do would be to not invite Dave and his partner. You know, we talked about that. My mother asked, "Well, how do you want to handle it?" I said, "Just like everybody else. You send an invitation for two, and if his partner doesn't want to come, that's fine; but make it be their decision and not ours, because I don't want to alienate them." And I think when they came to the wedding and my other friends saw that, they said, "Hmm, well if that jackass can do it . . ." or "If he has a friend who's gay, then maybe it's not that bad." I don't know if that's the case or not, but I suspect a lot of them were like that. So, I'm not going to claim that it made a big difference in any of their lives, but the fact that Dave and his partner came and nobody made a big deal out of it when I thought some of them would, I mean they all said great things, "Wow, what nice dudes." Maybe that was forwarding the process a bit. Nobody said anything bad; nobody made any remark* [Interviews 10B and 10C].

Recall that Mark's own attitudes toward gay men were challenged when Dave came out to him years after they first met and even lived together. Recognizing the change that he himself has gone through, he is much more conscious of the fact that a situation like the wedding he describes would pose a similar challenge for his straight, military buddies. He believes that, if he could change his own attitudes, then these other guys certainly should be able to as well.

Nicole, who is straight, provides another concrete example about how her friendship with Eva makes a difference.

*I think absolutely that friendships like ours make a difference. I think the fact that I'm friends with people who are straight, who maybe aren't aware that they know people who are gay, but they know me. And when it comes up, I share with them. "Hey . . . ," you know. This is my philosophy on that and I invite my gay friends to parties at my house with my straight friends, and maybe straight friends who haven't had gay friends in the past, but it forces some interaction and they meet new people. It starts to just raise awareness for people that, "Wow, I guess maybe I do know some gay people." I think it helps people to realize that there are gay people all around you and they're just like you. I think it's a big help and if people don't have friends who are different in that way, then society will never change. So, I think it definitely has an impact and makes it just seem more normal and makes people get more comfortable* [Interviews 36B & 36C].

Nicole recognizes the value of "cross-pollinating" different groups of people. When gays and straights get the opportunity to interact on a level playing field, they are given the chance to see each other as people very much like themselves. This in turn increases everyone's comfort level and opens the door for a change in attitudes that can further affect other social relations outside of that social circle, like ripples in a pond (Rude 2009). Therefore, what sets those who are optimistic about the impact of their friendships on the world around them apart is their awareness that, even within the confines of their own, limited social circles, they can make a wider difference in a kind of chain reaction. Within their own individual spheres of influence, they can make a difference in the attitudes of others; but the change does not necessarily stop there. It can keep going as these others change their own behavior, influencing their own social circles. This is known as the "extended contact effect" (Wright *et al.* 1997). Through such overlapping social circles, it is possible to create changes within the larger society. It may take time and it may be incremental, but they firmly believe that their friendships ultimately make a difference in the world, challenging the system of social stratification.

While discussed in the abstract, sociologists have largely neglected this challenge to the societal status quo posed by the informal social ties of friendship (Allan and Adams 1998).[10] The research presented here is intended to fill part of the gap by focusing on how these friendships counter the "wider divisions" present between diverse groups of people. These unlikely friendships represent a countervailing force against that "society of strangers" I described in my past research by establishing solidarity and social cohesion in the face of very real social boundaries within our stratified society.

Establishing the social affinity that is required for strong social bonds and bridging ties depends on establishing social consciousness, sentiment, and action (Vela-McConnell 1999), all of which are present in the diverse friendships studied. Educating and learning about one's friend and his or her experiences as a member of a socially constructed category raises our social consciousness regarding the social boundaries in our society and how those boundaries are experienced in individuals' day-to-day lives. As noted in chapter 4, this makes it possible to identify and empathize with one's friend, what Rude identifies as "racial empathy" (2009) and might be better labeled "empathy with diverse others" given the multiple boundaries included in this research. Such roletaking with a single, concrete other makes it possible to then empathize with the collective other—the entire group represented by that friend (Vela-McConnell 1999). In other words, it is possible to generalize our emotional connection with a single individual to an entire group of people, increasing the number of potential bridging ties. Finally, these diverse friends take action at multiple levels. At the most basic level, such learning is potentially transformative for the individual friend. As noted by Rawlins, "No learning of consequence occurs within [diverse] friendships without changes in the person involved—and there is no meaningful change in people without integrating new knowledge into our lives" (2009, 156). Moreover, the two friends model diverse friendships simply by existing and being witnessed by those around them, people who might not have thought such friendships likely or possible. At the most active end of the spectrum, one or another friend may actually intervene and challenge those who object to such friendships or the relevant out-group itself. In this way, this research confirms the claim Rawlins made in his discussion of the social change potential of friendships: "The personal *is* political. Our daily actions can promote freedom and justice in small and large ways" (2009, 193). These friendships bring social consciousness, sentiment, and action together, sparking social affinity and the creation of social ties that bridge socially constructed boundaries. In this way, the social cohesion that is fundamental to the health of society is strengthened.

Insofar as the majority of close friendships are between those who are demographically similar to each other, the social status differences between the diverse groups within the population are upheld and reinforced, sustaining our stratified social order. As observed by Allan and Adams, "Just as friendships take on characteristics of the cultural, economic, and social settings in which they arise, equally these ties are consequential in helping sustain the order there is within these settings. With changes in the dominant social formation, the patterns of friendship alter, and most significantly alter in ways which reflect the external changes occurring" (1998, 191). The fact that there are indications that friendships extending across at least some demographic categories are on the rise (see chapter 1) indicates, much like a barometer, that there are changes occurring within the social order of our society. At the same time, these friendships are in the minority and are bucking the larger trend that follows the pattern of segregation and social inequality. So these friendships pose a challenge to our social order insofar as it continues to distinguish status differences based on race, gender, sexual orientation, class, religion, age, and ability. This challenge arises out of the sense of equality that characterizes friendships: "Standing as equal embodies a challenge to hierarchical social structures" (Rawlins 2009, 194). These friendships then represent a counter-culture challenging the status quo (Pahl 2000), corroborating the idea that "friendships can motivate valuable social change" (Goering 2003, 406). As the counter culture gains ground, it is likely to further dismantle the stratification system within our society. The relationship between social context and individual choice is not a one-way street. Yes, it is true that individual "choices are not made in isolation" (Allan and Adams 1998, 190) and are thus significantly shaped through social context. These interpersonal relationships that challenge the socially constructed boundaries within society must be coupled with structural changes (Korgen 2002; Rude 2009) in order to be truly transformative. It is equally true that individual choices, when taken in their cumulative effect, are not without consequence. We cannot pretend that individual choices make no difference in the larger scheme of things. Taken separately, individual choices seem to be overwhelmed by more global social processes. Taken together, they form a pattern that, when large enough, may reach a "tipping point" (Gladwell 2002) and fundamentally alter the social context in which they occur.

In sociological terms, these optimistic friends recognize the interconnection between the micro and the macro social order such that what happens at one level of analysis will certainly reverberate within the other. Yes, this is a two-way street: these friendships are never removed from their larger social context. What happens in our social world—whether it be the Defense of Marriage kind of backlash we have seen in the last number of years, our perceptions of Muslims in a post-9/11 world, or a ruling by the Supreme Court on school integration—has ramifications for our personal lives and interpersonal relationships. Nevertheless, these research participants doggedly avoid a deterministic view of the world, a view in which individuals are merely swept along by larger social forces. Instead, they recognize the value of human agency, the ability of individuals to *act* in this world and, in so doing, to shape the world around them.[11] All friendships connect individuals to one another, "integrating individuals structurally" (Allan and Adams 1998, 184). The friendships studied here— friendships crossing socially constructed boundaries like race, gender, sexual orientation, class, religion, age, and ability—perhaps serve this structural integration function even more fully insofar as they connect those who are marginalized within our society to those in a position of privilege. As such, they represent a defense against the social disorganization feared by many sociologists, including myself. These unlikely friendships are like open arms, allowing the marginalized—those kept at the periphery of society—to become full and equal participants in that same society. Starting at the micro level of interpersonal relations, these friendships reverberate throughout society, posing a challenge to the system of social stratification that would keep these groups at the periphery.

# Notes

1. Forty-three of 80 responses, or 54.75 percent.
2. Representing 16.25 percent of the total responses (n=80).
3. Three out of 80 responses, or 3.75 percent.
4. Seventy percent of the 111 different responses.
5. Confronting the difference and allowing for one or both individuals to enter "the comfort zone" together account for an additional 14 percent of the 111 different responses.
6. Thirty-one percent of the 111 responses.
7. Thirty-nine percent of the 111 responses.
8. Out of the 111 responses, or 4 percent.
9. Only 17 percent (13 of 77 responses) felt that their friendships made no difference, while 43 percent (33 of 77 responses) thought that it did, at least within the limited circle of their lives. Another 36 percent (28 of 77 responses) fell somewhere in the middle, saying "it depends," "it's possible," or "I hope so," more tentative answers that still moved in the affirmative direction, expressing at least the potential for friendships like theirs to make a difference.
10. For example, Allan and Adams note that, "Outside childhood ties, sociologists have in the main failed to analyze at all fully how ethnicity affects informal solidarities, or indeed how informal relations of friendship help sustain or counter wider divisions" (1998, 185). Beyond race and ethnicity, I would add that research on how gender, sexual orientation, class, religion, age, and ability affect informal solidarities like friendship has also been neglected.
11. This view is consistent with the perspective of Allan and Adams, although these sociologists seem to give more weight to determinism rather than human agency: "[O]ne

of the key aspects of friendships is the way they serve to integrate individuals structurally . . . But if friendships play a part in integrating individuals structurally, they are in turn circumscribed by contextual factors. They cannot be socially significant without also being moulded by both the immediate and more abstracted environments in which they are developed and sustained" (1998, 184).

# *Afterword*

# "Some of My Best Friends Are . . ."

One of the ideas inspiring this research was the all-too-common phrase we hear tossed around in conversations having to do with diversity: "Some of my best friends are _____." Then we fill in the blank with whatever marginalized group happens to be the focus of the conversation. As a social psychologist, I have always found this phrase rather amusing given its not-so-subtle role in our efforts at impression management, particularly since it is usually intended to send one message ("See how open-minded I am.") but is often interpreted very differently: "Here's a person who's desperately trying to compensate for his or her racism, sexism, homophobia, or what have you." In this way, denials of prejudice are accomplished in an equivocating and vague manner, a rather common approach (van Dijk 1992 and Billig 1988; see also Barnes, Palmary, and Durrheim 2001). Given how much there is to say about the social psychology of using such a phrase, I thought it would be interesting to hear how the research participants reacted to its use. So, when concluding the paired interviews, I asked them what impression they had of those who use the phrase "some of my best friends are _____." While most had an immediate negative reaction, there were many nuanced responses as well. Here I will represent the full spectrum of their responses and include my own commentary on the use of that phrase.

Some of those interviewed found the phrase itself to be odd and wondered why anyone would say such a thing. Keosha simply comments, *"I don't understand why you would do that. I wouldn't, even though a lot of my friends are white, you know"* [Interview 18C]. And Katie says, *"That's a weird thing to say"* [Interview 4C]. Nikki takes this question one step further, wondering *"What's their point when they say that? Why point that out? Why say that? What's the basis of asking the question"* [Interview 3C]? All of these are good questions and valid observations about the use of the phrase. In responding to that question from a social psychological perspective, we recognize that what we say to others has more to say about ourselves and how we would like others to perceive us than the actual claim being made in the statement itself.

Our appearance and manner are very important aspects of our presentation of self to others (Goffman 1959) because they provide others—our audience—with an idea of who we are as a person. So, there's a lot we can do to convey information about ourselves simply by manipulating our appearance and manner. Still, there's some information that is difficult to convey in these ways. When we wish to convey information about ourselves that might otherwise remain hidden, we engage in "dramatic realization" (Lemert and Branaman 1997). The phrase "some of my best friends are . . ." represents an attempt at dramatic realization insofar as it is intended to signal the audience about our open-minded character. As noted by others who were interviewed, the function of saying such a thing is to make a claim about one's personal attitudes. Janice acknowledges that she does hear people say that and tries to be understanding of it.

> *[Those who say it are] trying to prove that they are open-minded. They want you to think well of them or something. You do hear it in conversations, so it's not like it's totally out of bounds; but still it's like somebody's putting forward a message that is trying to convince you of something* [Interview 22C].

Quinn points out that, if taken at face value, using the phrase "some of my best friends are . . ." lends some credibility to what the individual is saying.

> *If some of your best friends or a significant number of people that you associate with are of, you know, fill-in-the-blank group, I think it does give you more credibility in terms of speaking to what's going on. You certainly can't identify completely with that group because you're not part of it; but I do genuinely feel that it gives people more credibility. It doesn't give you license to be an offensive jerk, but . . . because you do have a certain relationship with a certain social group, you do know a bit more at least than somebody else* [Interview 16C].

The lingering question, and a question that is on many people's minds (the majority of those interviewed, for example), is whether the use of this phrase can ever be taken at face value.

What begins to cast doubt in our eyes is when people use the phrase as a sort of badge of honor that presumably elevates them higher than their audience members. Ann Marie literally describes it in this way: a badge of honor. *"Some people are like, 'I have friends that are gay' and it's like, you know, 'Good for you' kind of thing when some people are kind of wearing it as a badge, you know. Like, 'I'm so great, I have [gay friends]'"* [Interview 14C]. At this point, we begin to wonder how much of the claim is simply hollow pretense. Perhaps some of this doubt, as Sarah illustrates, stems from our knowledge of the times we've made such claims ourselves.

*I grew up in a pretty much all-white, Jewish neighborhood and I went to this camp and my best friend was this black kid. He was half black, half Jewish or something. But after that, in elementary school, I used to say, "Yeah, I have this black friend." I remember thinking it was cool that I had this one black friend. I've had experiences like that. I guess it's just, I don't know, I guess I just want to be proud of it almost. Like, "I know a black kid"* [Interview 2C].

When we recognize that we've made claims of our own that are blown out of proportion, we begin to wonder whether the person now making the same claim to us is doing the same thing. What makes this point evident is to ask yourself how ludicrous it would sound if someone said, "Some of my best friends are moms!" When this was pointed out, Emily and Jenna had the following exchange:

*EMILY: Why is it [that people do that]?*
*JENNA: When people say that, I think it's more about posturing really. Some of my best friends are . . . black.*
*EMILY: So, it's like name-dropping?*
*JENNA: Yeah, like name-dropping* [Interview 24C].

Ultimately, as a piece of our impression management, using the phrase "some of my best friends are . . ." is an attempt to solicit validation from the members of one's audience. In other words, while we can make claims about who we are as a person, in this case about our open-minded character, those around us actually have to accept us as such in order for the claim to be valid. Susan Condor and her associates have studied the denial of prejudice in dialogue and conclude that, "the success, or otherwise, of a claim to non-prejudiced character ultimately depends on its acceptance or rejection on the part of the audience. In this respect, prejudice denial and mitigation represents an essentially collaborative exercise" (Condor *et al.* 2006). So, if a person wants to be accepted by others as open-minded, she or he has to accurately play the part of such a person in her or his social circle. Any deviation from that, and your social identity as an open-minded individual is jeopardized (Lemert and Branaman 1997). Sam is the only one interviewed who was able to pick up on our need for validation from the audience.

*[If they are talking to] a black person and they say, "Some of my best friends are black," that is a pathetic attempt for that person to be like, "Hey, I can relate to you," you know. Like, "I should be cool with you," you know. It's ignorantly and inconceivably fishing for some kind of validation from that person. It's just dumb. Who gives a shit, you know* [Interview 30C]?

While Sam rhetorically and rather colorfully asks "who cares?" it is obvious that the person making the claim and donning the badge of honor cares very deeply about what others think. This is true of all of us as we engage in impression management. We employ what Goffman terms "facework" (Lemert and Branaman 1997), which involves the communication strategies we use to enact, support, or challenge our public image.

There are times when we are so conscious of our impression on others that we may stretch the truth a bit in our facework in order to be more acceptable to the members of our audience. In other words, there is a tendency for us to present idealized versions of ourselves to others. This idealization process (Lemert and Branaman 1997) includes concealing anything that is inconsistent with that ideal image we are attempting to create. Because there are times when we do this ourselves, we can't help but wonder when those around us are doing the same thing. So, when we hear somebody make the claim, "some of my best friends are . . . ," many of us question the legitimacy of that claim and believe that the person is trying to conceal some underlying feelings of prejudice. Sometimes we may even catch ourselves making a mistake in our facework, saying something that we suddenly realize others may see as offensive. At that point, we may try to fix the situation—corrective facework—by saying something like "some of my best friends are . . . ." At other times, we may anticipate that something we want to share may sound bad, so we try to make it sound better ahead of time—preventive facework. Again, one option would be to use the phrase "some of my best friends are . . . ." Since this phrase is so handy for corrective and preventive facework as well as idealization, it becomes immediately suspect when we hear it from others.

There were many, many examples of such a suspicious reaction on the part of those interviewed. Of course, much of the suspicion is based on their prior experiences, so there is some foundation for such a reaction. Here are two examples:

> BRAD: *Generally speaking, when somebody is making that statement, it certainly raises a red flag for me, indicating that somebody's having trouble with this particular issue: orientation or race or gender or whatever. So, usually when somebody says that, I'm pretty confrontational. If somebody's pretty strong on it and they try to defend it a bit more, I think that is within social protocol to allow the confrontation to be the learning experience and hope they think about it down the road* [Interview 7C].

> LAURA: *[When they say that], they're trying to say they're not racist or that they're not sexist or that they're not homophobic and you know damn well that they are or they wouldn't be saying that in the first place.*
> CHAD: *[It's just] like when someone says, "I'm not racist, but those Hmong people are just, they don't keep up their property very well."*
> LAURA: *"And don't confront me about racism because some of my best friends are black," that kind of shit.*
> CHAD: *Yeah.*
> LAURA: *So, it's something I try to avoid.*
> CHAD: *'Cause usually it's followed by something, some prejudiced or racist remark. You know, "I have friends who are women but, you know, these femi-*

*nists are just pushing the envelope . . ." It seems like [the phrase] is always fol-*
*lowed by a justification of prejudice.*
*LAURA: "Some of my best friends are men." Even if it's true, that doesn't*
*mean you can't be confronted* [Interview 9C].

Both Brad and Laura believe that it is possible to confront someone who says "some of my best friends are . . ." as a means of concealing some underlying prejudice even though the statement is often used as a means to avoid such a confrontation. Karen provides an example in which she actually confronts a co-worker.

*She thinks that she's not speaking badly about them and she is. I've called her*
*on it with gay people, too, because she thinks because she knows one that she*
*can say certain things. I have to tell her, "You don't know what you're talking*
*about," you know, and, "You're being very offensive." I think that she doesn't*
*walk on eggshells because she's too ignorant to realize what she's doing; but*
*it's really upsetting to hear anybody talk about any group of people like they're*
*this much below where I am* [Interview 12C].

Janine believes that, even if it is true, simply having such friends does not auto-matically mean one is a safe person. She wonders if there is more substance be-hind those words.

*By saying something like, "Oh, well I have black friends," I don't buy it. That*
*doesn't mean anything to me, you know. It doesn't mean squat to me. It's like,*
*"Okay, well then what do you do about it then?" I always want to know, "How*
*does that change your behavior? How does that change your way of thinking?*
*Do you think about what it means to be black and what your role is in that"*
*and stuff like that? I think that people believe that if they are friends with a per-*
*son who is different, that automatically makes them a safe person* [Interview
20C].

The questions raised by Janine are very perceptive. They highlight how the phrase "some of my best friends . . ." in and of itself can be a very shallow claim with no substance to back it up. Given that prejudice mitigation is a "collabora-tive exercise" depending on the willingness of the audience to accept claims of a non-prejudiced character (Condor *et al.* 2006), it appears that many of those who actually have diverse friends are highly skeptical of these claims and thus ac-tively prevent those who use such phrases from successfully identifying them-selves as non-prejudiced.

One reason that the phrase is perceived as such a shallow claim without substance is that it is used in a very reductionistic way. As observed by Rawlins, "A friend must be seen as a singular person—neither reduced to a token of race [or gender, or sexual orientation, and so on] nor expanded into a nondescript representative of the human condition" (2009, 152). It reduces the friends spoken of to a single, over-simplified category based on race, gender, sexual orientation, or what have you. As seen throughout this book, such reductionism is quite foreign to those I interviewed who actually did have a close, intimate friendship with someone who was demographically different from them. Melissa and Lenora recognize that identifying a friend based on one characteristic really does not say anything about that person.

> *MELISSA: Saying what race my friends are doesn't say anything about them. That's why it bothers me when people say stuff like that. It's just like, "So what?"*
> *LENORA: "Well, so is she nice or not? I'm not asking you her color"* [Interview 5C].

Jenna is also bothered by how such a phrase reduces the whole person to a tiny aspect of who they are, effectively dehumanizing them.

> *I have a problem with labels. And so to me, if I hear someone say that, I guess I think phony. I mean, these are your best friends. Your best friends are human. Your best friends are your best friends. Your best friends are so much more than just a one-word answer. I hate to say that, but that's just how I feel about it. I don't like that sort of naming because I don't feel like that. I identify as a lesbian, but it's not my number one identification for myself* [Interview 24C].

Human beings are multi-dimensional and there is much one can say about individuals, their identities, their qualities, their aspirations and dreams, their affiliations and beliefs, and so on. Simply identifying them in terms of a single characteristic flattens individuals out, reducing them to whatever preconceived image we have of people with that one characteristic. In effect, it wipes out their humanity.

The use of that phrase goes even a step further and strikes at the very heart of the theme of this book. By calling attention to that single quality of the individual—race, gender, sexual orientation, or what have you—the person saying it is sending a clear message that he or she is aware of the difference, and are drawing attention to it; in so doing he or she is actually *creating* the social boundary that separates the different groups. First of all, there is the awareness of the difference; in and of itself, that is not a bad thing. Color blindness, or blindness to any other demographic difference is less than ideal (Korgen 2002). Nevertheless, calling unnecessary attention to that difference is interpreted as being almost "hyper-aware" of it, thereby implying that it may be problematic for the speaker. This is the central point in what Miriam has to say in response to the question.

> *I mean if someone says that then I think that they're aware of that difference. You know, if I were to say I have a ton of friends that are men—unless we were specifically talking about men and we didn't have male friends or something— it would make me think well okay, then you're very aware of that difference.*

> *And not to say that you can't be friends and still be aware of the issue, but I think when I hear people say that, it says to me that they're aware of that difference* [Interview 8C].

Barbara agrees with Miriam's assessment when she says, *"By saying that, it's almost like saying I want to erase a line that is really there"* [Interview 22C]. Beyond demonstrating such hyper-awareness, using the phrase actually turns the difference being highlighted from something that could be completely neutral into an issue, as Jerry points out.

> *You know, it makes it an issue. And it really isn't, nor should it be. I think that sort of keeps perpetuating the whole gender bias and racism and all sorts of different stuff because people are still putting each other and other people into different groupings and categories when it's unnecessary. We're people. We're human beings who happen to be friends* [Interview 11C].

Maggie takes this point a step further and argues that using that phrase actually creates a barrier: *"You're creating a barrier by saying that just because you're saying, 'Well, there's this difference'"* [Interview 16C]. This is actually a very important sociological point. Saying, "Some of my best friends are . . ." effectively constructs a wall between "us" and "them," highlighting the fact that "they" are different from us. Such separation is fundamental to the creation of in-groups—the group *we* belong to or identify with—and out-groups—the group that is different and ultimately seen as deficient and even threatening (Allport 1954). It is in separating out these two groups—distinguishing between "us" and "them"—that we open the door to prejudice, discrimination, and even outright hostility. As we've seen throughout this book, socially constructed boundaries have very real consequences.

To be fair, it is important to acknowledge a key maxim in sociology that says, "context is everything." The words "some of my best friends are . . ." are one thing; the way they are said and the context in which the phrase comes up both have a tremendous impact on the way in which the phrase is interpreted and understood. In other words, the actual meaning of the phrase can vary widely depending on the circumstances in which it is uttered, how it is said, the relationship among the people having the conversation, the previous experiences of the audience members, and so on. This point was acknowledged without my prompting in half of the interviews.

In a minority of cases, those interviewed even argued that the phrase could be used to challenge people and their apparently bigoted attitudes or to demonstrate alliance in the face of prejudice. This was generally brought up when describing a situation in which the person being interviewed actually used the phrase or said something like it. Tom explains why he'd say such a thing, though he wouldn't phrase it as, "Some of my best friends are . . ."

> *I'm speaking up, I'm saying, "This isn't stuff to hide," but it is interesting be-*
> *cause it pushes and prods a little more. So there's a little more aggression in*
> *that way . . . I can't quite get the word . . . It's almost like an ally-ship. It's al-*
> *most, I know I'm ready to really go at it or something. I'm a little combative*
> *that way. The other is, though, I don't usually say it that way ["some of my best*
> *friends are . . ."]. There's a little more subtlety, but I do let people know.*
> *There's a sense in which I like to let other people know that I have friends who*
> *are different from me in a lot of ways that may not be socially acceptable, but*
> *that I think should be [socially acceptable]. It's a way of getting at that. I don't*
> *want to do it in the sense of "I'm cool because I have this exotic friend" or*
> *something. I want to get away from that; but I do want them to know and I want*
> *others to know I think it's important, that I have friends of different races, dif-*
> *ferent classes, different sexual orientations, and that's good. That's the way*
> *things should be. There's a sense that because we don't say it, we almost allow*
> *a silence to go on* [Interview 6C].

For Tom, it is much better to confront someone for his or her bigotry and risk appearing shallow by using the phrase or something like it than to allow the silence to continue, sending the message that such bigoted attitudes are acceptable. Dennis too explains how he's used the phrase, and it is much more directly confrontational.

> *You know, I think whenever I've heard it or said it, it's been more confronta-*
> *tional, that it's more of a way of saying, "Hold it. This is who I am and I'm tell-*
> *ing you that this particular person is a friend of mine, and what you need to*
> *think about is what you're going to say next. Because what you've already said*
> *has got me to the point where I'm speaking up. And now you should be listen-*
> *ing rather than talking." 'Cause if those words are coming out of my mouth,*
> *it's pretty tense. I'm scared and I'm terrified and I'm going to make a stand*
> [Interview 14C].

In both of these instances, the person who uses the phrase or something like it is intending to send a warning to those who have already demonstrated their own bigoted attitudes. Karen tells a much more specific story in which she did exactly that.

> *My boss was talking about a figure skater who is presumably gay from every-*
> *thing that we've heard. He said something like that, and I just flat out told him,*
> *"Some of my best friends are gay, and I find what you're saying very offen-*
> *sive." And he apologized to me, and he knows when we get in situations like*
> *that, he needs to hold his tongue because he does talk pretty freely about what*
> *his thoughts are on the issue; but he also knows that when he's in my company*
> *he needs to mind his P's and Q's. So I don't know, I think it's just that if some-*
> *body's using it, I hope it's in the right tone and the right way and that they're*
> *using it for education purposes kind of like I did* [Interview 12C].

Perhaps the most important function served by saying "some of my best friends are . . ." or something like it goes beyond the confrontation and includes the idea of "standing with" those who belong to a marginalized group, being their ally and their advocate; in this way, they are taking an active stance against bigotry, which is an outcome consistent with past research (Korgen 2002). Nancy states this most eloquently when she says, *"It becomes so important for people to say, 'I am this person's friend' and more than just, 'I support them,' but like, 'We're holding hands and marching.' It becomes really important to say, 'I have friends across these so-called boundaries'"* [Interview 23C]. For Nancy, it is certainly possible and even desirable to use the phrase to confront others in their own bigotry and to become an advocate for those who are marginalized. Notice, however, that this means the phrase is not simply dropped into the midst of a conversation without further elaboration. Instead, it is used as a sort of "teachable moment" and includes an explanation of why one is stopping the conversation to confront something that is considered offensive. As discussed in chapter 4, many friends have learned about socially constructed differences and the challenges that go with that. They then often "feel an impetus to act on this knowledge" (Korgen 2002, 72), becoming what Goffman (1963) identifies as a "model of normalization"—a person who demonstrates for others how members of a stigmatized or marginalized group should be treated as equals, effectively removing the stigma.

Overall, the use of the phrase "some of my best friends are . . ." has many negative connotations. More often than not, those who use the phrase are trying to manage their impression on others and create an image of being open-minded about some issue of diversity. Nonetheless, the opposite effect is often achieved among those who do have close friendships with diverse others, particularly when paired with an offensive comment or observation. Instead of demonstrating one's good qualities, it comes across as demeaning, reducing the individual to a single trait, and dehumanizing them in the process. It even creates the social boundaries that then have to be "crossed" or "bridged" in the first place. In some cases, the phrase may be used to confront the bigoted attitudes of others, but in those situations, the phrase is not simply tossed out and left to stand alone. Instead, it is followed up with a more direct explanation and challenge to the other person's attitudes. Regardless, the meanings associated with the use of this phrase, both the intended meaning on the part of the user and the interpretation on the part of the audience, are a collaborative exercise (Condor *et al.* 2006), much the same as the success of the friendships studied represent a collaborative exercise between two people who refuse to allow a socially constructed boundary to prevent them from establishing and sustaining a close relationship.

# Appendix A

# Researching Friendship Diversity

Many of my own friends who heard about this research project wondered not only about what I learned, but also about how the research was conducted. I found myself surprised by how interested they were in the methodology of the project, but then if they're not doing social science research themselves, it must be like getting the chance to look behind the curtain and see the everyday mechanics behind the finished product. Of course, in such conversations, I limited myself to a general description of the methodology, much as I did in the brief overview in the Preface. Here, however, I will provide more detail into the research procedures for those who are especially interested in the technicalities of a research project such as this. In doing so, I will cover the sampling procedure used and describe the interview and data analysis process. I will then briefly discuss the questions remaining unanswered by this project. Those who found the brief methodological overview in the Preface sufficient and who are less interested in such details may want to skip ahead to the last section of Appendix A in which I discuss the impact of the interview process on the individuals who participated in the research and on their friendships. This was an issue of particular fascination among my friends and colleagues alike.

## Sampling Procedure

To begin the data collection process, I mentioned the research project to friends, colleagues, and acquaintances and asked for referrals. I gave them a letter that provided an overview of the research purpose and procedures along with my contact information for them to pass along to their own friends. Then, after each interview was completed, I asked the research participants if they knew of anyone who also had diverse friends who might be interested in participating in the research. I gave them the same letter for them to pass along. Thus, the sampling procedure was a combination of a snowball and network approach. However, I also had specific categories to fill as I identified friendship pairs. As outlined in the Preface, my goal was to include ten friendships each focusing on race, gender, and sexual orientation as well as ten additional friendships focusing on a variety of other socially constructed boundaries.[1] The sample categories and sizes appear in Table P.1 in the Preface. Thus, I followed a purposive or "judgmental" sampling procedure that is actually rather common within qualitative research design (Bogden and Biklen 1992, 71-72). This sampling procedure is defined as "a type of nonprobability sample in which you select the units to be observed on the basis of your own judgment about which ones will be the most useful or representative" (Babbie 1992, G5). As discussed below, such a sampling procedure allows one "to select the widest variety of respondents to test the broad applicability" of, in this case, the emerging analysis (1992, 230). Moreover, it is particularly appropriate in situations where the population to be studied is "easily identified, but the enumeration of all of them would be nearly impossible," (1992, 230) thus eliminating random or systematic sampling as a viable option.

Relying on a snowball referral process certainly has its drawbacks. In the first place, I had to rely on those interviewed to take the lead in contacting the members of their social network. Then I had to rely on the individuals in their social network to take the initiative in contacting me if their names weren't passed along to me directly. Then, once a connection was made, the individual's friend also had to be interested and available to participate in the interview process.

I did include several overlapping friendships in which I interviewed a person on more than one occasion about different friendships. I also interviewed their different friends. The disadvantage of this approach is that there were fewer separate individuals in the overall sample. On the other hand, this technique had the advantage of allowing me to compare different friendships in the life of a single individual in order to see if there were significant differences. It became apparent that the same individual would approach each friendship differently and that it was the dynamics of the relationship *between* the individuals that guided the friendship rather than the personalities of the common individual who drove the dynamics of the friendship.

In addition to filling in the four categories of socially constructed boundaries crossed, it was my intent to maximize the sample diversity as much as possible. Using friendship networks in a snowball fashion often results in people of the same race, sexual orientation, and so on due to the reasons noted in chapter 2, so I elected to be more highly selective in the sampling process. Maximizing the friendship pair diversity within each category meant that not all cross-gender friendships would focus on heterosexuals or single people. Instead, I intentionally diversified it such that some pairs included a lesbian and a straight man or a gay man and straight woman or two single individuals, or a single and a married individual, and so on. I also attempted to maximize the race and gender composition of the sample for all categories. In the end, the sample was 44 percent male and 56 percent female (n = 80); it included a mix of races: 80 percent white, 10 percent black, 3.75 percent Latino, 3.75 percent Asian, 2.5 percent Native American and the sample represented a full spectrum of ages, from 20 to 65+ years of age. There was also variety in terms of the duration of the friendships, from a year to over 20 years. And there was some range in economic status although, as already discussed, this was minimal. While I started the sampling process in the upper Midwest, it resulted in the inclusion of individuals from across the country, including New England, Florida, Iowa, Colorado, and Washington. Some of these interviews were done by telephone while most were conducted face-to-face, as were all but one of the interviews conducted in the upper Midwest.

Filling each of the four social boundary categories while maximizing diversity within each became increasingly challenging as the data collection progressed. In the beginning, I could be quite flexible in selecting those to be included in the sample. As the categories filled up, my criteria for inclusion had to be increasingly specific so that by the end, far fewer friendship pairs qualified. For example, toward the end I needed to include another cross-gender friendship where both were single and heterosexual. I also needed a friendship between a gay man and straight man (finding lesbian/straight woman pairs was comparatively easy). Such pairs were not as easy to find as one might think.

By maximizing the diversity of the sample, one is simultaneously maximizing the possible permutations in the data. This technique is based on analytic induction in which the initial data gathered is analyzed and is then used to shape further sampling intended to diversify the sample itself (Bogden and Biklen 1992, 69-72). Subsequent cases are selected through the purposive sampling procedure described above. The idea here is that later interview participants will provide examples of *negative cases* for the developing analysis. Such negative cases help to expand the analysis in order to account for the variations found in the data, ultimately resulting in a stronger analysis. So, for example, after interviewing a gay man and straight woman about their gender-crossing friendship, it was found that there were no issues of jealousy by the intimate partner of either friend. The same was found when interviewing a lesbian and a straight man. However, by intentionally introducing cross-gender friendship pairs in which both individuals are straight and one or the other or both are married changes these friendship dynamics because of the reaction of the respective intimate partners. The developing analysis needs to be able to account for these variations in the data, so by diversifying the sample in this way it was possible to provide a more nuanced analysis of friendships crossing social boundaries.

This is also the logic for including friendships that cross gender, race, sexual orientation, class, religion, age, and ability all in the same study. If we examined only one of these socially constructed boundaries, as previous studies have done, then the analysis is limited to that one social boundary. By including multiple social boundaries, it is possible to develop a more general and nuanced analysis about bridging socially constructed boundaries in general regardless of the specific boundary in question. Moreover, this research structure allows the researcher to draw comparisons between the different social boundaries in order to see what makes one distinctive from another—that is, how is an interracial friendship different from a friendship crossing sexual orientation?

## Interview Procedures

The interviews conducted for this study followed a semi-structured format (Gordon 1992). There was a specific set of questions with suggestions for follow-up questions and, while it was desirable to cover all the questions on the interview schedule, they did not have to be asked in the exact order following the exact wording. Accordingly, the interview schedule served as a guide for an interview that was intended to be as conversational as possible. With this in mind, if the research participant brought up themes relevant to later sections of the interview, they could be pursued immediately rather than returning to them later when the interview schedule dictated. It was also possible to pursue lines of questioning inspired by what the participant said that were not planned in advance if they were deemed relevant to the research objectives. If such a line of questioning proved to be fruitful, it would be added to the interview schedule for subsequent interviews. The end effect was to create an interview environment that maintained a relaxed, conversational tone rather than a strict "Q & A" format with no flexibility.

The interview schedules covered several broad topics, starting with a history of the friendship and then focusing more specifically on the socially constructed boundary that was the focus of the interview and its relevance for and impact on the friendship. From there, we discussed the social boundary itself in relation to society. The interviews finished with a set of wrap-up questions intended to sum up the experiences of the research participants in their respective friendships. The one-on-one interviews included two additional broad topics. These interviews started with a set of warm-up questions focusing on the biography of the person being interviewed. Later, the individuals were asked about their own experiences as a member of whatever social category was our focus (i.e. their own experience of being a woman or a man, gay or straight, a racial or religious minority, and so on).

Again, I interviewed the two friends separately and followed this up with a paired interview in which I interviewed the two friends together. The one-on-one interview schedule was much more detailed and lengthy, resulting in interviews that averaged between two and three hours each, but ranging from one to six hours in length. If there was insufficient time to complete an interview in a single session, a follow-up session was immediately scheduled and we would resume the interview where left off. This only happened in several cases.

Naturally, the participants would be quite curious about what their friends said during their own interviews. For example, at the end of the paired interview, Allison said, *"I was always a little curious about what Keosha had said. How did Keosha respond to this question"* [Interview 18C]? This is where confidentiality was key. I had to be very careful to maintain confidentiality when conducting each of these interviews. This necessitated going so far as to convey ignorance of the friendship itself when interviewing the second individual. Of course, I knew the history of the friendship at least as the first of the friends remembered it, but I could not let on what I did and did not know when interviewing the second friend.

After each of the one-on-one interviews was completed, I would schedule the paired interview with both friends. In a few instances, the paired interviews closely followed the one-on-one interviews (within a day or two). At the other extreme, the paired interview occurred as much as a year later (because of difficulties in scheduling due to one of the friends being out of the country for an extended period of time). Most paired interviews fell within a couple weeks of the completion of the two one-on-one interviews. To continue maintaining confidentiality, I had to convey ignorance in the paired interview as well since there were many times when, during the one-on-one interview, one person would say something about the friendship that the other person did not and vice versa. Rather than keep all of that straight in my head for 120 interviews, I simply conveyed ignorance and had them tell me again. Of course, they knew this and I made light of it during the interview; but they accepted it with good humor and continued on. The other tricky part regarding confidentiality during the paired interview was the fact that, as the researcher, I was the only person required to maintain confidentiality regarding what was said during the interview. The two friends were not bound by professional standards of confidentiality. So, I made certain they understood that and told them that, if there was something said they wanted their friend to keep confidential they should be sure to say so.

For these paired interviews, the interview schedule was a streamlined version of the one-on-one interview schedule, focusing on the more central questions and adding a few additional questions that did not appear in the initial interviews. Allison, who expressed curiosity about what her friend Keosha said during her own interview, enjoyed participating in this paired interview and having the opportunity to hear the other person's perspective: *"I like the fact that we're sitting across from each other and we're listening to what each other has to say. It's more in-depth and now I can understand where she's coming from and how she feels about things instead of just going in and asking her some questions off the top of my head"* [Interview 18C]. Allison's observation hints at how the interview process itself often provided the friends participating in the research project the opportunity to directly talk about the dynamics of the friendship given the socially constructed boundary between them. This is a topic covered below.

In the meantime, I'll note that the purpose of these paired interviews was to create a discussion between the friends about the socially constructed boundary within the friendship. As the interviewer, I would act more as a facilitator of these discussions and become a witness to them. Sometimes this technique was highly effective and at other times it was not. In the latter case, the individuals could not get around their definition of the situation as an interview and regularly responded to me as if their friend was not even present, speaking of him or her in the third person. In these cases, the interview proceeded in a turn-taking style where first one friend and then the other would respond to each question I asked. While that defeated the purpose of creating a discussion, it still allowed me to compare answers with what they had said in their initial interviews for consistency and it allowed me to see what they chose not to say in their paired interview that they covered in the one-on-one interview and vice versa. In those cases where creating a discussion between the two friends was effective, they would turn to face each other, speaking directly to one another without having to use me as an intermediary. In fact, they often asked each other questions that were not on the interview schedule, and I encouraged this. As these conversations deepened, it was almost as if they forgot I was there for a few minutes. The strength of this method was that I got to see their friendship "in action" and would get a unique view into their friendship dynamics. On the downside, the friends would often "go down memory lane" and start talking about things that had no bearing on the research topic. However, I decided to let them go because this downside was far outweighed by the benefits. In the end, these paired interviews lasted just as long as the one-on-one interviews even though the interview schedule included only half as many questions.

The interview schedules contained a number of broad, open-ended questions. Researchers who adhere to a highly structured data collection philosophy that focuses on very specific questions would find such broad questions to be useless for their research purposes. In contrast, I find it highly valuable. As discussed in my earlier work (Vela-McConnell 1999), I prefer such broad questions because they allow the research participants to define the situation for me rather than imposing my own definition of the situation upon them. For example, friends and colleagues often asked how I defined close friendship and screened research participants based on that definition. My response was that I didn't. Instead, I simply sought out those individuals who saw themselves in a close friendship with another person who was different in terms of race, gender, sexuality, and so on. I let them decide who they considered to be a close friend and then I asked everyone I interviewed how they defined and understood friendship, how they distinguished a close friend from someone who was "just a friend," how close they were to their friend participating in the research project, and how they knew they were that close.

I did the same thing with regard to definitions of race, gender, sexuality, and so on. Rather than imposing my own, highly academic and sociological definition upon them, I asked them to tell me what race is, what gender is, what the differences are between the relevant categories and so on. Some academics might find this troubling because these definitions offered up by the research participants are not at all like our current sociological understanding of the nature of race, gender, sexuality, and so on. However, I again refuse to impose such definitions on the research participants because such academic understandings and interpretations are so far removed from their day-to-day experiences. Those I interviewed are those who live in the "real" world where non-academic definitions hold sway and influence the perceptions and experiences of themselves and everyone around them, where non-academic definitions of the situation shape the relationships that are formed between them. If I imposed my own sociological definitions upon them, I would have no idea how they themselves understood race or gender or sexuality or any of the other socially constructed boundaries I covered. Without this information, I would have no basis for accurately analyzing their experiences and instead would present a highly biased and even judgmental attitude toward the perceptions and experiences of the research participants, which I find to be the epitome of academic arrogance and the worst of the "ivory tower" stereotype. Imposing academic definitions rests on the assumption that the lived experiences and perceptions of those studied have no actual value or relevance. Instead, from a symbolic interactionist and phenomenological perspective, such everyday experiences and perceptions are crucial to understanding the phenomenon under study.

The use of broad, open-ended questions is in keeping with symbolic interactionism and phenomenology, both of which focus on the process by which internal, subjective feelings and perceptions are translated into external, objective social interactions and structures. Our subjective experience is based upon our perceptions of the surrounding social environment (Vela-McConnell 1999; Berger and Luckmann 1967). These perceptions shape our experience of the world and are also shaped by those experiences. Thus, what is understood to be "real" is based on one's direct experiences and perceptions and less on what academics define as reality. What academics have to say is often highly informative and theoretically valid, but it does not change the way in which individuals experience the social world in their daily lives. As one who is studying people's experiences of the world, I find that discovering how a person understands and perceives the world is central to a more accurate analysis of their experiences. Such discovery is made possible by allowing those perceptions free reign through the use of broad, open-ended questions. Of course, many follow-up questions are then required to get a more precise understanding of the individual's views, the vast majority of which can never be planned because one is not always able to anticipate the initial responses given. As a result, the majority of the questions actually asked never appear on an interview schedule.

There is also a need for more narrow and even closed-ended questions, many of which appear in the interview schedules as well. These questions allow me to determine the direction of a series of follow-up questions. However, these more narrow questions focus less on meanings, perception, and understanding and more on actual events and direct experiences. After getting an initial response, I then follow up with the more broad questions intended to elicit such perceptions and understandings.

## Data Analysis

Upon completion of each interview, I typed out a memo about the interview and what I learned from it. Each memo represented an initial attempt to answer the research questions based on what I had learned in that particular interview and in that interview together with all prior interviews. These memos became cumulative in that each one built upon, revised, and/or elaborated the analytical ideas developed in earlier memos. These memos also included any methodological issues that may have come up in the course of the research project and any general observations I had about the person being interviewed.

All interviews were recorded by me and then transcribed word-for-word by a professional transcriptionist, resulting in 7,953 double-spaced pages of text (averaging sixty-six pages per interview). They were then formatted for computerized data analysis using HyperResearch as a coding tool (see Hesse-Biber, DuPuis, and Kinder, 1990 for a description). The data analysis began with "initial coding" (Lofland and Lofland 1995, 192) focusing on the broad themes identified in the memos. These themes later served to delineate the different chapters of the book. At that point, I narrowed my focus to a single theme at a time and its corresponding chapter. I then engaged in "focused coding" (Lofland and Lofland 1995, 192-193), elaborating the details within each theme. The focused coding scheme then became the framework around which each chapter was organized and helped to outline the subsections within each chapter. Thus, the overall analysis was purely inductive in nature with the overall structure of the book being determined by the responses of those interviewed.

As the writing progressed, it was then necessary to select which quotations would appear in the text of each chapter. My selection criteria included (1) which quote(s) best represented the theme under discussion; (2) if multiple quotes were to be used, which quotes best complemented one another in order to provide a more full and nuanced picture of that theme; and (3) I made every attempt to ensure that the maximum number of friendship pairs were represented at some point in the text of the book (with quotes from one or another or both individuals). Naturally, some research participants provided more in-depth responses to the questions while others were rather sketchy. I still made an attempt to include the latter, but that was not possible in all cases. When the quotes to be included had been decided upon, I then "cleaned" them up, correcting the grammar, eliminating repetitions and false starts, deleting tangential information, and so on while maintaining the actual words, speaking style, and meaning of the research participants.

Given the fact that both friends within a friendship were interviewed, one might wonder, "What is the unit of analysis? What is a case?" For this study, there were two levels at which to look at the data. In other words, the unit of analysis could be the individuals who were interviewed about their friendships (resulting in eighty cases) or it could be the friendships themselves (resulting in forty cases). This research design allowed much flexibility for analysis. On the one hand, it was possible to analyze individual perceptions and experiences of their friendships. On the other hand, it was also possible to analyze the interactional dynamics within each friendship as a whole. Thus, the data analysis presented in the book seamlessly moves from one to the other level of analysis.

## Unanswered Questions

Despite the fact that multiple socially constructed boundaries were included in this research and quite a large amount of data collected, by necessity the research focus was limited. Because of limited resources, it was necessary to limit the total number of friendships to forty. Given that limitation, it did not make sense to include additional social boundaries because then all depth would have been sacrificed for breadth of coverage. For reasons noted above, race, gender, and sexual orientation became the central social boundaries covered while class, for example, was relegated to the comparison group of socially constructed boundaries. In the future, it would be advisable to expand the secondary social boundaries included in this project—class (especially given how pervasive class divisions are), religion, age, and ability—by interviewing more friendship pairs. It is evident from the analysis presented in this book that the experiences of those on different sides of these socially constructed boundaries were highly informative and had much to contribute. I would be interested to learn more about these social boundaries in the context of friendship.

Moreover, the social boundary of religion introduces a factor that goes beyond demographics, and that is difference based on values and belief systems. The reader will recall that a key factor in the success of many of these friendships was the fact that, despite their demographic differences, the friends shared many of the same values and beliefs—what is known as "value homophily" (McPherson, Smith-Lovin, and Cook 2001, 419). If value homophily was a contributing factor to the success of those unlikely friendships falling outside of the "status homophily" pattern (based on demographics), then what about those friendships that succeed despite falling outside of the "value homophily" pattern? What makes these friendships successful? Using religion as the central social boundary in a friendship would be one way to approach this question. However, as we saw in the friendship between Deborah and Fatima, they found that, despite the fact that one is Jewish and the other is Muslim, they still shared most of their underlying values and beliefs. Perhaps it would be better to focus in on another social boundary based on differences in values and belief systems, such as political differences and political party affiliation. What allows, for example, staunch conservatives and liberals to create and maintain successful, close relationships?

This project by necessity also focused in on the success cases: those who were able to create and maintain friendships despite social differences. Given the fact that these friendships are much less likely than homophilous friendships, perhaps we should also study failed friendships. We know that most friends demonstrate status homophily, but perhaps we could learn more about why—especially in instances where, at least initially, both parties were open to such a friendship—some of those friendships failed after they were initiated. Such an inquiry would focus on the friendship dynamics themselves and would go beyond the structural opportunities, values, and beliefs that prevent many of these friendships from ever starting.

As noted in chapter 1, my past research distinguished three variables that hindered social cohesion: social distance, spatial distance, and temporal distance (Vela-McConnell 1999). Social distance was, by far, the most influential of these three and so I made that the focus of the research presented in this current book. I also took spatial distance into account by examining the role of segregation between diverse groups. Still, what about those friendships spanning a geographic divide, where the friends live in different regions of the country or the world? Several of the friendships studied in this project have succeeded despite geographic separation although, because that was not the focus of this project, such separation was not pursued in adequate detail for presentation here. In the same vein, what about the use of technology to maintain such friendships? We've moved well beyond the telephone in terms of our ability to stay in touch with our friends. We now have e-mail, instant messaging, video-conferencing technology, and on-line communities. What are friendship opportunity structures like now that geographic separation is less and less relevant? How does such technology change the meaning of friendship? And with what consequences? We now live in a world where the word "friend" is a verb. What does that mean for the depth of our relationships with our friends? These and many other fascinating questions can be answered with additional research in the area of friendships and I find the prospects exciting.

## The Impact of Interviews on the Participants and Their Friendships

When speaking with friends and colleagues about my research on friendships, one of the most frequently asked questions—asked only partially in jest—was whether any of the friendships I studied ended because of the nature of the interview process. This is a highly interesting and relevant question to discuss when addressing research methods given that it focuses on the impact of the research process itself on those being studied. But let me start by saying that, to my knowledge none of the friendships has ended as a result of participating in this research process. In fact, in many cases, it is quite the opposite. Some have voluntarily contacted me and told me how much their friendship has grown as a result of participating. In fact, in a personal communication to me, Brad (friendship pair 7) indicated that participating was like going on a retreat and that he and his friend Eric are much closer as a result.

Knowing that the interview process could elicit much reflection on the part of those who participated, I concluded every paired interview by asking the participants whether they have "learned anything new about yourself, each other, or your friendship from having done these interviews? Did anything surprise you?" The most typical responses were similar to what Brad described: participation served to increase their appreciation for one another and deepened their friendship. (I'll provide additional examples below.) Only a minority of the responses to this question indicated that the participants learned nothing about themselves, each other, or their friendship. The rest of the responses were all quite positive, indicating that participation in this research did have a noticeable impact on the participants and one that they considered quite positive.

A few of those interviewed indicated that they had learned something previously unknown about their friend from having participated in the paired interview. The case of Janice and Barbara provides a good example. Barbara was taken by surprise finding out that Janice struggled with coming out to her.

*BARBARA: I never realized her struggles with telling me [that she's lesbian].* [Turning to Janice, she said:] *I mean, I knew you struggled with the sexuality issue, but I never knew of the struggle to tell me just in general. Not that it bothers me. It's just something I didn't know. And I imagine it gives me a better awareness of other friendships [I have] as well: just because I think it's a non-issue doesn't mean that it's a non-issue for the other person. I need to be more sensitive to that. It just didn't really occur to me. You can never be too sensitive.*
*JANICE: Well, you grew up with it* [referring to Barbara's gay brother]. *So for you it was just run of the mill while for me it's not run of the mill.*
*BARBARA: Right. And I think that's just as important with all types of relationships. Sometimes we forget that our worldview isn't the same as the other person's worldview. We need to remember that, realizing that I haven't lived the way you live. That's important in all relationships. It's also important for understanding prejudice and things like that, you know. Wow, my world has been different, sometimes better, sometimes worse, but definitely different. I think that's something that I don't think I would have an overt understanding of before this interview* [Interview 22C].

Barbara had an intellectual understanding that people had different experiences, but participating in the interview process brought home to her the idea that not all gays and lesbians have the same experience with coming out to themselves or to others and that she should use her past experiences with other people to judge how her friends have experienced sexual orientation.

For her part, Janice has also learned something from participating in the paired interview with Barbara:

> JANICE: *The only thing that surprised me about you was that you would let go of a friend who is homophobic. I don't know if I would call it quits on a friend who is racist per se, because of . . .*
> BARBARA: *Yeah, I know. It depends how long I've been their friend. You figure if I've known them for ten years, I would know they were homophobic. But if it was someone I just met, we would never be friends. We just wouldn't because of what it would tell me about him as a person. I'd do the same thing with a racist comment, too.*
> JANICE: *You know, I think I probably would. I'd have my guard up and I wouldn't get close to a person I think.*
> BARBARA: *You'd still talk to them. You wouldn't be mean to them.*
> JANICE: *Yeah, it depends on what you mean by friend. How's that for complexity* [Interview 22C]?

While what they learned may seem small to the outsider, the fact that both Barbara and Janice mentioned them indicates that they had some significance in further shaping how they perceive their friend.

When Barbara indicates that she learned how much Janice struggled with coming out to her, she also alludes to learning something about herself: the fact that she was taking something for granted by assuming that Janice's comfort level about being out would be the same as that of her brother. In this, she is not alone. Almost one quarter of the responses indicated that the individuals realized what they were taking for granted or that the interview process made them think about and evaluate themselves. This again highlights how the interviews served to spark a self-reflective process among many of the research participants. For example, Brad notes that

> What I really have learned about myself through this whole process is that I do some compartmentalizing [with my friends]. What I mean is that there are many things I would say to my other gay friends that I would not say to Eric. If I really were going to talk about a gay thing, I'd probably talk to my gay friends just because that's where I've put my mind. That's kind of a fascinating thought to me right now. Why do I do what I do within that context? Right now, at this moment, I can't think of a thing that I wouldn't say to Eric; but sometimes I just don't, you know [Interview 7B].

Brad begins to wonder why he doesn't share everything with his straight friend Eric, noticing that he relegates certain topics to conversations with certain friends. Personally, I think we all do this knowing that certain topics will resonate better with certain friends and not with others. The point, however, is that Brad is coming to that realization as a result of participating in the interview process.

Bao and Irene also came to understand that there are certain things that they have taken for granted, things toward which the interviews have drawn their attention.

> *BAO: I think doing my individual interview has helped me reflect a lot on the friendship I have with Irene . . . things that I might have taken for granted or that I might not have thought about.* [The interview process] *has challenged me to think about it more or go deeper into it and stuff like that.*
> *IRENE: Same for me. I understand more. I found that I'm taking some things for granted . . . or not really taking for granted, it's just that I hadn't really thought about it, you know, and the interview just gave me more of a chance to really think about it. Like why we're friends, you know?*
> *BAO: Yeah, it solidified why we're friends* [Interview 19C].

Notice how vague both Bao and Irene are about what they've taken for granted, at least until they get to the point of saying that the interviews helped to solidify why they became friends. Much of what the research participants talked about was a challenge for them to articulate because they've never really had to explain it to an outsider before. For many, it was something that they and their friends simply understood and therefore took for granted. So a number of the responses focused on the challenge they had in articulating what they've never before had to explain.

An additional one fifth of the responses expressed how the interviews provided a unique opportunity to think and talk about the differences between the friends. In the case of Maggie and Quinn, this conversation included a focus on the status of their friendship and helped to clarify some doubts Maggie had. (She wondered if they were friends simply because she is best friends with Quinn's now ex-girlfriend. While Maggie was abroad, Quinn had broken up with his girlfriend and this made Maggie wonder where she stood with him.) This was the one case where the paired interview occurred more than a year after the two one-on-one interviews were completed. Maggie had been out of the country and during that time she and Quinn had minimal contact with one another due in large part to the insecurity Maggie had in their friendship. However, when they finally did schedule their paired interview, they made a point to meet each other the week before and have an in-depth conversation about their friendship. In the end, they were both much closer and Maggie was certainly more secure in their relationship and where she stood with Quinn. Here is what they had to say at the end of their paired interview:

> *QUINN: We discussed this last week outside of the context of these interviews, but I think these interviews have kind of motivated our conversation in a way. I guess I hadn't realized to the level that Maggie somewhat felt like our friendship existed mainly because of my girlfriend. I feel like I've learned a bit about how she saw that and I think that's good. Because I had sort of seen it in a similar way, you know, but I'd also seen it as an independent friendship and*

*I'm just glad that it came up so we could resolve that and have an independent*
*friendship.*
*MAGGIE: Yeah, I would say the same. When we were talking about it last*
*week, we talked about whether we would have hung out ever just the two of us.*
*Was his ex-girlfriend an essential part of us interacting together? So just know-*
*ing that Quinn felt the same way, that it wasn't just because of her that we were*
*friends, just made me feel more confident in our friendship. Before that, I just*
*hadn't been sure where . . . because I had that third-wheel feeling sometimes.*
*So I just didn't know where that was and so we just cleared things up a lot* [In-
terview 16C].

Maggie and Quinn feel that they had this important conversation about the status
of their friendship because they were in a position of having scheduled the
paired interview that would focus on their friendship. They both thought it
would be important for them to clarify where they were each at with regard to
the other person before they were put in a position of having to talk about their
friendship with an outside party. The conversation they had helped them to solidify the foundation on which their friendship stands.

Again, strengthening the friendship was the most common response to my
question about what the participants learned as a result of the interview process,
with almost a third indicating that they have a renewed or increased appreciation
for their friendship and that the experience of talking about it with a third party
and with each other during the paired interview brought them closer together.
Here are a few poignant examples.

*DENNIS: I like myself a little bit more!*
*ANN MARIE: I'm like, "more people should be friends with me!" I don't think*
*I've learned anything that's really surprised me, but it's been cool to sit down*
*with this thing* [our friendship] *and spit and polish it and look at it from every*
*side. Last time* [during my one-on-one interview] *it was really interesting to*
*kind of walk through our friendship from day one to the present . . . where did*
*this relationship come from and how did it build and how did we get to where*
*we are? Once you put language to it and define what's going on, you're put in*
*a place where you just cherish it all the more. I knew how good friends we were*
*before we did this and knew how comfortable I was even entering a project like*
*this to talk about our relationship; but now that you've kind of looked at it front*
*ways and sideways and back ways, then you know what's going on there. You*
*hold on to it a little bit tighter.*
*DENNIS:* [Turning to me] *You should take this show on the road!*
*ANN MARIE: A lot of people would probably be pretty interested in our story.*
*DENNIS: Call Oprah* [Interview 14C]!

*EMILY: I've learned how special our friendship is. Deep. It's a deep friend-*
*ship.*
*JENNA: I came away from my individual interview with the sense that I really*
*am so fortunate, you know. I mean, I think it makes me more cognitively aware*
*of what we've done, what we've come through and how important you are to*
*me. Because I think you get into the daily grind and you get distracted with kid*

*stuff, the partner stuff, the work stuff and you forget how important the friendship is. But acknowledging together that we cannot always have contact or say these things to one another, we still have this underlying understanding that there's always going to be this friendship there and that we'll always give each other the benefit of the doubt. No matter what happens in Emily's life, I trust her and I love her.* [Turning to Emily:] *I love you and I just think that, whatever happens, I'm just always going to be there and support you and love you.*
*EMILY: Yeah, and that's how I feel, too.*
*JENNA: Yeah, but I don't know that we've ever said that to each other.*
*EMILY: No.*
*JENNA: That's funny. I mean it's like this . . .*
*EMILY: And it's easier for you to say that than it is for me. I don't know why. You'll say, "love you" on the phone and I'm like, I don't know if I can say that. I don't say that to anybody* [Interview 24C].

*EVA: You know, I've always felt very . . . I always treasure our friendship; but I think what has occurred for me during the first interview is just realizing how very rare it may be because I don't take it for granted. I really respect it and treasure it and yet I don't think I realized until we started really talking about these things that this may be a very rare relationship.*
*NICOLE: Yeah, I think it's an amazing thing to take the time, which we hardly ever—if ever—do, to really examine an important relationship in our life. Like Eva said, we don't take it for granted; but on some level we do. And taking the time to really think more deeply about what draws us to another person and what makes us want to make sure that that's a lasting relationship is something that doesn't happen often. When you get the chance to do that, when somebody kind of puts you in a situation where you really have to think about it and examine it, it just reinforces everything so you realize, "Wow," you know, "I'm really lucky to have this person in my life"* [Interview 36C].

It is well established that research has an impact on those being studied, for better or for worse. Most of our attention as researchers has been on the negative side, which has resulted in necessary advances in ethical standards for research involving people. We've also paid attention to how research impacts those studied and how this shapes and perhaps even distorts the results. While we pay lip service to the idea that research may actually be beneficial to those studied, I think it is clear from my experiences conducting this research project and from the responses and positive feelings of those who participated, that research has much potential for good, not just in the findings revealed but in the process of conducting research itself.

# Note

1. Some might wonder how these particular social boundaries were selected. In order to narrow the research scope so that the project was more manageable, I decided to

focus my primary attention on those social boundaries that are generally described as comprising an individual's *ascribed status*. That is, these social boundaries are based on characteristics that individuals are born with and/or imposed upon them and not voluntarily chosen or worked for (as in *achieved status*, like level of education). Individuals are born and immediately categorized by race and gender. Individuals cannot control their age, nor can they control their physical ability whether we are talking about an innate condition or one that develops as the result of a disease or accident. While still open to some debate, it is my experience that individuals are born with a particular sexual orientation. This criterion becomes a bit more cloudy with class and religion. Individuals are born into a particular class position and religious tradition and, while it is possible for these to change over the course of a person's lifetime, many individuals stay in the same category through processes like social reproduction (MacLeod 2008).

# Appendix B

## Friendship Pairs

| ID# | Friendship Pair | Primary Difference | Category | Additional Differences |
|---|---|---|---|---|
| 1A | Kelly | Race | White | Gender |
| 1B | Colin | | Black | Ability |
| 2A | Sarah | Sexual | Bisexual | Gender |
| 2B | Matt | Orientation | Straight | |
| 3A | Liz | Age | 40-49 | None |
| 3B | Nikki | | 20-25 | |
| 4A | Katie | Gender | Female | None |
| 4B | Ed | | Male | |
| 5A | Lenora | Race | Black | None |
| 5B | Melissa | | While | |
| 6A | Dave | Sexual | Gay | None |
| 6B | Tom | Orientation | Straight | |
| 7A | Eric | Sexual | Straight | None |
| 7B | Brad | Orientation | Gay | |
| 8A | Miriam | Gender | Female | Sexual |
| 8B | Dave | | Male | Orientation |
| 9A | Chad | Gender | Male | Sexual |
| 9B | Laura | | Female | Orientation |
| 10A | Dave | Sexual | Gay | None |
| 10B | Mark | Orientation | Straight | |
| 11A | Bob | Age | 65+ | None |
| 11B | Jerry | | 30-39 | |
| 12A | Bill | Sexual | Gay | Gender |
| 12B | Karen | Orientation | Straight | |
| 13A | Suzanne | Class | Upper-Middle | Race |
| 13B | Jenny | | Lower-Middle | |

| ID# | Friendship Pair | Primary Difference | Category | Additional Differences |
|---|---|---|---|---|
| 14A | Ann Marie | Gender | Female | Sexual Orientation |
| 14B | Dennis | | Male | |
| 15A | Quinn | Class | Working | Religion & Age |
| 15B | Mike | | Upper-Middle | |
| 16A | Maggie | Gender | Female | None |
| 16B | Quinn | | Male | |
| 17A | Deborah | Religion | Jewish | Nationality |
| 17B | Fatima | | Muslim | |
| 18A | Keosha | Race | Black | None |
| 18B | Allison | | White | |
| 19A | Bao | Race | Asian (Hmong) | Class |
| 19B | Irene | | Black | |
| 20A | Monica | Sexual Orientation | Straight | Race |
| 20B | Janine | | Lesbian | |
| 21A | Frank | Race | White | None |
| 21B | Wilson | | Black (biracial) | |
| 22A | Janice | Sexual Orientation | Lesbian | None |
| 22B | Barbara | | Straight | |
| 23A | Jessica | Age | 20-25 | None |
| 23B | Nancy | | 30-39 | |
| 24A | Jenna | Sexual Orientation | Lesbian | None |
| 24B | Emily | | Straight | |
| 25A | Tina | Religion | Christian | None |
| 25B | Jessi | | New Age | |
| 26A | Pam | Gender | Female | None |
| 26B | Tim | | Male | |
| 27A | Brianna | Class | Upper-Middle | None |
| 27B | Ruth | | Working | |
| 28A | Cynthia | Ability | Able-Bodied | Gender |
| 28B | Greg | | Wheelchair | |
| 29A | Melody | Race | White | None |
| 29B | Tenisha | | Black | |

| ID# | Friendship Pair | Primary Difference | Category | Additional Differences |
|-----|-----------------|--------------------|----------|------------------------|
| 30A | Sam | Race | White | Age |
| 30B | Rodney | | Native American | & Class |
| 31A | Patricia | Gender | Female | None |
| 31B | Adam | | Male | |
| 32A | Jeremiah | Religion | Christian | Race & |
| 32B | Adam | | Jewish | Nationality |
| 33A | Hugo | Gender | Male (Trans) | Race & |
| 33B | Debbie | | Female | Class |
| 34A | Christina | Race | Asian (Philippino) | Sexual Orientation |
| 34B | Ellen | | White | |
| 35A | Hugo | Race | Latino | Gender |
| 35B | Lisa | | Native American | |
| 36A | Eva | Sexual Orientation | Lesbian | None |
| 36B | Nicole | | Straight | |
| 37A | Kris | Gender | Male | None |
| 37B | Kim | | Female | |
| 38A | Jordan | Sexual Orientation | Bisexual | Class |
| 38B | Shawn | | Straight | |
| 39A | Caroline | Gender | Female | Sexual Orientation |
| 39B | Brian | | Male | |
| 40A | Ted | Race | Black | None |
| 40B | Jeremy | | White | |

# Bibliography

Aboud, Frances E., Morton J. Mendelson, and Kelly T. Purdy. "Cross-Race Peer Relations and Frienship Quality." *International Journal of Behavioral Development* 27, no. 2 (2003): 165.

Adams, Rebecca G. and Graham Allan, eds. *Placing Friendship in Context*. Cambridge, UK: Cambridge University Press, 1998.

Affifi, Walid, and Laura Guerrero. "Some Things Are Better Left Unsaid II: Topic Avoidance in Friendships." *Communication Quarterly* 46, no. 3 (1998): 231-49.

Allport, Gordon. *The Nature of Prejudice*. Reading, MA: Addison-Wesley Publishing Company, 1954.

Allan, Graham. *Friendship: Developing a Sociological Perspective*. Boulder, CO: Westview Press, 1990.

Allan, Graham and Rebecca G. Adams. "Reflections on Context." In *Placing Friendships in Context*, edited by Rebecca G. Adams and Graham Allan, 183-194. Cambridge, UK: Cambridge University Press, 1998.

Argyle, M., and M. Henderson. "The Rules of Friendship." *Journal of Social and Personal Relationships* 1 (1984): 211-237.

Atluri, Tara. "Lighten Up?! Humour, Race, and Da Off Colour Joke of Ali G." *Media, Culture & Society* 31, no. 2 (2009):197-214.

Babbie, Earl. *The Practice of Social Research*, 6th edition. Belmont, CA: Wadsworth Publishing Company, 1992.

Bacon, Sir Francis. "On Friendship." *Essays, Advancement of Learning, New Atlantis, and Other Pieces*. New York: Odyssey Press, 1937.

Barlow, Fiona Kate, Winnifred R. Louis, and Miles Hewstone. "Rejected! Cognitions of Rejection and Intergroup Anxiety as Mediators of the Impact of Cross-Group Friendships on Prejudice." *British Journal of Social Psychology* 48, no. 3 (2009): 389-405.

Barnes, Brendon, Ingrid Palmary, and Kevin Durrheim. "The Denial of Racism: The Role of Humor, Personal Experience, and Self-Censorship." *Journal of Language & Social Psychology* 20, no. 3 (2001): 321-338.

Baumann, Anja Esther. "Stigmatization, Social Distance and Exclusion Because of Mental Illness: The Individual with Mental Illness as a 'Stranger.'" *International Review of Psychiatry* 19, no. 2 (2007): 131-35.

Beck, Amanda. "Americans' Circle of Close Friends Shrinking." *Yahoo! News*, June 26, 2006.

Bell, Robert R. *Worlds of Friendship*. Beverly Hills: Sage Publications, 1981.

Beran, Nancy J. "Attitudes Toward Minorities: A Comparison of Homosexuals and the General Population" *Journal of Homosexuality* 23 (1992): 65-83.

Berger, Peter L. *Invitation to Sociology: A Humanistic Perspective*. New York: Anchor Books, 1963.

Berger, Peter and Thomas Luckmann. *The Social Construction of Reality: A Treatise in the Sociology of Knowledge*. New York: Anchor Books, 1967.

Billig, Michael. "The Notion of Prejudice: Rhetorical and Ideological Aspects." *Text* 8 (1988): 91-110.

Binder, Jens, Rupert Brown, Hanna Zagefka, Friedrich Funke, Thomas Kessler, Amelie Mummendey, Annemie Maquil, Stephanie Demoulin, and Jacques-Philippe Leyens. "Does Contact Reduce Prejudice or Does Prejudice Reduce Contact? A Longitudinal Test of the Contact Hypothesis Among Majority and Minority Groups in Three European Countries." *Journal of Personality & Social Psychology* 96, no. 4 (2009): 843-56.

Blieszner, Rosemary and Rebecca G. Adams. *Adult Friendship*. Newbury Park, CA: Sage Publications, 1992.

Blumer, Herbert. *Symbolic Interactionism: Perspective and Method*. Berkeley: University of California Press, 1986.

Blumer, Herbert. "Race Prejudice as a Sense of Group Position." *The Pacific Sociological Review* 1 (1958): 3-7.

Blumer, Herbert. "Reflections on Theory of Race Relations." In *Race Relations in World Perspective*, edited by A. W. Lind, 3-21. Honolulu: University of Hawaii Press, 1955.

Bobo, Lawrence D. "Prejudice as Group Position: Microfoundations of a Sociological Approach to Racism and Race Relations." *Journal of Social Issues* 55, no. 3 (1999): 445-45.

Bogdan, Robert C. and Sari Knopp Biklen. *Qualitative Research for Education: An Introduction to Theory and Methods*. Boston: Allyn and Bacon, 1992.

Bousfield, Catherine, and Paul Hutchison. "Contact, Anxiety, and Young People's Attitudes and Behavioral Intentions Towards the Elderly." *Educational Gerontology* 36, no. 6 (2010): 451-66.

Brain, Robert. *Friends and Lovers*. New York: Basic Books, 1976.

Butler, Judith. *Gender Trouble*. New York: Routledge, 1990.

Byrne, Donn. *The Attraction Paradigm*. New York: Academic Press, 1971.

Cameron, Lindsey, Adam Rutland, and Rupert Adam. "Promoting Children's Positive Intergroup Attitudes Towards Stigmatized Groups: Extended Contact and Multiple Classification Skills Training." *International Journal of Behavioral Development* 31, no. 5 (2007): 454-66.

Cameron, Lindsey, Adam Rutland, Rupert Brown, and Rebecca Douch. "Changing Children's Intergroup Attitudes Toward Refugees: Testing Different Models of Extended Contact." *Child Development* 77, no. 5 (2006): 1208-19.

Castelli, Luigi, Leyla De Amicis, and Steven J. Sherman. "The Loyal Member Effect: On the Preference for Ingroup Members Who Engage in Exclusive Relations with the Ingroup." *Developmental Psychology* 43, no. 6 (2007): 1347-59.

Coleman, Robin. *African American Viewers and the Black Situation Comedy: Situating Racial Humour*. New York: Garland, 2000.

Condor, Susan, Lia Figgou, Jackie Abell, Stephen Gibson, and Clifford Stevenson. "'They're Not Racist . . .' Prejudice Denial, Mitigation and Suppression in Dialogue." *British Journal of Social Psychology* 45, no. 3 (2006): 441-62.

Cooley, Charles Horton. *Social Organization*. New York: Scribner, 1909.

Cover, J. Daniel. "The Effects of Social Contact on Prejudice." *Journal of Social Psychology* 135, no. 3 (1995): 403-05.

Crystal, David S., Melanie Killen, and Martin Ruck. "It Is Who You Know That Counts: Intergroup Contact and Judgments About Race-Based Exclusion." *British Journal of Developmental Psychology* 26, no. 1 (2008): 51-70.

DeMott, Benjamin. *The Trouble With Friendship: Why Americans Can't Think Straight About Race*. New York: Atlantic Monthly Press, 1995.

de Souza Briggs, Xavier. "'Some of My Best Friends Are . . .': Interracial Friendships, Class, and Segregation in America." *City & Community* 6, no. 4 (2007): 263-90.

de Souza Briggs, Xavier. "Social Capital and Segregation: Race, Connections, and Inequality in America." Faculty Research Working Papers Series, John F. Kennedy School of Government, Harvard University, 2002.

de Tocqueville, Alexis. *Democracy in America*. London: Longman, Green and Co, 1889.

Dixon, Jeffrey C. "The Ties That Bind and Those That Don't: Toward Reconciling Group Threat and Contact Theories of Prejudice." *Social Forces* 84, no. 4 (2006): 2179-204.

DuBois, W. E. B. *The Souls of Black Folk: Essays and Sketches*. Greenwich, CT: Fawcett, 1961.

Durkheim, Émile. *The Elementary Forms of Religious Life*. Oxford University Press, 2008.

Durkheim, Émile. *The Division of Labor in Society*. New York: The Free Press, 1984.

Dwyer, Rachel E. "Poverty, Prosperity, and Place: The Shape of Class Segregation in the Age of Extremes." *Social Problems* 57, no. 1 (2010): 114-37.

Ellis, C., and A. Bochner. "Autoethnography, Personal Narrative, Reflexivity." In *Handbook of Qualitative Research, 2nd Ed.*, edited by Norman K. Denzin and Yvonna S. Lincoln, 733-68. Thousand Oaks, CA: Sage Publications, 2000.

Ellis, Robert A. "Social Stratification and Social Relations: An Empirical Test of the Disjunctiveness of Social Classes." *American Sociological Review* 22 (1957): 570-578.

Ellison, Christopher C., and Daniel A. Powers. "The Contact Hypothesis and Racial Attitudes among Black Americans." *Social Science Quarterly* 75, no. 2 (1994): 385-400.

Eve, Michael. "Is Friendship a Sociological Topic?" *European Journal of Sociology* 43 (2002): 386-409.

Feddes, Allard R., Peter Noack, and Adam Rutland. "Direct and Extended Friendship Effects on Minority and Majority Children's Interethnic Attitudes: A Longitudinal Study." *Child Development* 80, no. 2 (2009): 377-90.

Feld, Scott L. "Social Structural Determinants of Similarity Among Associates." *American Sociological Review* 47 (1982): 797-801.

Festinger, Leon, Stanley Schachter, and Kurt Back. *Social Pressures in Informal Groups: A Study of Human Factors in Housing*. London: Tavistock Publications, 1959.

Finchilescu, Gillian. "Meta-Stereotypes May Hinder Inter-Racial Contact." *South African Journal of Psychology* 35, no. 3 (2005): 460-72.

Fischer, Claude S. *To Dwell Among Friends: Personal Networks in Town and City*. Chicago: University of Chicago Press, 1982a.

Fischer, Claude S. "What Do We Mean by 'Friend'?" *Social Networks* 3 (1982b): 287-306.

Fischer, Mary J. "Does Campus Diversity Promote Friendship Diversity? A Look at Interracial Friendships in College." *Social Science Quarterly* 89, no. 3 (2008): 631-55.

Fisher, Bernice, and Roberta Galler. "Friendship and Fairness: How Disability Affects Friendship Between Women." In *Women with Disabilities: Essays in Psychology, Culture, and Politics*, edited by Michelle Fine and Adrienne Asch, 172-94. Philadelphia: Temple University Press, 1988.

Fossett, Mark. "Ethnic Preferences, Social Distance Dynamics, and Residential Segregation: Theoretical Explorations Using Simulation Analysis." *Journal of Mathematical Sociology* 30 (2006a): 185-274.

Fossett, Mark. "Including Preference and Social Distance Dynamics in Multi-Factor Theories of Segregation." *Journal of Mathematical Sociology* 30 (2006b): 289-98.

Gaertner, Samuel L., and John F. Dovidio. "Understanding and Addressing Contemporary Racism: From Aversive Racism to the Common Ingroup Identity Model." *Journal of Social Issues* 61, no. 3 (2005): 615-39.

Gans, Herbert J. Preface to *Cultivating Differences: Symbolic Boundaries and the Making of Inequality*, edited by Michéle Lamont and Marcel Fournier, xii-xv. Chicago: The University of Chicago Press, 1992.

Gee, Lisa. *Friends: Why Men and Women Are From the Same Planet*. New York: Bloomsbury, 2004.

Gibbons, Deborah and Paul M. Olk. "Individual and Structural Origins of Friendship and Social Position Among Professionals." *Journal of Personality and Social Psychology* 84 (2003): 340-351.

Gladwell, Malcolm. *The Tipping Point: How Little Things Can Make a Big Difference*. Boston: Back Bay Books, 2002.

Goering, S. "Choosing Our Friends: Moral Partiality and the Value of Diversity." *Journal of Social Philosophy* 34 (2003): 400-13.

Goff, Phillip Atiba, Claude M. Steele, and Paul G. Davies. "The Space Between Us: Stereotype Threat and Distance in Interracial Contexts." *Journal of Personality & Social Psychology* 94, no. 1 (2008): 91-107.

Goffman, Erving. *Interaction Ritual*. New York: Doubleday, 1967

Goffman, Erving. *The Presentation of Self in Everyday Life*. New York: Anchor Books, 1959.

Goffman, Erving. *Stigma: Notes on the Management of Spoiled Identity*. New York: Simon & Shuster, Inc, 1963.

Goldsmith, Pat Anténio. "Schools' Role in Shaping Race Relations: Evidence on Friendliness and Conflict." *Social Problems* 51, no. 4 (2004): 587-612.

Goldstein, Laurence. "Humor and Harm." *Sorites: Electronic Magazine of Analytical Philosophy*, issue #03, November 1995. http://www.ifs.csic.es/sorites /Issue_03/item4.htm (accessed February 15, 2007).

Gonzales, M. H., J. M. Davis, G. L. Loney, C. K. Lukens, and C. M. Junghans. "Interactional Approach to Interpersonal Attraction." *Journal of Personality and Social Psychology* 44 (1983): 1192-1197.

Gould, Allan. "No Laughing Matter: Those Racist and Sexist Jokes You Hear Are Dangerous." http://www.allangould.com/magazines/somefavourites/racisthumor /magazines_somefavouites_racisthumour.html (accessed February 15, 2007).

Greif, Geoffrey. *Buddy System: Understanding Male Friendships*. New York: Oxford University Press, 2009.

Hallinan, Maureen T. *The Structure of Positive Sentiment*. Elsevier Science Ltd., 1974.

Hallinan, Maureen T. and Ruy A. Teixeira. "Students' Interracial Friendships: Individual Characteristics, Structural Effects, and Racial Differences." *American Journal of Education* 85 (1987a): 563-583.

Hallinan, Maureen T. and Ruy A. Teixeira. "Opportunities and Constraints: Black-White Differences in the Formation of Interracial Friendships." *Child Development* 58 (1987b): 1358-1371.

Hamm, Jill V., B. Bradford Brown, and Daniel J. Heck. "Bridging the Ethnic Divide: Student and School Characteristics in African American, Asian-Descent, Latino, and White Adolescents' Cross-Ethnic Friend Nominations." *Journal of Research on Adolescence* 15, no. 1 (2005): 21-46.

Harwood, Jake, Miles Hewstone, Stefania Paolini, and Alberto Voci. "Grandparent-Grandchild Contact and Attitudes toward Older Adults: Moderator and Mediator Effects." *Personality and Social Psychology Bulletin* 31, no. 3 (2005): 393-406.

Heinze, Justin E., and Stacey S. Horn. "Intergroup Contact and Beliefs About Homosexuality in Adolescence." *Journal of Youth & Adolescence* 38, no. 7 (2009): 937-51.

Hesse-Biber, Sharlene, Paul DuPuis, and Scott Kinder. "HyperResearch: A Computer Program for the Analysis of Qualitative Data Using the Macintosh." *Qualitative Studies in Education* 3 (1990): 189-193.

Hewitt, John P. *Self and Society: A Symbolic Interactionist Social Psychology,* 8th edition. Boston: Allyn and Bacon, 2000.

Hipp, John R., and Andrew J. Perrin. "The Simultaneous Effect of Social Distance and Physical Distance on the Formation of Neighborhood Ties." *City & Community* 8, no. 1 (2009): 5-25.

Hsin-Chun Tsai, Jenny. "Xenophobia, Ethnic Community, and Immigrant Youths' Friendship Network Formation." *Adolescence* 41, no. 162 (2006): 285-98.

Hudson, J. Blaine, and Bonetta M. Hines-Hudson. "A Study of the Contemporary Racial Attitudes of Whites and African Americans." *Western Journal of Black Studies* 23 (1999): 22-34.

Hughes, Joanne. "Mediating and Moderating Effects of Inter-Group Contact: Case Studies from Bilingual/Bi-National Schools in Israel." *Journal of Ethnic & Migration Studies* 33, no. 3 (2007): 419-37.

Hutter, Horst. *Politics as Friendship.* Waterloo, Ontario: Wilfrid Laurier University Press, 1978.

Huxley, Aldous. *Brave New World: A Novel.* Garden City, NY: Doubleday, Doran & Company, Inc., 1932.

Jackman, Mary R., and Marie Crane. "'Some of My Best Friends Are Black . . .': Interracial Friendship and Whites' Racial Attitudes." *Public Opinion Quarterly* 50, no. 4 (1986): 459.

Jasínska-Kania, Aleksandra. "Exclusion from the Nation: Social Distances from National Minorities and Immigrants." *International Journal of Sociology* 39, no. 3 (2009): 15-37.

Johnsen, Eugene C. "Structure and Process: Agreement Models for Friendship Formation." *Social Networks* 8 (1986): 257-306.

Johnson, Martin A. "Variables Associated With Friendship in an Adult Population." *The Journal of Social Psychology* 129 (1989): 379-390.

Johnston, Ron, Michael Poulsen, and James Forrest. "The Geography of Ethnic Residential Segregation: A Comparative Study of Five Countries." *Annals of the Association of American Geographers* 97, no. 4 (2007): 713-38.

Jones, E. *Anansi Stories*. Concord, MA: Irwin Publishing, 1991.

Kawabata, Yoshito, and Nicki R. Crick. "The Role of Cross-Racial/Ethnic Friendships in Social Adjustment." *Developmental Psychology* 44, no. 4 (2008): 1177-83.

Korgen, Kathleen Odell. *Crossing the Racial Divide: Close Friendships Between Black and White Americans*. Praeger Publishers, 2002.

Korgen, Kathleen, and James A. Vela-McConnell. "Overcoming the Racial Divide: Bringing Together the Literature on Race, Friendships, and Social Affinity." Presented at *The 49th Annual Meeting of the Society for the Study of Social Problems*. Chicago, 1999.

Lamont, Michéle and Marcel Fournier, eds. *Cultivating Differences: Symbolic Boundaries and the Making of Inequality*. Chicago: The University of Chicago Press, 1992.

Lasch, Christopher. *The Culture of Narcissism*. New York: Norton, 1979.

Lauderdale, P., J. Parker, P. Smith-Cunnien, and J. Inverarity. "External Threat and the Definition of Deviance." *Journal of Personality and Social Psychology* 46 (1984): 1017-1028.

Laumann, Edward O. and Richard Senter. "Subjective Social Distance, Occupational Stratification, and Forms of Status and Class Consciousness: A Cross-National Replication and Extension." *American Journal of Sociology* 81 (1976): 1301-1338.

Lazarsfeld, Paul F. and Robert K. Merton. "Friendship as a Social Process: A Substantive and Methodological Analysis." In *Freedom and Control in Modern Society,* edited by Morroe Berger, Theodore Abel, and Charles H. Page, 18-66. New York: D. Van Nostrand Company, Inc, 1954.

Lemert, Charles and Ann Branaman. *The Goffman Reader*. Cambridge, MA: Blackwell, 1997.

Letki, Natalia. "Does Diversity Erode Social Cohesion? Social Capital and Race in British Neighbourhoods." *Political Studies* 56, no. 1 (2008): 99-126.

Levin, Shana, Colette Van Laar, and Jim Sidanius. "The Effects of Ingroup and Outgroup Friendships on Ethnic Attitudes in College: A Longitudinal Study." *Group Processes & Intergroup Relations* 6, no. 1 (2003): 76-92.

Lorber, Judith. *Paradoxes of Gender*. New Haven, CT: Yale University Press, 1994.

Lorde, Audre. *Sister Outsider*. Trumansburg, NY: The Crossing Press Feminist Series, 1984.

Markides, K. C., and S. F. Cohn. "External Conflict/Internal Cohesion: A Reevaluation of an Old Theory," *American Sociological Review* 47 (1982): 88-89.

Marsden, Peter V. "Homogeneity in Confiding Relations." *Social Networks* 10 (1988): 57-76.

Massey, Douglas, and Mary J. Fisher. "The Geography of Inequality in the United States, 1950-2000." In *Brookings-Wharton Papers on Urban Affairs 2003*, edited by W. G. Gale and J. T. Pack. Washington, D.C.: Brookings Institution, 2003.

McCullough, Mary W. *Black and White Women as Friends: Building Cross-Race Friendships*. Cresskill, NJ: Hampton Press, 1998.

McGlothlin, Heidi, and Melanie Killen. "Intergroup Attitudes of European American Children Attending Ethnically Homogeneous Schools." *Child Development* 77, no. 5 (2006): 1375-86.

McIntosh, Peggy. "White Privilege: Unpacking the Invisible Knapsack." Wellesley College, MA, 1988.

McPherson, J. Miller and Lynn Smith-Lovin. "Homophily in Voluntary Organizations: Status Distance and the Composition of Face-to-Face Groups." *American Sociological Review* 52 (1987): 370-379.

McPherson, Miller, Lynn Smith-Lovin, and Matthew E. Brashears. "Social Isolation in America: Changes in Core Discussion Networks Over Two Decades." *American Sociological Review* 71 (2006): 353-375.

McPherson, Miller, Lynn Smith-Lovin, and James M. Cook. "Birds of a Feather: Homophily in Social Networks." *Annual Review of Sociology* 27 (2001): 415-444.

McWilliams, Susan and Judith A. Howard. "Solidarity and Hierarchy in Cross-Sex Friendships." *Journal of Social Issues* 49 (1993): 191-203.

Mills, C. Wright. *The Sociological Imagination.* New York: Oxford University Press, 1959.

Mo, Timothy. *The Monkey King.* London: Abacus, 1991.

More, St. Thomas. *Utopia.* Edited by Edward Surtz, S.J. New Haven, CT: Yale University Press, 1964.

Moreland, R.L. "Social Categorization and the Assimilation of 'New' Group Members." *Journal of Personality and Social Psychology* 48 (1985): 1173-1190.

Nardi, Peter M. "That's What Friends Are For: Friends as Family in the Gay and Lesbian Community." In *Modern Homosexualities: Fragments of Lesbian and Gay Experience,* edited by Ken Plummer, 108-120. New York: Routledge, 1992a.

Nardi, Peter M. "Sex, Friendship, and Gender Roles Among Gay Men." In *Men's Friendships,* edited by Peter M. Nardi, 173-185. Newbury Park, CA: Sage Publications, 1992b.

Nardi, Peter M., ed. *Men's Friendships.* Newbury Park, CA: Sage Publications, 1992c.

Nardi, Peter M. *Gay Men's Friendships: Invincible Communities.* Chicago: University of Chicago Press, 1999.

Newcomb, Theodore M. "Stabilities Underlying Changes in Interpersonal Attraction." *Journal of Abnormal and Social Psychology* 66 (1963): 376-386.

Newcomb, Theodore M. *The Acquaintance Process.* New York: Holt, Rinehart and Winston, 1961.

Newcomb, Theodore M. "The Prediction of Interpersonal Attraction." *American Psychologist* 11 (1956): 575-586.

Ogburn, William Fielding. *Social Change With Respect to Culture and Original Nature.* New York: Viking Press, 1950.

Orfield, Gary. "Schools More Separate: Consequences of a Decade of Resegregation." The Civil Rights Project, http://www.civilrightsproject.ucla.edu/research/deseg /separate_schools01.php.

Ortiz, Michelle, and Jake Harwood. "A Social Cognitive Theory Approach to the Effects of Mediated Intergroup Contact on Intergroup Attitudes." *Journal of Broadcasting & Electronic Media* 51, no. 4 (2007): 615-31.

Pahl, Ray. *On Friendship.* Cambridge, UK: Polity Press, 2000.

Pahl, Ray. "Towards a More Significant Sociology of Friendship." *European Journal of Sociology* 43 (2002): 410-423.

Pahl, Ray and David J. Pevalin. "Between Family and Friends: A Longitudinal Study of Friendship Choice." *The British Journal of Sociology* 56 (2005): 433-450.

Park, Robert. "Introduction." In *The Marginal Man,* by Everett V. Stonequist. New York: Russell & Russell, 1937.

Passel, Jeffrey S., Wendy Wang, and Paul Taylor. "Marrying Out: One-in-Seven New U.S. Marriages Is Interracial or Interethnic." Pew Research Center, Social & Demographic Trends Project, 2010.

Pettigrew, Thomas F. "Generalized Intergroup Contact Effects on Prejudice." *Personality and Social Psychology Bulletin* 23 (1997): 173-185.

Pettigrew, Thomas F. "Intergroup Contact Theory." *Annual Review of Psychology* 49 (1998): 65-85.

Plummer, Ken, ed. *Modern Homosexualities: Fragments of Lesbian and Gay Experience.* New York: Routledge, 1992.

Prado, C. G. "Political Correctness." *Personal Ethics: Suite 101.* August 2, 2006. http://personalethics.suite101.com /print_article.cfm/political_correctness (accessed February 15, 2007).

Prado, C. G. "Racist and Sexist Humor." *Personal Ethics: Suite 101.* December 20, 2006. http://personalethics.suite101.com/print_article.cfm/racist_and_sexist_humor (accessed February 15, 2007).

Prestwich, Andrew, Jared B. Kenworthy, Michelle Wilson, and Natasha Kwan-Tat. "Differential Relations Between Two Types of Contact and Implicit and Explicit Racial Attitudes." *British Journal of Social Psychology* 47, no. 4 (2008): 575-88.

Price, Jammie. *Navigating Differences: Friendships Between Gay and Straight Men.* Binghamton, NY: Haworth Press, Inc, 1999.

Putnam, Robert D. *Bowling Alone: The Collapse and Revival of American Community.* New York: Simon & Schuster, 2000.

Rawlins, William K. *The Compass of Friendship: Narratives, Identities, and Dialogues.* Newbury Park, CA: Sage Publications, 2009.

Rawlins, William K. *Friendship Matters: Communication, Dialectics, and the Life Course.* New York: Aldine de Gruyter, 1992.

Raybon, Patricia. *My First White Friend: Confessions on Race, Love, and Forgiveness.* New York: Penguin Group, USA, 1997.

Reicher, Stephen. "Rethinking the Paradigm of Prejudice." *South African Journal of Psychology* 37, no. 4 (2007): 820-34.

Rheingold, H. *The Virtual Community: Homesteading on the Electronic Frontier.* Cambridge, MA: Perseus Books, 1993.

Rogin, Michael Paul. *Blackface, White Noise: Jewish Immigrants in the Hollywood Melting Pot.* Berkeley, CA: University of California Press, 1996.

Rothenberg, Paula S. *White Privilege: Essential Readings on the Other Side of Racism.* New York: Worth Publishers, 2004.

Rubin, Lillian B. *Just Friends: The Role of Friendship in Our Lives.* New York: Harper & Row, Publishers, 1985.

Rubington, Earl and Martin S. Weinberg. *The Study of Social Problems: Seven Perspectives, 5th ed.* New York: Oxford University Press, 1995.

Rude, Jesse D. "Interracial Friendships in Context: Their Formation, Development, and Impact." Dissertation, University of California—Davis, 2009.

Ryan, Allan J. *The Trickster Shift: Humour and Irony in Contemporary Native Art.* Vancouver: University of British Columbia Press, 1999.

Saenz, Victor B., Hoi Ning Ngai, and Sylvia Hurtado. "Factors Influencing Positive Interactions Across Race for African American, Asian American, Latino, and White College Students." *Research in Higher Education* 48, no. 1 (2007): 1-38.

Samter, Wendy, and William Cupach. "Friendly Fire: Topical Variation in Conflict Among Same and Cross-Sex Friends." *Communication Studies* 49, no. 42 (1998): 121-38.

Scheff, Thomas J. *Microsociology: Discourse, Emotion, and Social Structure*. Chicago: The University of Chicago Press, 1990.

Segal, M. W. "Alphabet and Attraction: An Unobtrusive Measure of the Effect of Propinquity in Field Training." *Journal of Personality and Social Psychology* 30 (1974): 654-657.

Sherif, Muzafer. "Experiments in Group Conflict." *Scientific American* (1956): 195.

Sherif, M., O. J. Harvey, B. J. White, W. R. Hood, and C. W. Sherif. *Intergroup Conflict and Cooperation: The Robbers Cave Experiment*. Norman: Institute of Group Relations, University of Oklahoma, 1961.

Shibutani, T. and K. M. Kwan. *Ethnic Stratification*. New York: Macmillan, 1965.

Shook, Natalie J., and Russell H. Fazio. "Interracial Roommate Relationships: An Experimental Field Test of the Contact Hypothesis." *Psychological Science* 19, no. 7 (2008): 717-23.

Sigelman, Carol K., Jennifer L. Howell, David P. Cornell, John D. Cutright, and Janine C. Dewey. "Courtesy Stigma: The Social Implications of Associating with a Gay Person." *Journal of Social Psychology* 131, no. 1 (1991): 45-56.

Simkus, Albert and Bogdan Mach. "Analyses of Social Distances Among Classes: Detailed Analyses for Hungary and Poland." *International Journal of Sociology* 25 (1995): 25-42.

Simmel, Georg. *On Individuality and Social Forms*. Donald N. Levine, ed. Chicago: The University of Chicago Press, 1971.

Simmel, Georg. *The Sociology of Georg Simmel*. Translated by Kurt H. Wolff. New York: The Free Press, 1950.

Speier, H. "The Social Types of War." *American Journal of Sociology* 46 (1941): 445-454.

Spencer, Liz and Ray Pahl. *Rethinking Friendship: Hidden Solidarities Today*. Princeton, NJ: Princeton University Press, 2006.

Steinberg, Stephen. *The Ethnic Myth: Race, Ethnicity, and Class in America*. Boston: Beacon Press, 2001.

Stolle, Dietlind, Stuart Soroka, and Richard Johnston. "When Does Diversity Erode Trust? Neighborhood Diversity, Interpersonal Trust and the Mediating Effect of Social Interactions." *Political Studies* 56, no. 1 (2008): 57-75.

Suitor, Jill and Shirley Keeton. "Once a Friend, Always a Friend? Effects of Homophily on Women's Support Networks Across a Decade." *Social Networks* 19 (1997): 51-62.

Tajfel, Henri, Michael Billig, R. P. Bundy, and Claude Flament. "Social Categorization and Intergroup Behavior." *European Journal of Social Psychology* 1 (1971): 149-77.

Thaler, Kai. "Confusion Blemished Parody's Reception." *Yale Daily News*, September 27, 2006, http://www.yaledailynews.com/articles/view/18112 (accessed February 15, 2007).

Thomas, William I. *The Child in America: Behavior Problems and Programs*. New York: Knopf, 1928.

Tönnies, Ferdinand. *Community and Society*. New Brunswick, NJ: Transaction Books, 1988.

Towles-Schwen, Tamara, and Russell H. Fazio. "Automatically Activated Racial Attitudes as Predictors of the Success of Interracial Roommate Relationships." *Journal of Experimental Social Psychology* 42, no. 5 (2006): 698-705.

Trail, Thomas E., J. Nicole Shelton, and Tessa V. West. "Interracial Roommate Relationships: Negotiating Daily Interactions." *Personality and Social Psychology Bulletin*

35 (2009): 671-84.

Tredoux, Colin, and Gillian Finchilescu. "The Contact Hypothesis and Intergroup Relations 50 Years On: Introduction to the Special Issue." *South African Journal of Psychology* 37, no. 4 (2007): 667-78.

Tropp, Linda. "Perceived Discrimination and Interracial Contact: Predicting Interracial Closeness Among Black and White Americans." *Social Psychology Quarterly* 70 (2007): 70-81.

Turner, Rhiannon N., Miles Hewstone, Alberto Voci, Stefania Paolini, and Oliver Christ. "Reducing Prejudice Via Direct and Extended Cross-Group Friendship." *European Review of Social Psychology* 18 (2007): 212-55.

Turner, Rhiannon N., and Richard J. Crisp. "Imagining Intergroup Contact Reduces Implicit Prejudice." *British Journal of Social Psychology* 49, no. 1 (2010): 129-42.

Vanderpool, Tim. "Secession of the Successful: Homeowners' Associations Turn Neighborhoods Into Islands." *Utne Reader,* November/December 1995.

Vander Zanden, James W. *Social Psychology,* 4th ed. New York: Random House, 1987.

van Dijk, T. A. "Discourse and the Denial of Racism." *Discourse and Society* 3 (1992): 87-118.

Vela-McConnell, James A. *Who Is My Neighbor? Social Affinity in a Modern World.* New York: State University of New York Press, 1999.

Verbrugge, Lois M. "The Structure of Adult Friendship Choices." *Social Forces* 56 (1977): 576-597.

Vitak, Jessica M. "Facebook 'Friends': How Online Identities Impact Offline Relationships." Master's Thesis, Georgetown University, 2008.

Voci, Alberto, and Miles Hewstone. "Intergroup Contact and Prejudice toward Immigrants in Italy: The Mediational Role of Anxiety and the Moderational Role of Group Salience." *Group Processes & Intergroup Relations* 6, no. 1 (2003): 37-54.

Vonofakou, Christiana, Miles Hewstone, and Alberto Voci. "Contact with Out-Group Friends as a Predictor of Meta-Attitudinal Strength and Accessibility of Attitudes Toward Gay Men." *Journal of Personality & Social Psychology* 92, no. 5 (2007): 804-20.

Vonofakou, Christiana, Miles Hewstone, Alberto Voci, Stefania Paolini, Rhiannon N. Turner, Nicole T. Tausch, Tania Tam, Jake Harwood, and Ed Cairns. "The Impact of Direct and Extended Cross-Group Friendships on Improving Intergroup Relations." In *Improving Intergroup Relations: Building on the Legacy of Thomas F. Pettigrew,* 107-23. Malden, MA: Blackwell Publishers, 2008.

Waters, Mary C. "Optional Ethnicities: For Whites Only." In *Origins and Destinies,* edited by Sylvia Pedraza & Ruben G. Rumbaut, 444-454. Belmont, CA: Wadsworth Publishing Company, 1996.

Weeks, Jeffrey, Brian Heaphy, and Catherine Donovan. *Same Sex Intimacies: Families of Choice and Other Life Experiments.* New York: Routledge, 2001.

Weiss, Lawrence and Marjorie Fiske Lowenthal. "Life Course Perspectives on Friendship." In *Four Stages of Life,* edited by Marjorie Fiske Lowenthal, Majda Thurnher and David Chiriboga, 48-61. San Francisco: Jossey-Bass, 1975.

Wellman, B., and M. Gulia. "Virtual Communities as Communities: Net Surfers Don't Ride Alone." In *Communities in Cyberspace,* edited by M. Smith and P. Kollock, 167-94. London: Routledge, 1999.

West, Cornel. *Race Matters.* New York: Vintage Books, 1993.

Wilder, David A. and Peter N. Shapiro. "Role of Out-Group Cues in Determining Social Identity." *Journal of Personality and Social Psychology* 47 (1984): 342-348.

Wilmott, P. *Friendship Networks and Social Support.* London: Policy Studies Institute, 1987.

Wiseman, Jacqueline P. "Friendship: Bonds and Binds in a Voluntary Relationship." *Journal of Social & Personal Relationships* 3 (1986): 191-211.

Wittig, Monique. *The Straight Mind.* Boston: Beacon Press, 1992.

White, A. "'You've Got a Friend': African American Men's Cross-Sex Feminist Friendships and Their Influence on Perceptions of Masculinity and Women." *Journal of Social and Personal Relationships* 23 (2006): 523-42.

White, Michael J., Ann H. Kim, and Jennifer E. Glick. "Mapping Social Distance: Ethnic Residential Segregation in a Multiethnic Metro." *Sociological Methods & Research* 34, no. 2 (2005): 173-203.

Wolfe, Alan. *Whose Keeper? Social Science and Moral Obligation.* Berkeley: The University of California Press, 1989.

Wolff, Kurt H., ed. *The Sociology of Georg Simmel.* New York: The Free Press of Glencoe, 1950.

Wright, Stephen C., Arthur Aron, Tracy McLaughlin-Volpe, and Stacy A. Ropp. "The Extended Contact Effect: Knowledge of Cross-Group Friendships and Prejudice." *Journal of Personality & Social Psychology* 73, no. 1 (1997): 73-90.

Yancey, George. "An Examination of the Effects of Residential and Church Integration on Racial Attitudes of Whites." *Sociological Perspectives* 42, no. 2 (1999): 279-304.

Zinn, Howard. *You Can't Be Neutral on a Moving Train: A Personal History of Our Times.* Boston: Beacon Press, 1994.

# Index

ability, 5, 10, 33–34, 108, 110, 116, 118, 119, 120, 136–37

acquaintance, 6, 17–18, 24, 29, 50, 86–87, 205

Adam, 103, 113, 119, 184, 188, 223

age, 5, 10, 31, 41n11, 57–58, 96–97, 104, 106, 109–10, 116, 118, 119, 120, 121

Allison, 209, 222

Ann Marie, 175, 196, 218, 222

attraction, 6, 25, 51–54, 65–69, 100n6, 105, 113, 134, 137–39, 187

Bao, 45–46, 50, 80, 108, 130–32, 133, 141, 162, 171–72, 186, 217, 222

Barbara, 69–71, 72, 76, 85–86, 138–39, 162–63, 184–85, 201, 215–16, 222

Bill, 15, 18, 103–5, 122, 172–73, 178, 221

Bob, 57–58, 96–97, 106, 121, 182–83, 221

boundaries, socially constructed. *See* socially constructed boundaries

Brad, 64, 75, 92, 114, 189, 198, 199, 215, 216, 221

Brian, 66–67, 174, 223

Brianna, 73, 222

bridging ties, 7–8, 11, 12, 12n3, 16, 34–38, 39, 92, 94–95, 99, 101, 124, 144, 148, 151, 160, 167, 173–82, 191–92, 208. *See also* social capital

Caroline, 49–50, 66–67, 174, 223

Chad, 95, 198–99, 221

changeability, 119–22, 127, 128n4

Christina, 96, 107, 141–42, 223

Colin, 52, 62, 100n4, 108, 109, 123–25, 144–46, 151–52, 185–86, 221

contact theory. *See* intergroup contact theory

context, friendship, 3, 8, 37, 43n26, 48, 84, 102, 148, 150–51, 155–57, 161, 164, 165n7, 167, 213

context, group, 11, 23, 43n26, 47, 61–76, 83, 99, 174–75; accepting those who have crossed category lines, 74–76; extended family and other friends, 62–64; partner or spouse, 65–73

context, individual, 11, 76–99; comfort and familiarity, 88–93; perception, 93–99; personal experiences, 83–87; sense of disconnection, 79–83; similar personal qualities, 77–79

context, institutional, 11, 19, 23, 47, 54–61, 76, 99, 99–100nn2–3, 174–75

context, social, 3–6, 9, 17, 22, 23, 25, 28, 41n10, 43n26, 45–48, 61, 65, 78, 99n1, 142, 151, 179, 201

context, socio-cultural, 11, 17, 23, 47, 48–54, 76, 78, 99, 174–75

class, 5, 9–10, 21, 26, 32–33, 55–57,
    101, 104, 110–12, 116, 118, 119,
    122, 137, 146–47, 170–71, 177,
    179
Cynthia, 108, 119, 136–37, 222

Dave, 17–18, 74–75, 78, 84, 90–91,
    98, 110, 115, 120, 122, 126–27,
    134–35, 153–57, 162, 169–70,
    176–77, 188, 189–90, 221
Debbie, 51, 63–64, 77, 120, 176, 223
Deborah, 58–59, 84, 132–33, 135–36,
    140–41, 185, 213, 222
Dennis, 175, 218, 202, 222
dyadic relationships, 19, 21–23, 41n9,
    47, 61, 180

Ed, 24, 138, 221
Ellen, 96, 107, 141–42, 223
Emily, 71–72, 76, 197, 219–19, 222
Eric, 64, 75, 92, 114, 189, 215, 216,
    221
Eva, 62–63, 84, 168, 174, 178, 190,
    219, 223

facework, 198
Fatima, 58–59, 83–84, 132–33,
    135–36, 140–41, 144
Frank, 142–43, 144, 157–59, 160, 188,
    222
friendship: as a counter culture, 21,
    41n7, 183, 191, 192, 193n10; cul-
    ture of, 41n7, 153, 157, 161, 163;
    defining, 9, 11, 16–18, 40n1,
    40nn3–4, 137–38; equality within,
    16, 18, 19, 20–21, 22, 36, 41n6,
    41n8, 43n26, 57, 60, 130, 175,
    182–83, 192, 193, 203; formation
    of, 26–27, 28–30, 42n14, 57, 181,
    183;heterogeneity within, 1–3, 8–9,
    13n4, 21, 27, 31, 32, 35–40,
    42nn15–16, 43nn25–26; homoge-
    neity within, 5, 7, 11, 16, 21,
    26–27, 28–29, 30–34, 64, 179; pat-
    terns of, 1–2, 3–7, 20, 22–23,
    26–27, 30–34, 35–36, 41n8; per-
    sonal significance of, 136, 167–73;
    potential, 36–37, 180; and social
    bonds, 11, 16, 21–22, 23–31,
    34–38, 39, 102, 103–5, 107, 116,
    117, 124, 132, 133, 160–61, 164,
    167; and social context, 11, 18, 20,
    41n10, 192–93; sociological rele-
    vance of, 8, 16, 18–23, 34–38;
    stages of, 12, 122–27; stratification
    and, 12, 16, 19, 21–23, 30, 33–34,
    41n6, 183, 193n10; voluntary na-
    ture of, 12n2, 15–16, 18, 19–20,
    21, 22, 35, 41n5
friendship network, 33, 34, 48, 60, 64,
    184, 206

gender, 6–7, 10, 31–32, 33, 39, 43n26,
    48–55, 67–69, 82, 95, 103–5, 106,
    107, 116, 117, 119–20, 125, 134,
    137–38, 139–40, 152, 159–60,
    176–77, 184, 185. *See also* attrac-
    tion
Greg, 108, 119, 136–37, 222

heterosexism, 51, 53, 149
homogeneity: within institutions, 27;
    within neighborhoods, 26–27. *See
    also* friendship homogeneity; social
    network
homophily, 7, 8, 25, 27, 31, 33, 42n15,
    46, 61, 77, 214; and ability, 33; and
    age, 31; and class, 32–33; explana-
    tions for, 25–27, 29; and gender,
    31–32; and race, 31; and religion,
    32; and sexual orientation, 33;
    status, 25, 41n12, 77, 213, 214;
    value, 41n12, 77, 213
homophobia, 58, 63, 169, 175, 186,
    187, 195
Hugo, 51, 63, 77, 82–83, 86, 120,
    173–74, 176, 177, 223

impact of socially constructed bounda-
    ries, 10, 11–12, 98–99, 102–15,
    184; being mindful, 104, 109–12,
    115, 116, 117; eye opening, 103–6,
    107, 117, 118; initial hesitation,
    104, 109–10, 115, 116, 117, 121,
    123–24, 126; less understanding,
    104, 109, 113–15, 116, 117; nega-
    tive impact, 109–15; no impact,
    107–9, 129; positive impact,

103–7, 129, 132; respect, 103, 104, 105, 106–7, 116, 117; some discomfort, 104, 109, 112–14, 115, 116, 117, 118, 125; source of bonding, 102, 103–5, 107, 116, 117, 124
in-group, 29–30, 34–35, 36–37, 42n24, 59, 76, 87, 148, 179, 180–81, 201
intergroup contact theory, 36–37, 40, 42n22, 42n24, 54, 92, 132, 148, 180–81, 183
interpersonal techniques for managing differences, 8, 12, 98, 127, 129–30, 164, 173, 178, 181; educating one's friend, 130, 144–48, 191; focusing on hidden commonalities, 130–34, 173; meeting one's friend "more than half way," 130, 139–44; taking care, 130, 134–39; use of humor, 130, 148–64, 173
Irene, 45–46, 80–81, 83, 100n4, 108, 130–32, 133, 141, 162, 171, 186, 217, 222

Janice, 69–71, 72, 76, 85, 86, 138–39, 162, 196, 215–16, 222
Janine, 184, 199, 222
Jenna, 71–72, 76, 197, 200, 218–19, 222
Jenny, 110–11, 120, 137, 146–48, 187, 221
Jeremiah, 113, 223
Jeremy, 152–53, 165n8, 223
Jerry, 57–58, 96–97, 106, 121, 182–83, 201, 221
Jessi, 105–6, 120, 222
Jessica, 222
Jordan, 65–66, 100n6, 112–13, 122, 142, 144, 223

Karen, 103, 105, 122, 172–73, 178, 199, 202, 221
Katie, 24, 138, 195, 221
Kelly, 52, 62, 100n4, 108, 109, 123–25, 144–46, 151–52, 185, 221
Keosha, 195, 209, 222
Kim, 52–53, 72–73, 76, 77, 185, 223
Kris, 52–53, 72–73, 76, 77, 185, 223

Laura, 64, 95, 198–99, 221

Lenora, 89–90, 91, 97–98, 110, 120, 125, 126, 143, 168–69, 187, 188–89, 200, 221
Lisa, 86–87, 89, 173, 223
Liz, 221

Mark, 115, 120, 122, 153–57, 162, 169–70, 189–90, 221
Matt, 64, 176, 221
Melissa, 81, 83, 89–90, 91, 92, 97–98, 110, 120, 125, 126, 143, 168–69, 176, 187, 188–89, 200, 221
Melody, 169, 222
Miriam, 78, 134–35, 176–77, 200–201, 221
Monica, 222

Nancy, 203, 222
Nicole, 62–63, 84, 168, 174, 178, 190, 223
Nikki, 195, 221

out-group, 12n3, 29–30, 35, 36, 37–38, 42nn24–25, 59, 87, 148, 171, 181, 191, 201

Pam, 67–69, 72, 76, 106, 139–40, 144, 159–60, 222
Patricia, 103, 119, 223
proximity, 24–25, 28, 100n9

Quinn, 55–57, 77–78, 101, 107, 111, 119, 170–71, 177, 196, 217–18, 222

race, 2, 4–5, 6, 7, 10, 26–27, 31–32, 42n16, 45–46, 48–49, 54–55, 75, 80–82, 83, 86–87, 93–96, 97, 100n4, 104, 107–10, 116, 117–18, 119, 120, 123–25, 127n3, 141–43, 145–46, 148–53, 157–59, 171–72, 185–89, 199–200
racism, 2, 48, 58, 86, 94, 144, 149–51, 153–54, 157, 175, 186–87, 195, 198–99, 201, 216
relational boundaries, 124, 137–39
religion, 5, 10, 32, 42n18, 47, 54, 56, 58–59, 60, 84, 104, 105–6, 107, 113, 116, 117–18, 119, 120–22,

132–33, 135–36, 160, 170–71, 185, 213

Rodney, 86, 162, 223

Ruth, 222

Sam, 86, 162, 187, 197, 223

Sarah, 64, 82, 176, 196–97, 221

segregation, 5–6, 7, 10, 25–28, 30–34, 35, 37–38, 41n13, 54–61, 99n2, 141, 179–81, 192, 214. *See also* self-segregation

self-segregation, 32, 37, 55, 57–61, 180–81

sexism, 149–50, 153, 159–60, 175, 186, 187, 195, 198

sexual orientation, 4–5, 6, 10, 65–67, 69–72, 83–86, 91–92, 98, 100n6, 103–5, 109–10, 112–13, 115, 116, 117–18, 119–20, 122, 125–27, 127n2, 137–39, 152, 155–57, 174, 178–79, 184–85, 189–90, 215–16. *See also* attraction

Shawn, 65–66, 112–13, 122, 142, 144, 223

similarity, 1, 5, 7, 21, 25, 28–30, 31, 33, 38, 41n12, 50, 56, 58, 59, 61, 64, 70, 75, 77–79, 81, 82, 89–90, 93, 96, 98, 100n9, 105–6, 110, 125, 126, 130–34, 138–39, 145, 154, 192

social affinity, 24–25, 30, 36, 41n11, 148, 179–80, 191–92

social bonds, 7–8, 24, 30–31, 34–38, 39, 40n1, 54, 70, 79, 148, 180, 191. *See also* friendship and social bonds

social capital, 16, 34–36, 179–80

social cohesion, 11, 12, 16, 23–30, 34–36, 38, 148, 160, 167, 179–80, 191, 192, 214

social distance, 1, 3, 25, 28–30, 36–37, 164, 181, 214

social network, 17, 19, 27, 31, 34–35, 42nn16–17, 47–48, 61–62, 65, 76, 100n7, 112, 125, 180, 206. *See also* friendship network

socially constructed boundaries, 1–3, 8, 28–30, 34, 38, 57, 78–79, 200, 201, 203, 209, 219n1; comparison of, 115–18; breaking down, 3, 8, 34, 36, 38–39, 173–93; and perception, 93–99. *See also* ability; age; change ability; class; gender; impact of socially constructed boundaries; interpersonal techniques for managing differences; race; religion; sexual orientation; visibility

sociological imagination, 3–4, 7, 46–47, 95, 99

spatial distance, 25–28, 30, 179, 214

Suzanne, 110–11, 120–21, 137, 146–47, 148, 187

Ted, 152–53, 165n8, 223

Tenisha, 222

Tim, 67–69, 72, 76, 106, 139–40, 144, 159–60, 222

Tina, 105–6, 120, 222

visibility, 57, 88, 91, 95, 111, 119–22, 123, 125, 127, 128n4, 179, 184–85, 186

Wilson, 142–43, 144, 157–59, 160, 222

## About the Author

James A. Vela-McConnell is associate professor of sociology at Augsburg College in Minneapolis, Minnesota. He received his PhD and MA in sociology from Boston College and his BA in sociology from Loyola University, New Orleans. He specializes in social psychology, social inequality, and qualitative research methodology. In addition, Vela-McConnell teaches in the areas of social problems and violence. His prior work includes *Who Is My Neighbor?: Social Affinity in a Modern World* and contributions to *Sex, Media, Religion*; *What's Left?: Radical Politics in the Postcommunist Era*; and *The Human Experience Reader: Selections from Sociology.*

Breinigsville, PA USA
03 December 2010
250517BV00003B/4/P